An Introduction to Microeconomics and Finance Theories and economics Methods

An Introduction to Microeconomics and Finance: Theories and Economics Methods

Pankaj Gupta

CYBER TECH PUBLICATIONS
4264/3, Ansari Road, Daryaganj, New Delhi-110002 (India)
Ph.: 011-23244078, 011-43559448 Fax: 011-23280028
E-Mail: cyberpublicationsdelhi@yahoo.com
cyberpublications@gmail.com
Website: www.cybertechpublications.com

An introduction to Microeconomics and finance Theories and Economics Methods

Pankaj Gupta

2012 Edition

Asian Offset Printers

Published by
G.S. Rawat for Cyber Tech Publications
4264/3, Ansari Road, Daryaganj, New Delhi-110002 (India)
Ph.: 011-23244078, 011-43559448 Fax: 011-23280028
E-Mail: cyberpublicationsdelhi@yahoo.com
cyberpublications@gmail.com
Website: www.cybertechpublications.com

Preface

Dr. Alfred Marshall, one of the greatest economists of the nineteenth century, writes "Economics is a study of man's actions in the ordinary business of life: it enquires how he gets his income and how he uses it". Thus, it is one side, a study of wealth; and on the other, and more important side; it is the study of man. As Marshall observed, the chief aim of economics is to promote 'human welfare', but not wealth. Economics is a study of human activity both at individual and national level. The economists of early age treated economics merely as the science of wealth. The reason for this is clear. Every one of us in involved in efforts aimed at earning money and spending this money to satisfy our wants such as food, Clothing, shelter, and others. Such activities of earning and spending money are called "Economic activities". It was only during the eighteenth century that Adam Smith, the Father of Economics, defined economics as the study of nature and uses of national wealth'.

The study of an individual consumer or a firm is called microeconomics (also called the *Theory of Firm*). Micro means 'one millionth'. Microeconomics deals with behavior and problems of single individual and of micro organization. Managerial economics has its roots in microeconomics and it deals with the micro or individual enterprises. It is concerned with the application of the concepts such as price theory, Law of Demand and theories of market structure and so on.

The study of 'aggregate' or total level of economics activity in a country is called *macroeconomics*. It studies the flow of economics resources or factors of production (such as land, labour, capital, organisation and technology) from the resource owner to the business firms and then from the business firms to the households. It deals with total aggregates, for instance, total national income total employment, output and total investment. It studies the interrelations among various aggregates and examines their nature and behaviour, their determination and causes of fluctuations in the. It deals with the price level in general, instead of studying the prices of individual commodities. It is concerned with the level of employment in the economy. It discusses aggregate consumption, aggregate investment, price level, and payment, theories of employment, and so on.

Though macroeconomics provides the necessary framework in term of government policies etc., for the firm to act upon dealing with analysis of business conditions, it has less direct relevance in the study of theory of firm.

Management is the science and art of getting things done through people in formally organized groups. It is necessary that every organisation be well managed to enable it to achieve its desired goals. Management includes a number of functions: *Planning, organizing, staffing, directing, and controlling*. The manager while directing the efforts of his staff *communicates* to them the goals, objectives, policies, and procedures; *coordinates* their efforts; *motivates* them to sustain their enthusiasm; and *leads* them to achieve the corporate goals.

—*Author*

CONTENTS

1

Introduction to Economics

Economics is a study of human activity both at individual and national level. The economists of early age treated economics merely as the science of wealth. The reason for this is clear. Every one of us in involved in efforts aimed at earning money and spending this money to satisfy our wants such as food, Clothing, shelter, and others. Such activities of earning and spending money are called

"Economic activities". It was only during the eighteenth century that Adam Smith, the Father of Economics, defined economics as the study of nature and uses of national wealth'.

Dr. Alfred Marshall, one of the greatest economists of the nineteenth century, writes "Economics is a study of man's actions in the ordinary business of life: it enquires how he gets his income and how he uses it". Thus, it is one side, a study of wealth; and on the other, and more important side; it is the study of man. As Marshall observed, the chief aim of economics is to promote 'human welfare', but not wealth.

The definition given by AC Pigou endorses the opinion of Marshall. Pigou defines Economics as "the study of economic welfare that can be brought directly and indirectly, into relationship with the measuring rod of money".

Prof. Lionel Robbins defined Economics as "the science, which studies human behaviour as a relationship between ends and scarce means which have alternative uses". With this, the focus of economics shifted from 'wealth' to human behaviour'.

Lord Keynes defined economics as 'the study of the administration of scarce means and the determinants of employments and income".

MICROECONOMICS

The study of an individual consumer or a firm is called microeconomics (also called the *Theory of Firm*). Micro means 'one millionth'. Microeconomics deals with behavior and problems of single individual and of micro organization. Managerial economics has its roots in microeconomics and it deals with the micro or individual enterprises. It is concerned with the application of the concepts such as price theory, Law of Demand and theories of market structure and so on.

Macroeconomics

The study of 'aggregate' or total level of economics activity in a country is called *macroeconomics*. It studies the flow of economics resources or factors of production (such as land, labour, capital, organisation and technology) from the resource owner to the business firms and then from the business firms to the households. It deals with total aggregates, for instance, total national income total employment, output and total investment. It studies the interrelations among various aggregates and examines their nature and behaviour, their determination and causes of fluctuations in the. It deals with the price level in general, instead of studying the prices of individual commodities. It is concerned with the level of employment in the economy. It discusses aggregate consumption, aggregate investment, price level, and payment, theories of employment, and so on.

Though macroeconomics provides the necessary framework in term of government policies etc., for the firm to act upon dealing with analysis of business conditions, it has less direct relevance in the study of theory of firm.

Management

Management is the science and art of getting things done through people in formally organized groups. It is necessary that every organisation be well managed to enable it to achieve its desired goals. Management includes a number of functions: *Planning, organizing, staffing, directing, and controlling*. The manager while directing the efforts of his staff *communicates* to them the goals, objectives, policies, and procedures; *coordinates* their efforts; *motivates* them to sustain their enthusiasm; and *leads* them to achieve the corporate goals.

Welfare Economics

Welfare economics is that branch of economics, which primarily deals with taking of poverty, famine and distribution of wealth in an economy. This is also called *Development Economics.* The central focus of welfare economics is to assess how well things are going for the members of the society. If certain things have gone terribly bad in some situation, it is necessary to explain why things have gone wrong. Prof. Amartya Sen was awarded the Nobel Prize in Economics in 1998 in recognition of his contributions to welfare economics. Prof. Sen gained recognition for his studies of the 1974 famine in Bangladesh. His work has challenged the common view that food shortage is the major cause of famine.

In the words of Prof. Sen, famines can occur even when the food supply is high but people cannot buy the food because they don't have money. There has never been a famine in a democratic country because leaders of those nations are spurred into action by politics and free media. In undemocratic countries, the rulers are unaffected by famine and there is no one to hold them accountable, even when millions die.

Welfare economics takes care of what managerial economics tends to ignore. In other words, the growth for an economic growth with societal upliftment is countered productive. In times of crisis, what comes to the rescue of people is their won literacy, public health facilities, a system of food distribution, stable democracy, social safety, (that is, systems or policies that take care of people when things go wrong for one reason or other).

MANAGERIAL ECONOMICS

Managerial Economics as a subject gained popularity in USA after the publication of the book "Managerial Economics" by Joel Dean in 1951. Managerial Economics refers to the firm's decision making process. It could be also interpreted as "Economics of Management" or "Economics of Management". Managerial Economics is also called as "Industrial Economics" or "Business Economics". As Joel Dean observes managerial economics shows how economic analysis can be used in formulating polices.

Meaning & Definition

In the words of E. F. Brigham and J. L. Pappas Managerial Economics is "the applications of economics theory and methodology to business administration practice". Managerial Economics bridges the gap between traditional economics theory and real business practices in two days.

First it provides a number of tools and techniques to enable the manager to become more competent to take decisions in real and practical situations. Secondly it serves as an integrating course to show the interaction between various areas in which the firm operates.

C. I. Savage & T. R. Small therefore believes that managerial economics "is concerned with business efficiency".

M. H. Spencer and Louis Siegelman explain the "Managerial Economics is the integration of economic theory with business practice for the purpose of facilitating decision making and forward planning by management".

It is clear, therefore, that managerial economics deals with economic aspects of managerial decisions of with those managerial decisions, which have an economics contest. Managerial economics may therefore, be defined as a body of knowledge, techniques and practices which give substance to those economic concepts which are useful in deciding the business strategy of a unit of management.

Managerial economics is designed to provide a rigorous treatment of those aspects of economic theory and analysis that are most use for managerial decision analysis says J. L. Pappas and E. F. Brigham.

Managerial Economics, therefore, focuses on those tools and techniques, which are useful in decision-making.

NATURE OF MANAGERIAL ECONOMICS

Managerial economics is, perhaps, the youngest of all the social sciences. Since it originates from Economics, it has the basis features of economics, such as assuming that other things remaining the same (or the Latin equivalent ceteris paribus). This assumption is made to simplify the complexity of the managerial phenomenon under study in a dynamic business environment so many things are changing simultaneously. This set a limitation that we cannot really hold other things remaining the same. In such a case, the observations made out of such a study will have a limited purpose or value. Managerial economics also has inherited this problem from economics.

Further, it is assumed that the firm or the buyer acts in a rational manner (which normally does not happen). The buyer is carried away by the advertisements, brand loyalties, incentives and so on, and, therefore, the innate behaviour of the consumer will be rational is not a realistic assumption. Unfortunately, there are no other alternatives to understand the subject other than by making such assumptions. This is because the behaviour of a firm or a consumer is a complex phenomenon.

The other features of managerial economics are explained as below:

(a) *Close to microeconomics*: Managerial economics is concerned with finding the solutions for different managerial problems of a particular firm. Thus, it is more close to microeconomics.

(b) *Operates against the backdrop of macroeconomics*: The macroeconomics conditions of the economy are also seen as limiting factors for the firm to operate. In other words, the managerial economist has to be aware of the limits set by the macroeconomics conditions such as government industrial policy, inflation and so on.

(c) *Normative statements*: A normative statement usually includes or implies the words 'ought' or 'should'. They reflect people's moral attitudes and are expressions of what a team of people ought to do. For instance, it deals with statements such as 'Government of India should open up the economy. Such statement are based on value judgments and express views of what is 'good' or 'bad', 'right' or ' wrong'. One problem with normative statements is that they cannot to verify by looking at the facts, because they mostly deal with the future. Disagreements about such statements are usually settled by voting on them.

(d) *Prescriptive actions*: Prescriptive action is goal oriented. Given a problem and the objectives of the firm, it suggests the course of action from the available alternatives for optimal solution. If does not merely mention the concept, it also explains whether the concept can be applied in a given context on not. For instance, the fact that variable costs are marginal costs can be used to judge the feasibility of an export order.

(e) *Applied in nature*: 'Models' are built to reflect the real life complex business situations and these models are of immense help to managers for decision-making. The different areas where models are extensively used include inventory control, optimization, project management etc. In managerial economics, we also employ case study methods to conceptualize the problem, identify that alternative and determine the best course of action.

(f) *Offers scope to evaluate each alternative*: Managerial economics provides an opportunity to evaluate each alternative in terms of its costs and revenue. The managerial economist can decide which is the better alternative to maximize the profits for the firm.

(g) *Interdisciplinary*: The contents, tools and techniques of managerial economics are drawn from different subjects such as economics, management, mathematics, statistics, accountancy, psychology, organizational behavior, sociology and etc.

(h) *Assumptions and limitations*: Every concept and theory of managerial economics is based on certain assumption and as such their validity is not universal. Where there is change in assumptions, the theory may not hold good at all.

SCOPE OF MANAGERIAL ECONOMICS

The scope of managerial economics refers to its area of study. Managerial economics refers to its area of study. Managerial economics, Provides management with a strategic planning tool that can be used to get a clear perspective of the way the business world works and what can be done to maintain profitability in an ever-changing environment. Managerial economics is primarily concerned with the application of economic principles and theories to five types of resource decisions made by all types of business organizations.

a. The selection of product or service to be produced.

b. The choice of production methods and resource combinations.

c. The determination of the best price and quantity combination

d. Promotional strategy and activities.

e. The selection of the location from which to produce and sell goods or service to consumer.

The production department, marketing and sales department and the finance department usually handle these five types of decisions. The scope of managerial economics covers two areas of decision making

a. Operational or Internal issues

b. Environmental or External issues.

Operational Issues

Operational issues refer to those, which wise within the business organization and they are under the control of the management. Those are:

1. Theory of demand and Demand Forecasting
2. Pricing and Competitive strategy
3. Production cost analysis
4. Resource allocation
5. Profit analysis
6. Capital or Investment analysis
7. Strategic planning.

Demand Analyses and Forecasting

A firm can survive only if it is able to the demand for its product at the right time, within the right quantity. Understanding the basic concepts of demand is essential for demand forecasting. Demand analysis should be a basic activity of the firm because many of the other activities of the firms depend upon the outcome of the demand fore cost. Demand analysis provides:

1. The basis for analyzing market influences on the firms; products and thus helps in the adaptation to those influences.
2. Demand analysis also highlights for factors, which influence the demand for a product. This helps to manipulate demand. Thus demand analysis studies not only the price elasticity but also income elasticity, cross elasticity as well as the influence of advertising expenditure with the advent of computers, demand forecasting has become an increasingly important function of managerial economics.

Pricing and competitive strategy

Pricing decisions have been always within the preview of managerial economics. Pricing policies are merely a subset of broader class of managerial economic problems. Price theory helps to explain how prices are determined under different types of market conditions. Competitions analysis includes the anticipation of the response of competitions the firm's pricing, advertising and marketing strategies. Product line pricing and price forecasting occupy an important place here.

Production and cost analysis

Production analysis is in physical terms. While the cost analysis is in monetary terms cost concepts and classifications, cost-out-put relationships, economies and diseconomies of scale and production functions are some of the points constituting cost and production analysis.

Resource Allocation

Managerial Economics is the traditional economic theory that is concerned with the problem of optimum allocation of scarce resources. Marginal analysis is applied to the problem of determining the level of output, which maximizes profit. In this respect linear programming techniques has been used to solve optimization problems. In fact lines programming is one of the most practical and powerful managerial decision making tools currently available.

Profit analysis

Profit making is the major goal of firms. There are several constraints here an account of competition from other products, changing input prices and changing business environment hence in spite of careful planning, there is always certain risk involved. Managerial economics deals with techniques of averting of minimizing risks. Profit theory guides in the measurement and management of profit, in calculating the pure return on capital, besides future profit planning.

Capital or investment analyses

Capital is the foundation of business. Lack of capital may result in small size of operations. Availability of capital from various sources like equity capital, institutional finance etc. may help to undertake large-scale operations. Hence efficient allocation and management of capital is one of the most important tasks of the managers. The major issues related to capital analysis are:

1. The choice of investment project
2. Evaluation of the efficiency of capital
3. Most efficient allocation of capital.

Knowledge of capital theory can help very much in taking investment decisions. This involves, capital budgeting, feasibility studies, analysis of cost of capital etc.

Strategic planning

Strategic planning provides management with a framework on which long-term decisions can be made which has an impact on the behavior of the firm. The firm sets certain long-term goals and objectives and selects the strategies to achieve the same. Strategic planning is now a new addition to the scope of managerial economics with the emergence of multinational corporations. The perspective of strategic planning is global.

It is in contrast to project planning which focuses on a specific project or activity. In fact the integration of managerial economics and strategic planning has given rise to be new area of study called corporate economics.

ENVIRONMENTAL OR EXTERNAL ISSUES

An environmental issue in managerial economics refers to the general business environment in which the firm operates. They refer to general economic, social and political atmosphere within which the firm operates. A study of economic environment should include:

a. The type of economic system in the country.
b. The general trends in production, employment, income, prices, saving and investment.
c. Trends in the working of financial institutions like banks, financial corporations, insurance companies
d. Magnitude and trends in foreign trade;
e. Trends in labour and capital markets;
f. Government's economic policies viz. industrial policy monetary policy, fiscal policy, price policy etc.

The social environment refers to social structure as well as social organization like trade unions, consumer's co-operative etc. The Political environment refers to the nature of state activity, chiefly states' attitude towards private business, political stability etc.

The environmental issues highlight the social objective of a firm i.e.; the firm owes a responsibility to the society. Private gains of the firm alone cannot be the goal.

The environmental or external issues relate managerial economics to macro economic theory while operational issues relate the scope to micro economic theory. The scope of managerial economics is ever widening with the dynamic role of big firms in a society.

MANAGERIAL ECONOMICS RELATIONSHIP WITH OTHER DISCIPLINES

Many new subjects have evolved in recent years due to the interaction among basic disciplines. While there are many such new subjects in natural and social sciences, managerial economics can be taken as the best example of such a phenomenon among social sciences. Hence it is necessary to trace its roots and relation ship with other disciplines.

Relationship with economics

The relationship between managerial economics and economics theory may be viewed form the point of view of the two approaches to the subject Viz. Micro Economics and Marco Economics. Microeconomics is the study of the economic behavior of individuals, firms and other such micro organizations. Managerial economics is rooted in Micro Economic theory. Managerial Economics makes use to several Micro Economic concepts such as marginal cost, marginal revenue, elasticity of demand as well as price theory and theories of market structure to name only a few. Macro theory on the other hand is the study of the economy as a whole. It deals with the analysis of national income, the level of employment, general price level, consumption and investment in the economy and even matters related to international trade, Money, public finance, etc.

The relationship between managerial economics and economics theory is like that of engineering science to physics or of medicine to biology. Managerial economics has an applied bias and its wider scope lies in applying economic theory to solve real life problems of enterprises. Both managerial economics and economics deal with problems of scarcity and resource allocation.

Management theory and accounting

Managerial economics has been influenced by the developments in management theory and accounting techniques. Accounting refers to the recording of pecuniary transactions of the firm in certain books.

A proper knowledge of accounting techniques is very essential for the success of the firm because profit maximization is the major objective of the firm.

Managerial Economics requires a proper knowledge of cost and revenue information and their classification. A student of managerial economics should be familiar with the generation, interpretation and use of accounting data. The focus of accounting within the firm is fast changing from the concepts of store keeping to that if managerial decision making, this has resulted in a new specialized area of study called "Managerial Accounting".

Managerial Economics and mathematics

The use of mathematics is significant for managerial economics in view of its profit maximization goal long with optional use of resources. The major problem of the firm is how to minimize cost, hoe to maximize profit or how to optimize sales. Mathematical concepts and techniques are widely used in economic logic to solve these problems. Also mathematical methods help to estimate and predict the economic factors for decision making and forward planning.

Mathematical symbols are more convenient to handle and understand various concepts like incremental cost, elasticity of demand etc., Geometry, Algebra and calculus are the major branches of mathematics which are of use in managerial economics. The main concepts of mathematics like logarithms, and exponentials, vectors and determinants, input-output models etc., are widely used. Besides these usual tools, more advanced techniques designed in the recent years viz. linear programming, inventory models and game theory fine wide application in managerial economics.

Managerial Economics and Statistics

Managerial Economics needs the tools of statistics in more than one way. A successful businessman must correctly estimate the demand for his product.

He should be able to analyses the impact of variations in tastes. Fashion and changes in income on demand only then he can adjust his output. Statistical methods provide and sure base for decision-making. Thus statistical tools are used in collecting data and analyzing them to help in the decision making process.

Statistical tools like the theory of probability and forecasting techniques help the firm to predict the future course of events. Managerial Economics also make use of correlation and multiple regressions in related variables like price and demand to estimate the extent of dependence of one variable on the other. The theory of probability is very useful in problems involving uncertainty.

Managerial Economics and Operations Research

Taking effectives decisions is the major concern of both managerial economics and operations research. The development of techniques and concepts such as linear programming, inventory models and game theory is due to the development of this new subject of operations research in the postwar years. Operations research is concerned with the complex problems arising out of the management of men, machines, materials and money.

Operation research provides a scientific model of the system and it helps managerial economists in the field of product development, material management, and inventory control, quality control, marketing and demand analysis. The varied tools of operations Research are helpful to managerial economists in decision-making.

Managerial Economics and the theory of Decision- making

The Theory of decision-making is a new field of knowledge grown in the second half of this century. Most of the economic theories explain a single goal for the consumer i.e., Profit maximization for the firm. But the theory of decision-making is developed to explain multiplicity of goals and lot of uncertainty.

As such this new branch of knowledge is useful to business firms, which have to take quick decision in the case of multiple goals. Viewed this way the theory of decision making is more practical and application oriented than the economic theories.

Managerial Economics and Computer Science

Computers have changes the way of the world functions and economic or business activity is no exception. Computers are used in data and accounts maintenance, inventory and stock controls and supply and demand predictions. What used to take days and months is done in a few minutes or hours by the computers. In fact computerization of business activities on a large scale has reduced the workload of managerial personnel. In most countries a basic knowledge of computer science, is a compulsory programme for managerial trainees.

To conclude, managerial economics, which is an offshoot traditional economics, has gained strength to be a separate branch of knowledge. It strength lies in its ability to integrate ideas from various specialized subjects to gain a proper perspective for decision-making.

A successful managerial economist must be a mathematician, a statistician and an economist. He must be also able to combine philosophic methods with historical methods to get the right perspective only then; he will be good at predictions. In short managerial practices with the help of other allied sciences.

THE ROLE OF MANAGERIAL ECONOMIST

Making decisions and processing information are the two primary tasks of the managers. Managerial economists have gained importance in recent years with the emergence of an organizational culture in production and sales activities.

A management economist with sound knowledge of theory and analytical tools for information system occupies a prestigious place among the personnel. A managerial economist is nearer to the policy-making. Equipped with specialized skills and modern techniques he analyses the internal and external operations of the firm. He evaluates and helps in decision making regarding sales, Pricing financial issues, labour relations and profitability. He helps in decision-making keeping in view the different goals of the firm.

His role in decision-making applies to routine affairs such as price fixation, improvement in quality, Location of plant, expansion or contraction of output etc. The role of managerial economist in internal management covers wide areas of production, sales and inventory schedules of the firm.

The most important role of the managerial economist relates to demand forecasting because an analysis of general business conditions is most vital for the success of the firm. He prepares a short-term forecast of general business activity and relates general economic forecasts to specific market trends.

Most firms require two forecasts one covering the short term (for nest three months to one year) and the other covering the long term, which represents any period exceeding one-year. He has to be ever alert to gauge the changes in tastes and preferences of the consumers.

He should evaluate the market potential. The need to know forecasting techniques on the part of the managerial economics means, he should be adept at market research. The purpose of market research is to provide a firm with information about current market position as well as present and possible future trends in the industry. A managerial economist who is well equipped with this knowledge can help the firm to plan product improvement, new product policy, pricing, and sales promotion strategy.

The fourth function of the managerial economist is to undertake an economic analysis of the industry. This is concerned with project evaluation and feasibility study at the firm level i.e., he should be able to judge on the basis of cost benefit analysis, whether it is advisable and profitable to go ahead with the project.

The managerial economist should be adept at investment appraisal methods. At the external level, economic analysis involves the knowledge of competition involved, possibility of internal and foreign sales, the general business climate etc.

• Another function is security management analysis. This is very important in the case of defense-oriented industries, power projects, and nuclear plants where security is very essential. Security management means, also that the production and trade secrets concerning technology, quality and other such related facts should not be leaked out to others. This security is more necessary in strategic and defense-oriented projects of national importance; a managerial economist should be able to manage these issues of security management analysis.

The sixth function is an advisory function. Here his advice is required on all matters of production and trade. In the hierarchy of management, a managerial economist ranks next to the top executives or the policy maker who may be doyens of several projects. It is the managerial economist of each firm who has to advise them on all matters of trade since they are in the know of actual functioning of the unit in all aspects, both technical and financial.

Another function of importance for the managerial economist is a concerned with pricing and related problems. The success of the firm depends upon a proper pricing strategy. The pricing decision is one of the most difficult decisions to be made in business because the information required is never fully available. Pricing of established products is different from new products.

He may have to operate in an atmosphere constrained by government regulation. He may have to anticipate the reactions of competitors in pricing. The managerial economist has to be very alert and dynamic to take correct pricing decision in changing environment.

Finally the specific function of a managerial economist includes an analysis of environment issues. Modern theory of managerial economics recognizes the social responsibility of the firm. It refers to the impact of a firm on environmental factors. It should not have adverse impact on pollution and if possible try to contribute to environmental preservation and protection in a positive way.

The role of management economist lies not in taking decision but in analyzing, concluding and recommending to the policy maker. He should have the freedom to operate and analyze and must possess full knowledge of facts. He has to collect and provide the quantitative data from within the firm. He has to get information on external business environment such as general market conditions, trade cycles, and behavior pattern of the consumers. The managerial economist helps to co-ordinate policies relating to production, investment, inventories and price.

He should have equanimity to meet crisis. He should act only after analysis and discussion with relevant departments. He should have diplomacy to act in advisory capacity to the top executive as well as getting co-operation from different departments for his economic analysis. He should do well to have intuitive ability to know what is good or bad for the firm.

He should have sound theoretical knowledge to take up the challenges he has to face in actual day to day affairs. "BANMOL" referring to the role of managerial economist points out. "A managerial economist can become a for more helpful member of a management group by virtue of studies of economic analysis, primarily because there he learns to become an effective model builder and because there he acquires a very rich body of tools and techniques which can help to deal with the problems of the firm in a far more rigorous, a far more probing and a far deeper manner".

2

Demand Analysis

INTRODUCTION & MEANING:

Demand in common parlance means the desire for an object. But in economics demand is something more than this. According to Stonier and Hague, "Demand in economics means demand backed up by enough money to pay for the goods demanded". This means that the demand becomes effective only it if is backed by the purchasing power in addition to this there must be willingness to buy a commodity.

Thus demand in economics means the desire backed by the willingness to buy a commodity and the purchasing power to pay. In the words of "Benham" "The demand for anything at a given price is the amount of it which will be bought per unit of time at that Price". (Thus demand is always at a price for a definite quantity at a specified time.) Thus demand has three essentials - price, quantity demanded and time. Without these, demand has to significance in economics.

LAW of Demand

Law of demand shows the relation between price and quantity demanded of a commodity in the market. In the words of Marshall, "the amount demand increases with a fall in price and diminishes with a rise in price".

A rise in the price of a commodity is followed by a reduction in demand and a fall in price is followed by an increase in demand, if a condition of demand remains constant.

The law of demand may be explained with the help of the following demand schedule.

Demand Schedule.

Price of Appel (In. Rs.)	*Quantity Demanded*
10	1
8	2
6	3
4	4
2	5

When the price falls from Rs. 10 to 8 quantity demand increases from 1 to 2. In the same way as price falls, quantity demand increases on the basis of the demand schedule we can draw the demand curve.

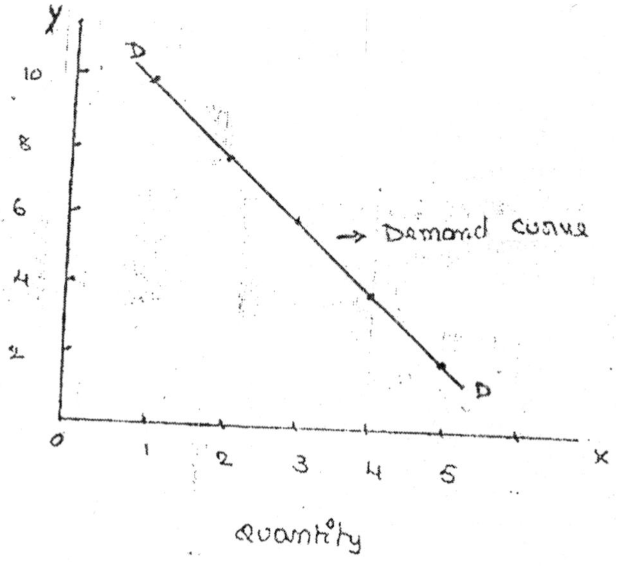

PRICE

The demand curve DD shows the inverse relation between price and quantity demand of apple. It is downward sloping.

Assumptions

Law is demand is based on certain assumptions:

1. This is no change in consumers taste and preferences.
2. Income should remain constant.

3. Prices of other goods should not change.
4. There should be no substitute for the commodity
5. The commodity should not confer at any distinction
6. The demand for the commodity should be continuous
7. People should not expect any change in the price of the commodity

Exceptional demand curve

Some times the demand curve slopes upwards from left to right. In this case the demand curve has a positive slope.

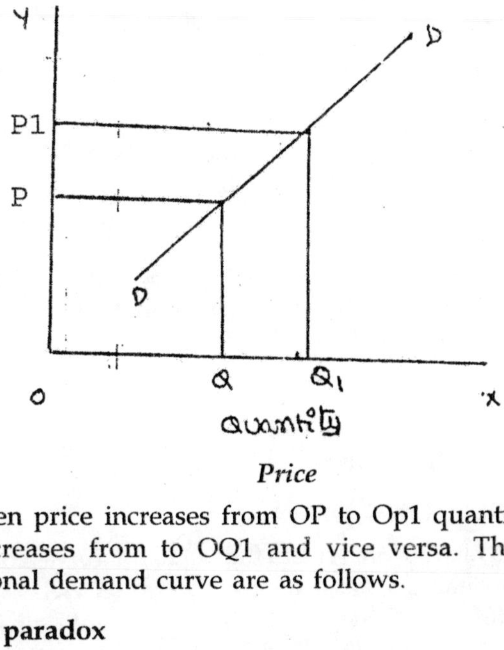

Price

When price increases from OP to Op1 quantity demanded also increases from to OQ1 and vice versa. The reasons for exceptional demand curve are as follows.

Giffen paradox

The Giffen good or inferior good is an exception to the law of demand. When the price of an inferior good falls, the poor will buy less and vice versa. For example, when the price of maize falls, the poor are willing to spend more on superior goods than on maize if the price of maize increases, he has to increase the quantity of money spent on it. Otherwise he will have to face starvation. Thus a fall in price is followed by reduction in quantity demanded and vice versa. "Giffen" first explained this and therefore it is called as Giffen's paradox.

Veblen or Demonstration effect

'Veblan' has explained the exceptional demand curve through his doctrine of conspicuous consumption. Rich people buy certain good because it gives social distinction or prestige for example diamonds are bought by the richer class for the prestige it possess. It the price of diamonds falls poor also will buy is hence they will not give prestige. Therefore, rich people may stop buying this commodity.

Ignorance

Sometimes, the quality of the commodity is Judge by its price. Consumers think that the product is superior if the price is high. As such they buy more at a higher price.

Speculative effect

If the price of the commodity is increasing the consumers will buy more of it because of the fear that it increase still further, Thus, an increase in price may not be accomplished by a decrease in demand.

Fear of shortage

During the times of emergency of war People may expect shortage of a commodity. At that time, they may buy more at a higher price to keep stocks for the future.

Necessaries

In the case of necessaries like rice, vegetables etc. people buy more even at a higher price.

FACTORS AFFECTING DEMAND

There are factors on which the demand for a commodity depends. These factors are economic, social as well as political factors. The effect of all the factors on the amount demanded for the commodity is called Demand Function.

These factors are as follows:

Price of the Commodity: The most important factor-affecting amount demanded is the price of the commodity. The amount of a commodity demanded at a particular price is more properly called price demand. The relation between price and demand is called the Law of Demand. It is not only the existing price but also the expected changes in price, which affect demand.

Income of the Consumer: The second most important factor influencing demand is consumer income. In fact, we can establish a relation between the consumer income and the demand at different levels of income, price and other things remaining the same. The demand for a normal commodity goes up when income rises and falls down when income falls. But in case of Giffen goods the relationship is the opposite.

Prices of related goods: The demand for a commodity is also affected by the changes in prices of the related goods also. Related goods can be of two types:

(i) Substitutes which can replace each other in use; for example, tea and coffee are substitutes. The change in price of a substitute has effect on a commodity's demand in the same direction in which price changes. The rise in price of coffee shall raise the demand for tea;

(ii) Complementary foods are those which are jointly demanded, such as pen and ink. In such cases complementary goods have opposite relationship between price of one commodity and the amount demanded for the other. If the price of pens goes up, their demand is less as a result of which the demand for ink is also less. The price and demand go in opposite direction. The effect of changes in price of a commodity on amounts demanded of related commodities is called Cross Demand.

Tastes of the Consumers: The amount demanded also depends on consumer's taste. Tastes include fashion, habit, customs, etc. A consumer's taste is also affected by advertisement. If the taste for a commodity goes up, its amount demanded is more even at the same price. This is called increase in demand. The opposite is called decrease in demand.

Wealth: The amount demanded of commodity is also affected by the amount of wealth as well as its distribution. The wealthier are the people; higher is the demand for normal commodities. If wealth is more equally distributed, the demand for necessaries and comforts is more. On the other hand, if some people are rich, while the majorities are poor, the demand for luxuries is generally higher.

Population: Increase in population increases demand for necessaries of life. The composition of population also affects demand. Composition of population means the proportion of young and old and children as well as the ratio of men to women. A change in composition of population has an effect on the nature of demand for different commodities.

Government Policy: Government policy affects the demands for commodities through taxation. Taxing a commodity increases its price and the demand goes down. Similarly, financial help from the government increases the demand for a commodity while lowering its price.

Expectations regarding the future

If consumers expect changes in price of commodity in future, they will change the demand at present even when the present price remains the same. Similarly, if consumers expect their incomes to rise in the near future they may increase the demand for a commodity just now.

Climate and weather: The climate of an area and the weather prevailing there has a decisive effect on consumer's demand. In cold areas woolen cloth is demanded. During hot summer days, ice is very much in demand. On a rainy day, ice cream is not so much demanded.

State of business: The level of demand for different commodities also depends upon the business conditions in the country. If the country is passing through boom conditions, there will be a marked increase in demand. On the other hand, the level of demand goes down during depression.

3

Elasticity of Demand

Elasticity of demand explains the relationship between a change in price and consequent change in amount demanded. "Marshall" introduced the concept of elasticity of demand. Elasticity of demand shows the extent of change in quantity demanded to a change in price.

In the words of "Marshall", "The elasticity of demand in a market is great or small according as the amount demanded increases much or little for a given fall in the price and diminishes much or little for a given rise in Price"

Elastic demand: A small change in price may lead to a great change in quantity demanded. In this case, demand is elastic.

In-elastic demand: If a big change in price is followed by a small change in demanded then the demand in "inelastic".

TYPES OF ELASTICITY OF DEMAND:

There are three types of elasticity of demand:

1. Price elasticity of demand
2. Income elasticity of demand
3. Cross elasticity of demand.

Price elasticity of demand

Marshall was the first economist to define price elasticity of demand. Price elasticity of demand measures changes in quantity demand to a change in Price. It is the ratio of percentage change in quantity demanded to a percentage change in price.

$$\text{Price elasticity} = \frac{\text{Proportionate change in the quantity demand of commodity}}{\text{Proportionate change in the price of commodity}}$$

There are five cases of price elasticity of demand:

A. ***Perfectly elastic demand:*** When small change in price leads to an infinitely large change is quantity demand, it is called perfectly or infinitely elastic demand. In this case E="

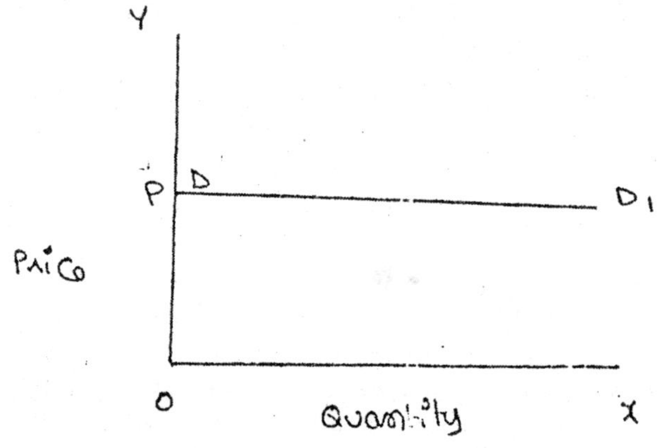

The demand curve DD1 is horizontal straight line. It shows the at "OP" price any amount is demand and if price increases, the consumer will not purchase the commodity.

B. ***Perfectly Inelastic Demand*** **:** In this case, even a large change in price fails to bring about a change in quantity demanded.

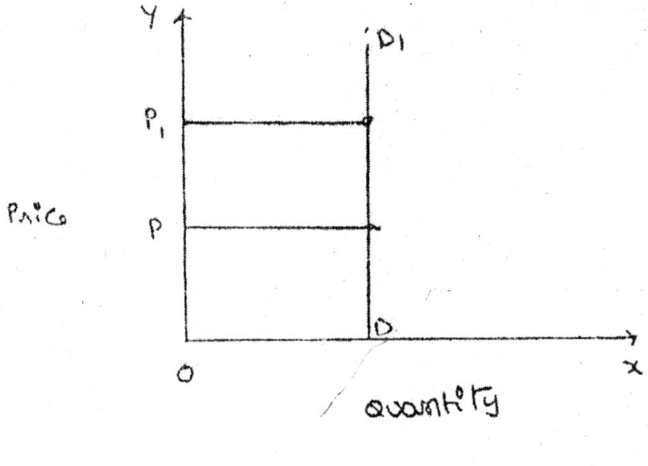

When price increases from 'OP' to 'OP', the quantity demanded remains the same. In other words the response of demand to a change in Price is nil. In this case 'E'=0.

C. Relatively elastic demand: Demand changes more than proportionately to a change in price. i.e. a small change in price loads to a very big change in the quantity demanded. In this case

E > 1. This demand curve will be flatter.

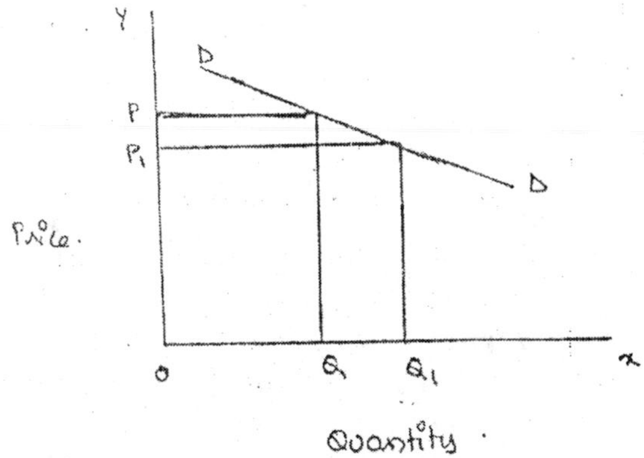

When price falls from 'OP' to 'OP', amount demanded in crease from "OQ' to "OQ1' which is larger than the change in price.

D. Relatively in-elastic demand. Quantity demanded changes less than proportional to a change in price. A large change in price leads to small change in amount demanded. Here E < 1. Demanded carve will be steeper.

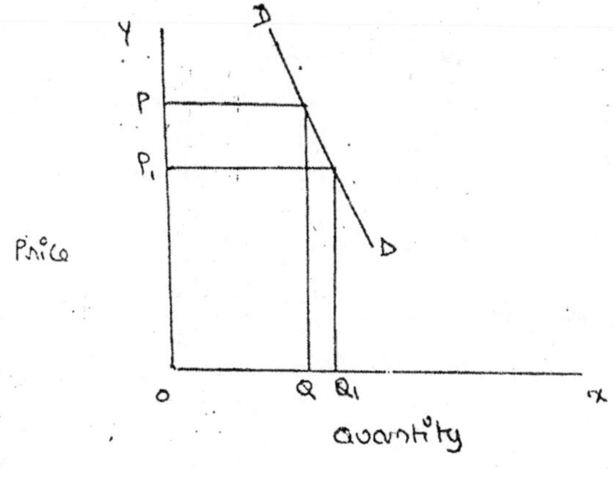

When price falls from "OP' to 'OP1 amount demanded increases from OQ to OQ1, which is smaller than the change in price.

E. Unit elasticity of demand: The change in demand is exactly equal to the change in price. When both are equal E=1 and elasticity if said to be unitary.

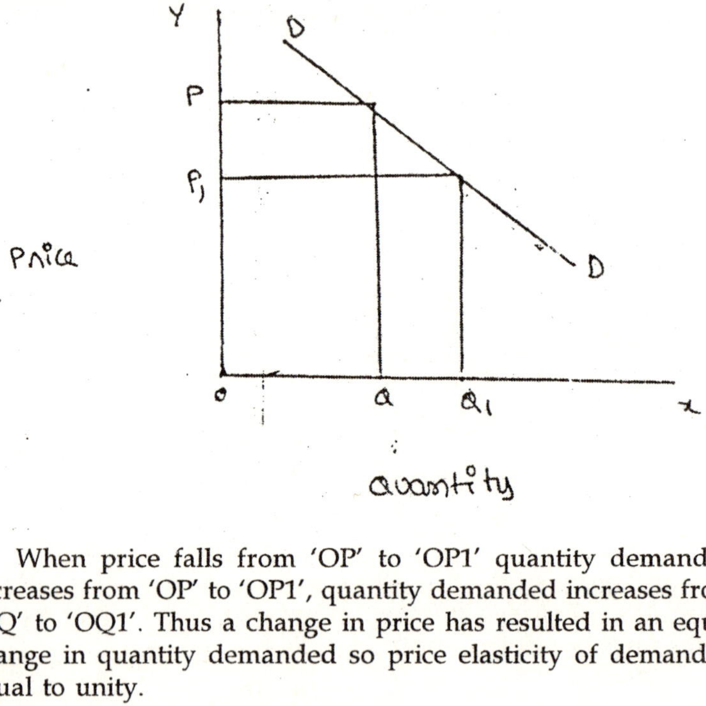

When price falls from 'OP' to 'OP1' quantity demanded increases from 'OP' to 'OP1', quantity demanded increases from 'OQ' to 'OQ1'. Thus a change in price has resulted in an equal change in quantity demanded so price elasticity of demand is equal to unity.

Income elasticity of demand:

Income elasticity of demand shows the change in quantity demanded as a result of a change in income. Income elasticity of demand may be slated in the form of a formula.

$$\text{Income Elasticity} = \frac{\text{Proportionate change in the quantity demand of commodity}}{\text{Proportionate change in the income of the people}}$$

Income elasticity of demand can be classified in to five types.

A. Zero income elasticity: Quantity demanded remains the same, even though money income increases. Symbolically, it can be expressed as Ey=0. It can be depicted in the following way:

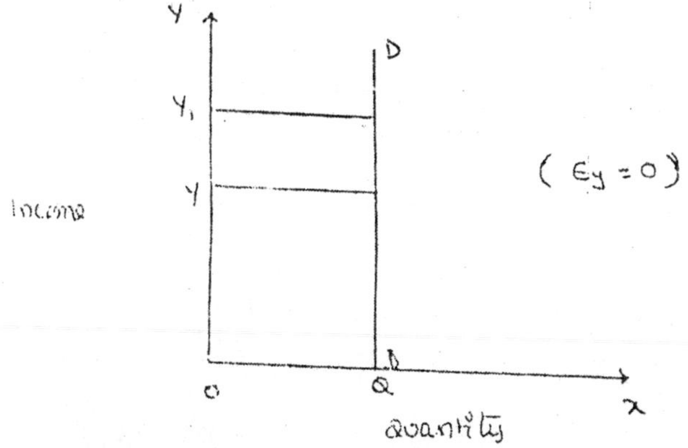

As income increases from OY to OY1, quantity demanded never changes.

B. Negative Income elasticity: When income increases, quantity demanded falls. In this case, income elasticity of demand is negative. i.e., Ey < 0.

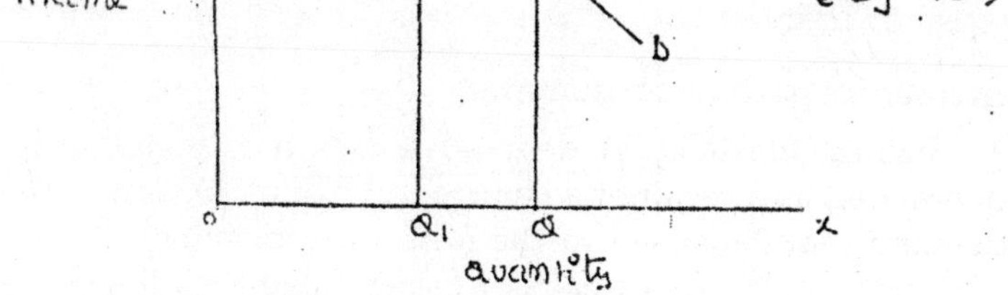

When income increases from OY to OY1, demand falls from OQ to OQ1.

c. Unit income elasticity: When an increase in income brings about a proportionate increase in quantity demanded, and then income elasticity of demand is equal to one. Ey = 1

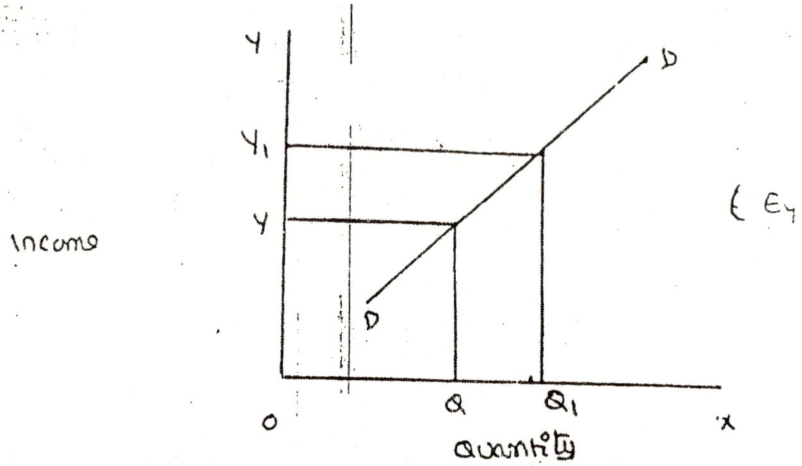

When income increases from OY to OY1, Quantity demanded also increases from OQ to OQ1.

d. Income elasticity greater than unity: In this case, an increase in come brings about a more than proportionate increase in quantity demanded. Symbolically it can be written as Ey > 1.

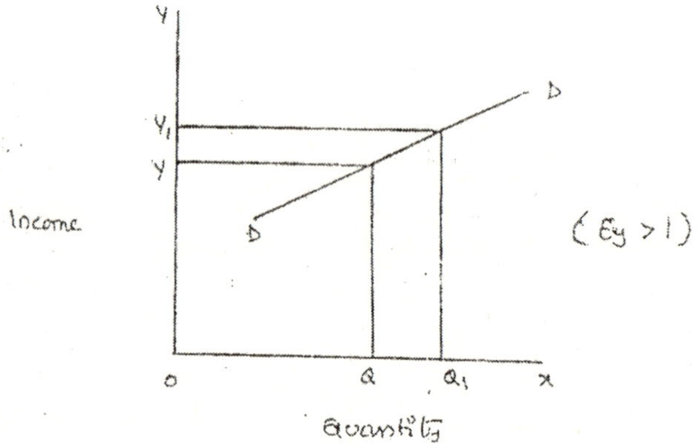

It shows high-income elasticity of demand. When income increases from OY to OY1, Quantity demanded increases from OQ to OQ1.

E. Income elasticity leas than unity: When income increases quantity demanded also increases but less than proportionately. In this case E < 1.

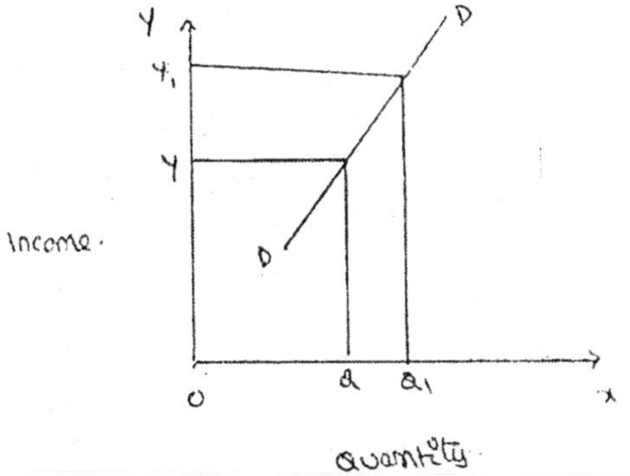

An increase in income from OY to OY, brings what an increase in quantity demanded from OQ to OQ1, But the increase in quantity demanded is smaller than the increase in income. Hence, income elasticity of demand is less than one.

Cross elasticity of Demand:

A change in the price of one commodity leads to a change in the quantity demanded of another commodity. This is called a cross elasticity of demand. The formula for cross elasticity of demand is:

$$\text{Cross elasticity} = \frac{\text{Proportionate change in the quantity demand of commodity "X"}}{\text{Proportionate change in the price of commodity "Y"}}$$

a. In case of substitutes, cross elasticity of demand is positive. Eg: Coffee and Tea. When the price of coffee increases, Quantity demanded of tea increases. Both are substitutes.

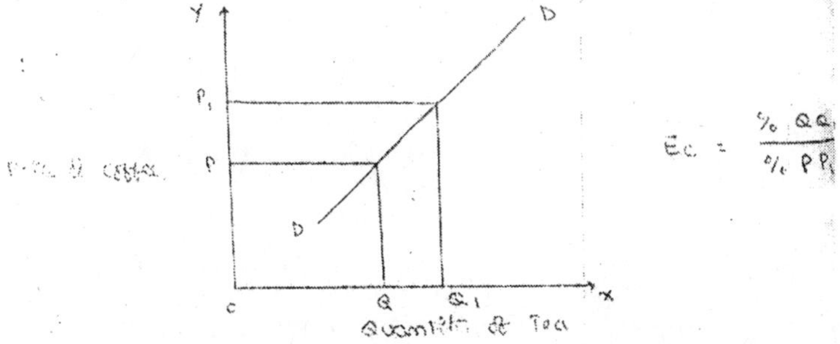

Price of Coffee

b. Incase of compliments, cross elasticity is negative. If increase in the price of one commodity leads to a decrease in the quantity demanded of another and vice versa.

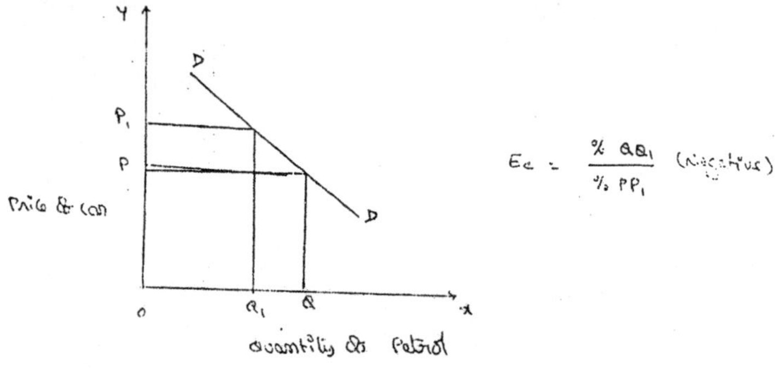

When price of car goes up from OP to OP!, the quantity demanded of petrol decreases from OQ to OQ!. The cross-demanded curve has negative slope.

c. In case of unrelated commodities, cross elasticity of demanded is zero. A change in the price of one commodity will not affect the quantity demanded of another.

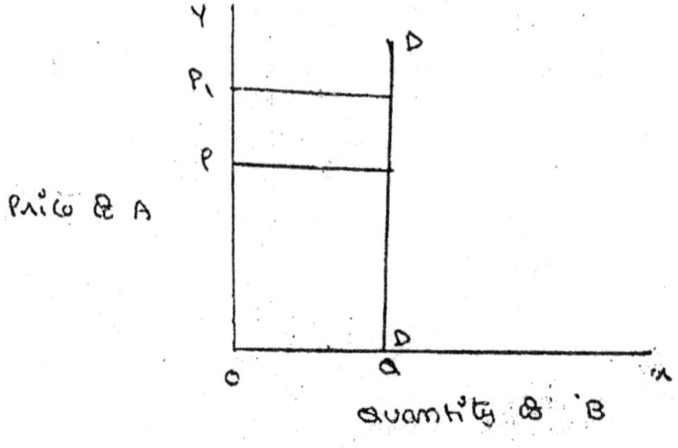

Quantity demanded of commodity "b" remains unchanged due to a change in the price of 'A', as both are unrelated goods.

FACTORS INFLUENCING THE ELASTICITY OF DEMAND

Elasticity of demand depends on many factors.

1. Nature of commodity: Elasticity or in-elasticity of demand depends on the nature of the commodity i.e. whether a commodity is a necessity, comfort or luxury, normally; the demand for Necessaries like salt, rice etc is inelastic. On the other band, the demand for comforts and luxuries is elastic.
2. Availability of substitutes: Elasticity of demand depends on availability or non-availability of substitutes. In case of commodities, which have substitutes, demand is elastic, but in case of commodities, which have no substitutes, demand is in elastic.
3. Variety of uses: If a commodity can be used for several purposes, than it will have elastic demand. i.e. electricity. On the other hand, demanded is inelastic for commodities, which can be put to only one use.
4. Postponement of demand: If the consumption of a commodity can be postponed, than it will have elastic demand. On the contrary, if the demand for a commodity cannot be postpones, than demand is in elastic. The demand for rice or medicine cannot be postponed, while the demand for Cycle or umbrella can be postponed.
5. Amount of money spent: Elasticity of demand depends on the amount of money spent on the commodity. If the consumer spends a smaller for example a consumer spends a little amount on salt and matchboxes. Even when price of salt or matchbox goes up, demanded will not fall. Therefore, demand is in case of clothing a consumer spends a large proportion of his income and an increase in price will reduce his demand for clothing. So the demand is elastic.
6. Time: Elasticity of demand varies with time. Generally, demand is inelastic during short period and elastic during the long period. Demand is inelastic during short period because the consumers do not have enough time to know about the change is price. Even if they are aware of the price change, they may not immediately switch over to a new commodity, as they are accustomed to the old commodity.

7. Range of Prices: Range of prices exerts an important influence on elasticity of demand. At a very high price, demand is inelastic because a slight fall in price will not induce the people buy more. Similarly at a low price also demand is inelastic. This is because at a low price all those who want to buy the commodity would have bought it and a further fall in price will not increase the demand. Therefore, elasticity is low at very him and very low prices.

Importance of Elasticity of Demand

The concept of elasticity of demand is of much practical importance.

1. Price fixation: Each seller under monopoly and imperfect competition has to take into account elasticity of demand while fixing the price for his product. If the demand for the product is inelastic, he can fix a higher price.
2. Production: Producers generally decide their production level on the basis of demand for the product. Hence elasticity of demand helps the producers to take correct decision regarding the level of cut put to be produced.
3. Distribution: Elasticity of demand also helps in the determination of rewards for factors of production. For example, if the demand for labour is inelastic, trade unions will be successful in raising wages. It is applicable to other factors of production.
4. International Trade: Elasticity of demand helps in finding out the terms of trade between two countries. Terms of trade refers to the rate at which domestic commodity is exchanged for foreign commodities. Terms of trade depends upon the elasticity of demand of the two countries for each other goods.
5. Public Finance: Elasticity of demand helps the government in formulating tax policies. For example, for imposing tax on a commodity, the Finance Minister has to take into account the elasticity of demand.
6. Nationalization: The concept of elasticity of demand enables the government to decide about nationalization of industries.

4

Demand Forecasting

INTRODUCTION

The information about the future is essential for both new firms and those planning to expand the scale of their production. Demand forecasting refers to an estimate of future demand for the product.

It is an 'objective assessment of the future course of demand". In recent times, forecasting plays an important role in business decision-making. Demand forecasting has an important influence on production planning. It is essential for a firm to produce the required quantities at the right time.

It is essential to distinguish between forecasts of demand and forecasts of sales. Sales forecast is important for estimating revenue cash requirements and expenses. Demand forecasts relate to production, inventory control, timing, reliability of forecast etc. However, there is not much difference between these two terms.

Types of demand Forecasting

Based on the time span and planning requirements of business firms, demand forecasting can be classified in to 1. Short-term demand forecasting and 2. Long - term demand forecasting.

Short-term demand forecasting

Short-term demand forecasting is limited to short periods, usually for one year. It relates to policies regarding sales, purchase, price and finances. It refers to existing production capacity of the firm. Short-term forecasting is essential for formulating is essential for formulating a suitable price policy. If the business people expect of rise in the prices of raw materials of shortages, they may buy early. This price forecasting helps in sale policy formulation. Production may be undertaken based on expected sales and not on actual sales. Further, demand forecasting assists in financial forecasting also. Prior information about production and sales is essential to provide additional funds on reasonable terms.

Long - term forecasting

In long-term forecasting, the businessmen should now about the long-term demand for the product. Planning of a new plant or expansion of an existing unit depends on long-term demand. Similarly a multi product firm must take into account the demand for different items. When forecast are mode covering long periods, the probability of error is high. It is vary difficult to forecast the production, the trend of prices and the nature of competition. Hence quality and competent forecasts are essential.

Prof. C. I. Savage and T.R. Small classify demand forecasting into time types. They are 1. Economic forecasting, 2. Industry forecasting, 3. Firm level forecasting. Economics forecasting is concerned with the economics, while industrial level forecasting is used for inter-industry comparisons and is being supplied by trade association or chamber of commerce. Firm level forecasting relates to individual firm.

METHODS OF FORECASTING

Several methods are employed for forecasting demand. All these methods can be grouped under survey method and statistical method. Survey methods and statistical methods are further subdivided in to different categories.

Survey Method

Under this method, information about the desires of the consumer and opinion of exports are collected by interviewing them. Survey method can be divided into four type's viz., Option survey method; expert opinion; Delphi method and consumers interview methods.

Opinion survey method

This method is also known as sales-force composite method (or) collective opinion method. Under this method, the company asks its salesman to submit estimate of future sales in their respective territories. Since the forecasts of the salesmen are biased due to their optimistic or pessimistic attitude ignorance about economic developments etc. these estimates are consolidated, reviewed and adjusted by the top executives. In case of wide differences, an average is struck to make the forecasts realistic.

This method is more useful and appropriate because the salesmen are more knowledge. They can be important source of information. They are cooperative. The implementation within unbiased or their basic can be corrected.

Expert opinion method

Apart from salesmen and consumers, distributors or outside experts may also e used for forecasting. In the United States of America, the automobile companies get sales estimates directly from their dealers. Firms in advanced countries make use of outside experts for estimating future demand. Various public and private agencies all periodic forecasts of short or long term business conditions.

Delphi Method

A variant of the survey method is Delphi method. It is a sophisticated method to arrive at a consensus. Under this method, a panel is selected to give suggestions to solve the problems in hand. Both internal and external experts can be the members of the panel.

Panel members one kept apart from each other and express their views in an anonymous manner. There is also a coordinator who acts as an intermediary among the panelists. He prepares the questionnaire and sends it to the panelist. At the end of each round, he prepares a summary report. On the basis of the summary report the panel members have to give suggestions. This method has been used in the area of technological forecasting. It has proved more popular in forecasting. It has provided more popular in forecasting non-economic rather than economic variables.

Consumers interview method

In this method the consumers are contacted personally to know about their plans and preference regarding the consumption of the product. A list of all potential buyers would be drawn and each buyer will be approached and asked how much he plans to buy the listed product in future. He would be asked the proportion in which he intends to buy. This method seems to be the most ideal method for forecasting demand.

STATISTICAL METHODS

Statistical method is used for long run forecasting. In this method, statistical and mathematical techniques are used to forecast demand. This method relies on post data.

Time series analysis or trend projection methods

A well-established firm would have accumulated data. These data are analyzed to determine the nature of existing trend. Then, this trend is projected in to the future and the results are used as the basis for forecast. This is called as time series analysis. This data can be presented either in a tabular form or a graph. In the time series post data of sales are used to forecast future.

Barometric Technique

Simple trend projections are not capable of forecasting turning paints. Under Barometric method, present events are used to predict the directions of change in future. This is done with the help of economics and statistical indicators. Those are (1) Construction Contracts awarded for building materials (2) Personal income (3) Agricultural Income. (4) Employment (5) Gross national income (6) Industrial Production (7) Bank Deposits etc.

Regression and correlation method

Regression and correlation are used for forecasting demand. Based on post data the future data trend is forecasted. If the functional relationship is analyzed with the independent variable it is simple correction. When there are several independent variables it is multiple correlation. In correlation we analyze the nature of relation between the variables while in regression; the extent of relation between the variables is analyzed. The results are expressed in mathematical form. Therefore, it is called as econometric model building. The main advantage of this method is that it provides the values of the independent variables from within the model itself.

5

Production Function

Introduction: The production function expresses a functional relationship between physical inputs and physical outputs of a firm at any particular time period. The output is thus a function of inputs. Mathematically production function can be written as

Q= f (A, B, C, D)

Where "Q" stands for the quantity of output and A, B, C, D are various input factors such as land, labour, capital and organization. Here output is the function of inputs. Hence output becomes the dependent variable and inputs are the independent variables. The above function does not state by how much the output of "Q" changes as a consequence of change of variable inputs. In order to express the quantitative relationship between inputs and output, Production function has been expressed in a precise mathematical equation i.e.

Y= a+b(x)

Which shows that there is a constant relationship between applications of input (the only factor input 'X' in this case) and the amount of output (y) produced. Importance:

1. When inputs are specified in physical units, production function helps to estimate the level of production.
2. It becomes is equates when different combinations of inputs yield the same level of output.
3. It indicates the manner in which the firm can substitute on input for another without altering the total output.
4. When price is taken into consideration, the production function helps to select the least combination of inputs for the desired output.

5. It considers two types' input-output relationships namely 'law of variable proportions' and 'law of returns to scale'. Law of variable propositions explains the pattern of output in the short-run as the units of variable inputs are increased to increase the output. On the other hand law of returns to scale explains the pattern of output in the long run as all the units of inputs are increased.
6. The production function explains the maximum quantity of output, which can be produced, from any chosen quantities of various inputs or the minimum quantities of various inputs that are required to produce a given quantity of output.

Production function can be fitted the particular firm or industry or for the economy as whole. Production function will change with an improvement in technology.

Assumptions

Production function has the following assumptions.

1. The production function is related to a particular period of time.
2. There is no change in technology.
3. The producer is using the best techniques available.
4. The factors of production are divisible.
5. Production function can be fitted to a short run or to long run.

COBB-DOUGLAS PRODUCTION FUNCTION

Production function of the linear homogenous type is invested by Junt wicksell and first tested by C. W. Cobb and P. H. Dougles in 1928. This famous statistical production function is known as Cobb-Douglas production function. Originally the function is applied on the empirical study of the American manufacturing industry. Cabb – Douglas production function takes the following mathematical form.

$Y = (AK^{X} L^{1-x})$

Where Y=output

K=Capital

L=Labour

A, "=positive constant

Assumptions

It has the following assumptions

1. The function assumes that output is the function of two factors viz. capital and labour.
2. It is a linear homogenous production function of the first degree
3. The function assumes that the logarithm of the total output of the economy is a linear function of the logarithms of the labour force and capital stock.
4. There are constant returns to scale
5. All inputs are homogenous
6. There is perfect competition
7. There is no change in technology

ISOQUANTS

The term Isoquants is derived from the words 'iso' and 'quant' – 'Iso' means equal and 'quent' implies quantity. Isoquant therefore, means equal quantity. A family of iso-product curves or isoquants or production difference curves can represent a production function with two variable inputs, which are substitutable for one another within limits.

Iqoquants are the curves, which represent the different combinations of inputs producing a particular quantity of output. Any combination on the isoquant represents the some level of output.

For a given output level firm's production become,

$Q= f (L, K)$

Where 'Q', the units of output is a function of the quantity of two inputs 'L' and 'K'.

Thus an isoquant shows all possible combinations of two inputs, which are capable of producing equal or a given level of output. Since each combination yields same output, the producer becomes indifferent towards these combinations.

Assumptions

1. There are only two factors of production, viz. labour and capital.

2. The two factors can substitute each other up to certain limit
3. The shape of the isoquant depends upon the extent of substitutability of the two inputs.
4. The technology is given over a period.

An isoquant may be explained with the help of an arithmetical example.

Combinations	*Labour (units)*	*Capital (Units)*	*Output (quintals)*
A	1	10	50
B	2	7	50
C	3	4	50
D	4	4	50
E	5	1	50

Combination 'A' represent 1 unit of labour and 10 units of capital and produces '50' quintals of a product all other combinations in the table are assumed to yield the same given output of a product say '50' quintals by employing any one of the alternative combinations of the two factors labour and capital. If we plot all these combinations on a paper and join them, we will get continues and smooth curve called Iso-product curve as shown below.

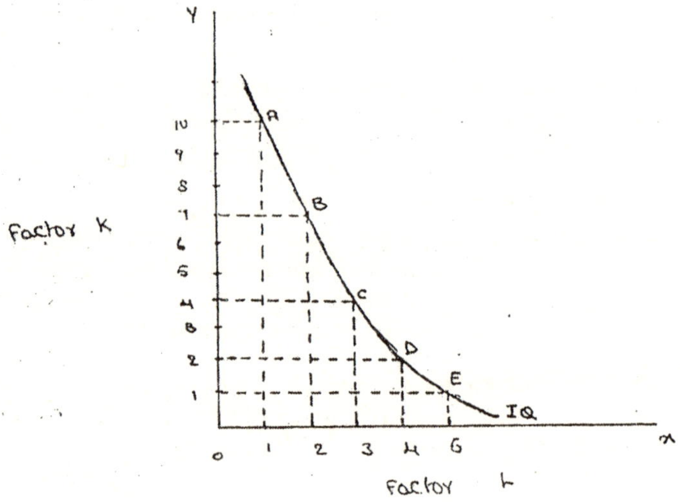

Labour is on the X-axis and capital is on the Y-axis. IQ is the ISO-Product curve which shows all the alternative combinations A, B, C, D, E which can produce 50 quintals of a product.

Producer's Equilibrium

The tem producer's equilibrium is the counter part of consumer's equilibrium. Just as the consumer is in equilibrium when be secures maximum satisfaction, in the same manner, the producer is in equilibrium when he secures maximum output, with the least cost combination of factors of production.

The optimum position of the producer can be found with the help of iso-product curve. The Iso-product curve or equal product curve or production indifference curve shows different combinations of two factors of production, which yield the same output. This is illustrated as follows.

Let us suppose. The producer can produces the given output of paddy say 100 quintals by employing any one of the following alternative combinations of the two factors labour and capital computation of least cost combination of two inputs.

It is clear from the above that 10 units of 'L' combined with 45 units of 'K' would cost the producer Rs. 20/-. But if 17 units reduce 'K' and 10 units increase 'L', the resulting cost would be Rs. 172/-. Substituting 10 more units of 'L' for 12 units of 'K' further reduces cost pf Rs. 154/-/However, it will not be profitable to continue this substitution process further at the existing prices since the rate of substitution is diminishing rapidly. In the above table the least cost combination is 30 units of 'L' used with 16 units of 'K' when the cost would be minimum at Rs. 154/-. So this is they stage "the producer is in equilibrium".

LAW OF PRODUCTION

Production analysis in economics theory considers two types of input-output relationships.

1. When quantities of certain inputs, are fixed and others are variable and
2. When all inputs are variable.

These two types of relationships have been explained in the form of laws.

i) Law of variable proportions

ii) Law of returns to scale

Law of variable proportions

The law of variable proportions which is a new name given to old classical concept of "Law of diminishing returns has played a vital role in the modern economics theory. Assume that a firms production function consists of fixed quantities of all inputs (land, equipment, etc.) except labour which is a variable input when the firm expands output by employing more and more labour it alters the proportion between fixed and the variable inputs. The law can be stated as follows:

"When total output or production of a commodity is increased by adding units of a variable input while the quantities of other inputs are held constant, the increase in total production becomes after some point, smaller and smaller".

"If equal increments of one input are added, the inputs of other production services being held constant, beyond a certain point the resulting increments of product will decrease i.e. the marginal product will diminish". (G. Stigler)

"As the proportion of one factor in a combination of factors is increased, after a point, first the marginal and then the average product of that factor will diminish". (F. Benham)

The law of variable proportions refers to the behaviour of output as the quantity of one Factor is increased Keeping the quantity of other factors fixed and further it states that the marginal product and average product will eventually do cline. This law states three types of productivity an input factor - Total, average and marginal physical productivity.

Assumptions of the Law: The law is based upon the following assumptions:

i) The state of technology remains constant. If there is any improvement in technology, the average and marginal out put will not decrease but increase.

ii) Only one factor of input is made variable and other factors are kept constant. This law does not apply to those cases where the factors must be used in rigidly fixed proportions.

iii) All units of the variable factors are homogenous.

Three stages of law

The behaviors of the Output when the varying quantity of one factor is combines with a fixed quantity of the other can be divided in to three district stages. Total product is maximum when the farmer employs 6th worker, nothing is produced by the 7th worker and its marginal productivity is zero, whereas marginal product of 8th worker is '-10', by just creating credits 8th worker not only fails to make a positive contribution but leads to a fall in the total output.

Production function with one variable input and the remaining fixed inputs is illustrated as below

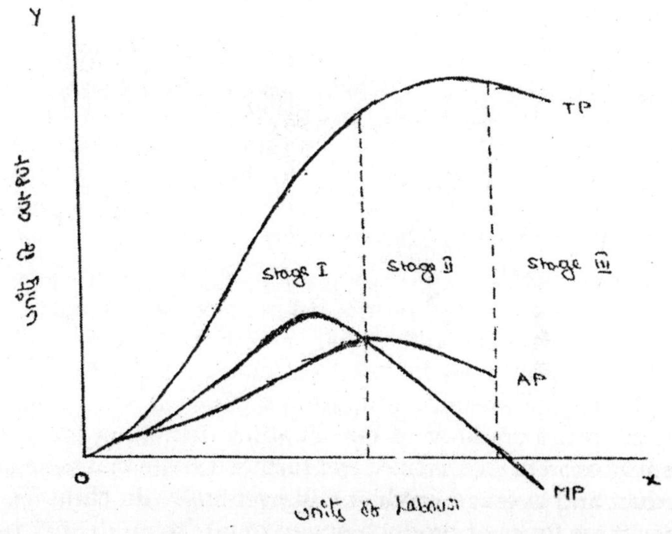

From the above graph the law of variable proportions operates in three stages. In the first stage, total product increases at an increasing rate. The marginal product in this stage increases at an increasing rate resulting in a greater increase in total product. The average product also increases. This stage continues up to the point where average product is equal to marginal product. The law of increasing returns is in operation at this stage. The law of diminishing returns starts operating from the second stage awards. At the second stage total product increases only at a diminishing rate. The average product also declines. The second stage comes to an end where total product becomes maximum and marginal product becomes zero. The marginal product becomes negative in the third stage. So the total product also declines. The average product continues to decline.

We can sum up the above relationship thus when 'A.P.' is rising, "M. P.' rises more than " A. P; When 'A. P." is maximum and constant, 'M. P.' becomes equal to 'A. P.' when 'A. P.' starts falling, 'M. P.' falls faster than ' A. P.'.

Thus, the total product, marginal product and average product pass through three phases, viz., increasing diminishing and negative returns stage. The law of variable proportion is nothing but the combination of the law of increasing and demising returns.

LAW OF RETURNS OF SCALE

The law of returns to scale explains the behavior of the total output in response to change in the scale of the firm, i.e., in response to a simultaneous to changes in the scale of the firm, i.e., in response to a simultaneous and proportional increase in all the inputs. More precisely, the Law of returns to scale explains how a simultaneous and proportionate increase in all the inputs affects the total output at its various levels.

The concept of variable proportions is a short-run phenomenon as in these period fixed factors can not be changed and all factors cannot be changed. On the other hand in the long-term all factors can be changed as made variable. When we study the changes in output when all factors or inputs are changed, we study returns to scale. An increase in the scale means that all inputs or factors are increased in the same proportion. In variable proportions, the cooperating factors may be increased or decreased and one faster (Ex. Land in agriculture (or) machinery in industry) remains constant so that the changes in proportion among the factors result in certain changes in output. In returns to scale all the necessary factors or production are increased or decreased to the same extent so that whatever the scale of production, the proportion among the factors remains the same.

When a firm expands, its scale increases all its inputs proportionally, then technically there are three possibilities. (i) The total output may increase proportionately (ii) The total output may increase more than proportionately and (iii) The total output may increase less than proportionately. If increase in the total output is proportional to the increase in input, it means constant returns to scale. If increase in the output is greater than the proportional increase in the inputs, it means increasing return to scale. If increase in the output is less than proportional increase in the inputs, it means diminishing returns to scale.

Let us now explain the laws of returns to scale with the help of isoquants for a two-input and single output production system.

ECONOMIES OF SCALE

Production may be carried on a small scale or o a large scale by a firm. When a firm expands its size of production by increasing all the factors, it secures certain advantages known as economies of production. Marshall has classified these economies of large-scale production into internal economies and external economies.

Internal economies are those, which are opened to a single factory or a single firm independently of the action of other firms. They result from an increase in the scale of output of a firm and cannot be achieved unless output increases. Hence internal economies depend solely upon the size of the firm and are different for different firms.

External economies are those benefits, which are shared in by a number of firms or industries when the scale of production in an industry or groups of industries increases. Hence external economies benefit all firms within the industry as the size of the industry expands.

Causes of internal economies

Internal economies are generally caused by two factors

1. Indivisibilities
2. Specialization.

Indivisibilities

Many fixed factors of production are indivisible in the sense that they must be used in a fixed minimum size. For instance, if a worker works half the time, he may be paid half the salary. But he cannot be chopped into half and asked to produce half the current output. Thus as output increases the indivisible factors which were being used below capacity can be utilized to their full capacity thereby reducing costs. Such indivisibilities arise in the case of labour, machines, marketing, finance and research.

Specialization

Division of labour, which leads to specialization, is another cause of internal economies. Specialization refers to the limitation of activities within a particular field of production. Specialization may be in labour, capital, machinery and place. For example, the production process may be split into four departments relation to manufacturing, assembling, packing and marketing under the charge of separate managers who may work under the overall charge of the general manger and coordinate the activities of the for departments. Thus specialization will lead to greater productive efficiency and to reduction in costs.

INTERNAL ECONOMIES

Internal economies may be of the following types.

Technical Economies

Technical economies arise to a firm from the use of better machines and superior techniques of production. As a result, production increases and per unit cost of production falls. A large firm, which employs costly and superior plant and equipment, enjoys a technical superiority over a small firm. Another technical economy lies in the mechanical advantage of using large machines. The cost of operating large machines is less than that of operating mall machine. More over a larger firm is able to reduce it's per unit cost of production by linking the various processes of production. Technical economies may also be associated when the large firm is able to utilize all its waste materials for the development of by-products industry. Scope for specialization is also available in a large firm. This increases the productive capacity of the firm and reduces the unit cost of production.

Managerial Economies

These economies arise due to better and more elaborate management, which only the large size firms can afford. There may be a separate head for manufacturing, assembling, packing, marketing, general administration etc. Each department is under the charge of an expert. Hence the appointment of experts, division of administration into several departments, functional specialization and scientific co-ordination of various works make the management of the firm most efficient.

Marketing Economies

The large firm reaps marketing or commercial economies in buying its requirements and in selling its final products. The large firm generally has a separate marketing department. It can buy and sell on behalf of the firm, when the market trends are more favorable.

In the matter of buying they could enjoy advantages like preferential treatment, transport concessions, cheap credit, prompt delivery and fine relation with dealers. Similarly it sells its products more effectively for a higher margin of profit.

Financial Economies

The large firm is able to secure the necessary finances either for block capital purposes or for working capital needs more easily and cheaply. It can barrow from the public, banks and other financial institutions at relatively cheaper rates. It is in this way that a large firm reaps financial economies.

Risk bearing Economies

The large firm produces many commodities and serves wider areas. It is, therefore, able to absorb any shock for its existence. For example, during business depression, the prices fall for every firm. There is also a possibility for market fluctuations in a particular product of the firm. Under such circumstances the risk-bearing economies or survival economies help the bigger firm to survive business crisis.

Economies of Research

A large firm possesses larger resources and can establish it's own research laboratory and employ trained research workers. The firm may even invent new production techniques for increasing its output and reducing cost.

Economies of welfare

A large firm can provide better working conditions in-and out-side the factory.

Facilities like subsidized canteens, crèches for the infants, recreation room, cheap houses, educational and medical facilities tend to increase the productive efficiency of the workers, which helps in raising production and reducing costs.

EXTERNAL ECONOMIES

Business firm enjoys a number of external economies, which are discussed below:

Economies of Concentration

When an industry is concentrated in a particular area, all the member firms reap some common economies like skilled labour, improved means of transport and communications, banking and financial services, supply of power and benefits from subsidiaries. All these facilities tend to lower the unit cost of production of all the firms in the industry.

Economies of Information

The industry can set up an information centre which may publish a journal and pass on information regarding the availability of raw materials, modern machines, export potentialities and provide other information needed by the firms. It will benefit all firms and reduction in their costs.

Economies of Welfare

An industry is in a better position to provide welfare facilities to the workers. It may get land at concessional rates and procure special facilities from the local bodies for setting up housing colonies for the workers.

It may also establish public health care units, educational institutions both general and technical so that a continuous supply of skilled labour is available to the industry. This will help the efficiency of the workers.

Economies of Disintegration

The firms in an industry may also reap the economies of specialization. When an industry expands, it becomes possible to spilt up some of the processes which are taken over by specialist firms. For example, in the cotton textile industry, some firms may specialize in manufacturing thread, others in printing, still others in dyeing, some in long cloth, some in dhotis, some in shirting etc. As a result the efficiency of the firms specializing in different fields increases and the unit cost of production falls.

Thus internal economies depend upon the size of the firm and external economies depend upon the size of the industry.

DISECONOMIES OF LARGE SCALE PRODUCTION

Internal and external diseconomies are the limits to large-scale production. It is possible that expansion of a firm's output may lead to rise in costs and thus result diseconomies instead of economies. When a firm expands beyond proper limits, it is beyond the capacity of the manager to manage it efficiently. This is an example of an internal diseconomy. In the same manner, the expansion of an industry may result in diseconomies, which may be called external diseconomies. Employment of additional factors of production becomes less efficient and they are obtained at a higher cost. It is in this way that external diseconomies result as an industry expands.

The major diseconomies of large-scale production are discussed below:

INTERNAL DISECONOMIES

Financial Diseconomies

For expanding business, the entrepreneur needs finance. But finance may not be easily available in the required amount at the appropriate time. Lack of finance retards the production plans thereby increasing costs of the firm.

Managerial diseconomies

There are difficulties of large-scale management. Supervision becomes a difficult job. Workers do not work efficiently, wastages arise, decision-making becomes difficult, coordination between workers and management disappears and production costs increase.

Marketing Diseconomies

As business is expanded, prices of the factors of production will rise. The cost will therefore rise. Raw materials may not be available in sufficient quantities due to their scarcities. Additional output may depress the price in the market. The demand for the products may fall as a result of changes in tastes and preferences of the people. Hence cost will exceed the revenue.

Technical Diseconomies

There is a limit to the division of labour and splitting down of production pOrocesses. The firm may fail to operate its plant to its maximum capacity. As a result cost per unit increases. Internal diseconomies follow.

Diseconomies of Risk-taking

As the scale of production of a firm expands risks also increase with it. Wrong decision by the management may adversely affect production. In large firms are affected by any disaster, natural or human, the economy will be put to strains.

External Diseconomies

When many firm get located at a particular place, the costs of transportation increases due to congestion. The firms have to face considerable delays in getting raw materials and sending finished products to the marketing centers. The localization of industries may lead to scarcity of raw material, shortage of various factors of production like labour and capital, shortage of power, finance and equipments. All such external diseconomies tend to raise cost per unit.

6

Cost Analysis

Profit is the ultimate aim of any business and the long-run prosperity of a firm depends upon its ability to earn sustained profits. Profits are the difference between selling price and cost of production. In general the selling price is not within the control of a firm but many costs are under its control. The firm should therefore aim at controlling and minimizing cost. Since every business decision involves cost consideration, it is necessary to understand the meaning of various concepts for clear business thinking and application of right kind of costs.

COST CONCEPTS

A managerial economist must have a clear understanding of the different cost concepts for clear business thinking and proper application. The several alternative bases of classifying cost and the relevance of each for different kinds of problems are to be studied. The various relevant concepts of cost are:

Opportunity costs and outlay costs

Out lay cost also known as actual costs obsolete costs are those expends which are actually incurred by the firm these are the payments made for labour, material, plant, building, machinery traveling, transporting etc., These are all those expense item appearing in the books of account, hence based on accounting cost concept. On the other hand opportunity cost implies the earnings foregone on the next best alternative, has the present option is undertaken. This cost is often measured by assessing the alternative, which has to be scarified if the particular line is followed.

The opportunity cost concept is made use for long-run decisions. This concept is very important in capital expenditure budgeting. This concept is very important in capital expenditure budgeting. The concept is also useful for taking short-run decisions opportunity cost is the cost concept to use when the supply of inputs is strictly limited and when there is an alternative. If there is no alternative, Opportunity cost is zero. The opportunity cost of any action is therefore measured by the value of the most favorable alternative course, which had to be foregoing if that action is taken.

Explicit and implicit costs

Explicit costs are those expenses that involve cash payments. These are the actual or business costs that appear in the books of accounts. These costs include payment of wages and salaries, payment for raw-materials, interest on borrowed capital funds, rent on hired land, Taxes paid etc.

Implicit costs are the costs of the factor units that are owned by the employer himself. These costs are not actually incurred but would have been incurred in the absence of employment of self - owned factors. The two normal implicit costs are depreciation, interest on capital etc. A decision maker must consider implicit costs too to find out appropriate profitability of alternatives.

Historical and Replacement costs

Historical cost is the original cost of an asset. Historical cost valuation shows the cost of an asset as the original price paid for the asset acquired in the past. Historical valuation is the basis for financial accounts.

A replacement cost is the price that would have to be paid currently to replace the same asset. During periods of substantial change in the price level, historical valuation gives a poor projection of the future cost intended for managerial decision. A replacement cost is a relevant cost concept when financial statements have to be adjusted for inflation.

Short - run and long - run costs

Short-run is a period during which the physical capacity of the firm remains fixed. Any increase in output during this period is possible only by using the existing physical capacity more extensively. So short run cost is that which varies with output when the plant and capital equipment in constant.

Long run costs are those, which vary with output when all inputs are variable including plant and capital equipment. Long-run cost analysis helps to take investment decisions.

Out-of pocket and books costs

Out-of pocket costs also known as explicit costs are those costs that involve current cash payment. Book costs also called implicit costs do not require current cash payments. Depreciation, unpaid interest, salary of the owner is examples of back costs.

But the book costs are taken into account in determining the level dividend payable during a period. Both book costs and out-of-pocket costs are considered for all decisions. Book cost is the cost of self-owned factors of production.

Fixed and variable costs

Fixed cost is that cost which remains constant for a certain level to output. It is not affected by the changes in the volume of production. But fixed cost per unit decrease, when the production is increased. Fixed cost includes salaries, Rent, Administrative expenses depreciations etc.

Variable is that which varies directly with the variation is output. An increase in total output results in an increase in total variable costs and decrease in total output results in a proportionate decline in the total variables costs. The variable cost per unit will be constant. Ex: Raw materials, labour, direct expenses, etc.

Post and Future costs

Post costs also called historical costs are the actual cost incurred and recorded in the book of account these costs are useful only for valuation and not for decision making.

Future costs are costs that are expected to be incurred in the futures. They are not actual costs. They are the costs forecasted or estimated with rational methods. Future cost estimate is useful for decision making because decision are meant for future.

Traceable and common costs

Traceable costs otherwise called direct cost, is one, which can be identified with a products process or product. Raw material, labour involved in production is examples of traceable cost.

Common costs are the ones that common are attributed to a

particular process or product. They are incurred collectively for different processes or different types of products. It cannot be directly identified with any particular process or type of product.

Avoidable and unavoidable costs

Avoidable costs are the costs, which can be reduced if the business activities of a concern are curtailed. For example, if some workers can be retrenched with a drop in a product - line, or volume or production the wages of the retrenched workers are escapable costs.

The unavoidable costs are otherwise called sunk costs. There will not be any reduction in this cost even if reduction in business activity is made. For example cost of the ideal machine capacity is unavoidable cost.

Controllable and uncontrollable costs

Controllable costs are ones, which can be regulated by the executive who is in change of it. The concept of controllability of cost varies with levels of management. Direct expenses like material, labour etc. are controllable costs.

Some costs are not directly identifiable with a process of product. They are appointed to various processes or products in some proportion. This cost varies with the variation in the basis of allocation and is independent of the actions of the executive of that department. These apportioned costs are called uncontrollable costs.

Incremental and sunk costs

Incremental cost also known as different cost is the additional cost due to a change in the level or nature of business activity. The change may be caused by adding a new product, adding new machinery, replacing a machine by a better one etc.

Sunk costs are those which are not altered by any change - They are the costs incurred in the past. This cost is the result of past decision, and cannot be changed by future decisions. Investments in fixed assets are examples of sunk costs.

Total, average and marginal costs

Total cost is the total cash payment made for the input needed for production. It may be explicit or implicit. It is the sum total of the fixed and variable costs. Average cost is the cost per unit of output. If is obtained by dividing the total cost (TC) by the total quantity produced (Q)

$$\text{Average cost} = \frac{TC}{Q}$$

Marginal cost is the additional cost incurred to produce and additional unit of output or it is the cost of the marginal unit produced.

Accounting and Economics costs

Accounting costs are the costs recorded for the purpose of preparing the balance sheet and profit and ton statements to meet the legal, financial and tax purpose of the company. The accounting concept is a historical concept and records what has happened in the post.

Economics concept considers future costs and future revenues, which help future planning, and choice, while the accountant describes what has happened, the economics aims at projecting what will happen.

COST-OUTPUT RELATIONSHIP

A proper understanding of the nature and behavior of costs is a must for regulation and control of cost of production. The cost of production depends on money forces and an understanding of the functional relationship of cost to various forces will help us to take various decisions. Output is an important factor, which influences the cost.

The cost-output relationship plays an important role in determining the optimum level of production. Knowledge of the cost-output relation helps the manager in cost control, profit prediction, pricing, promotion etc. The relation between cost and its determinants is technically described as the cost function.

C= f (S, O, P, T ....)

Where;

C= Cost (Unit or total cost)

S= Size of plant/scale of production

O= Output level

P= Prices of inputs

T= Technology

Considering the period the cost function can be classified as (a) short-run cost function and (b) long-run cost function. In economics theory, the short-run is defined as that period during which the physical capacity of the firm is fixed and the output can be increased only by using the existing capacity allows to bring changes in output by physical capacity of the firm.

Cost-Output Relation in the short-run

The cost concepts made use of in the cost behavior are total cost, Average cost, and marginal cost.

Total cost is the actual money spent to produce a particular quantity of output. Total cost is the summation of fixed and variable costs.

TC=TFC+TVC

Up to a certain level of production total fixed cost i.e., the cost of plant, building, equipment etc, remains fixed. But the total variable cost i.e., the cost of labour, raw materials etc., Vary with the variation in output. Average cost is the total cost per unit. It can be found out as follows.--------

$$AC=\frac{TC}{Q}$$

Q

The total of average fixed cost (TFC/Q) keep coming down as the production is increased and average variable cost (TVC/Q) will remain constant at any level of output.

Marginal cost is the addition to the total cost due to the production of an additional unit of product. It can be arrived at by dividing the change in total cost by the change in total output.

In the short-run there will not be any change in total fixed cost. Hence change in total cost implies change in total variable cost only.

Cost - output relations

And later rises. But the rise in AC is felt only after the start rising. In the table 'AVC' starts rising from the 5th unit onwards whereas the 'AC' starts rising from the 6th unit only so long as 'AVC' declines 'AC' also will decline. 'AFC' continues to fall with an increase in Output. When the rise in 'AVC' is more than the decline in 'AFC', the total cost again begin to rise. Thus there will be a stage where the 'AVC', the total cost again begin to rise thus there will be a stage where the 'AVC' may have started rising, yet the 'AC' is still declining because the rise in 'AVC' is less than the droop in 'AFC'.

Thus the table shows an increasing returns or diminishing cost in the first stage and diminishing returns or diminishing cost in the second stage and followed by diminishing returns or increasing cost in the third stage.

The short-run cost-output relationship can be shown graphically as follows.

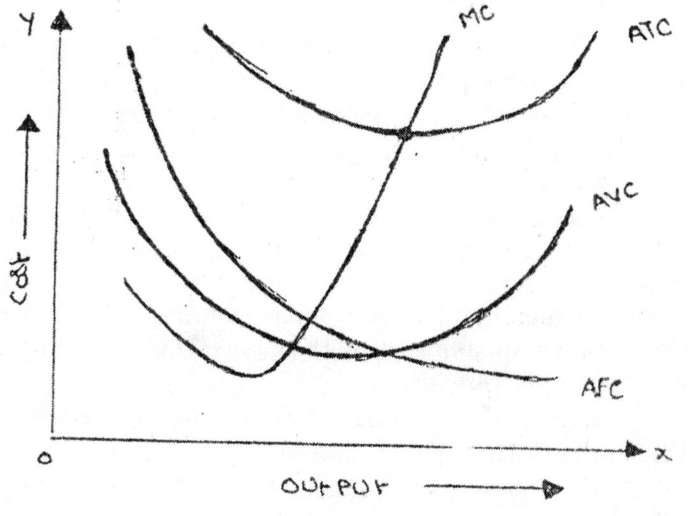

In the above graph the "AFC' curve continues to fall as output rises an account of its spread over more and more units Output. But AVC curve (i.e. variable cost per unit) first falls and than rises due to the operation of the law of variable proportions. The behavior of "ATC' curve depends upon the behavior of 'AVC' curve and 'AFC' curve. In the initial stage of production both 'AVC' and 'AFC' decline and hence 'ATC' also decline. But after a certain point 'AVC' starts rising. If the rise in variable cost is less than the decline in fixed cost, ATC will still continue to decline otherwise AC begins to rise. Thus the lower end of 'ATC' curve thus turns up and gives it a U-shape. That is why 'ATC' curve are U-shaped. The lowest point in 'ATC' curve indicates the least-cost combination of inputs. Where the total average cost is the minimum and where the "MC' curve intersects 'AC' curve, It is not be the maximum output level rather it is the point where per unit cost of production will be at its lowest.

The relationship between 'AVC', 'AFC' and 'ATC' can be summarized up as follows:

1. If both AFC and 'AVC' fall, 'ATC' will also fall.
2. When 'AFC' falls and 'AVC' rises
   a. 'ATC' will fall where the drop in 'AFC' is more than the raise in 'AVC'.
   b. 'ATC' remains constant is the drop in 'AFC' = rise in 'AVC'
   c. 'ATC' will rise where the drop in 'AFC' is less than the rise in 'AVC'

b. Cost-output Relationship in the long-run:

Long run is a period, during which all inputs are variable including the one, which are fixes in the short-run. In the long run a firm can change its output according to its demand. Over a long period, the size of the plant can be changed, unwanted buildings can be sold staff can be increased or reduced. The long run enables the firms to expand and scale of their operation by bringing or purchasing larger quantities of all the inputs. Thus in the long run all factors become variable.

The long-run cost-output relations therefore imply the relationship between the total cost and the total output. In the long-run cost-output relationship is influenced by the law of returns to scale.

In the long run a firm has a number of alternatives in regards to the scale of operations. For each scale of production or plant size, the firm has an appropriate short-run average cost curves. The short-run average cost (SAC) curve applies to only one plant whereas the long-run average cost (LAC) curve takes in to consideration many plants.

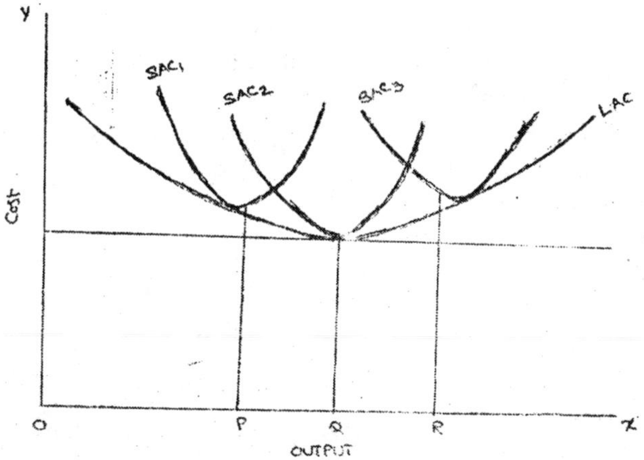

The long-run cost-output relationship is shown graphically with the help of "LCA' curve.

To draw on 'LAC' curve we have to start with a number of 'SAC' curves. In the above figure it is assumed that technologically there are only three sizes of plants - small, medium and large, 'SAC', for the small size, 'SAC2' for the medium size plant and 'SAC3' for the large size plant.

If the firm wants to produce 'OP' units of output, it will choose the smallest plant.

For an output beyond 'OQ' the firm wills optimum for medium size plant. It does not mean that the OQ production is not possible with small plant. Rather it implies that cost of production will be more with small plant compared to the medium plant.

For an output 'OR' the firm will choose the largest plant as the cost of production will be more with medium plant. Thus the firm has a series of 'SAC' curves.

The 'LCA' curve drawn will be tangential to the entire family of 'SAC' curves i.e. the 'LAC' curve touches each 'SAC' curve at one point, and thus it is known as envelope curve.

It is also known as planning curve as it serves as guide to the entrepreneur in his planning to expand the production in future. With the help of 'LAC' the firm determines the size of plant which yields the lowest average cost of producing a given volume of output it anticipates.

BREAKEVEN ANALYSIS

The study of cost-volume-profit relationship is often referred as BEA. The term BEA is interpreted in two senses. In its narrow sense, it is concerned with finding out BEP; BEP is the point at which total revenue is equal to total cost. It is the point of no profit, no loss. In its broad determine the probable profit at any level of production.

Assumptions:

1. All costs are classified into two - fixed and variable.
2. Fixed costs remain constant at all levels of output.
3. Variable costs vary proportionally with the volume of output.
4. Selling price per unit remains constant in spite of competition or change in the volume of production.
5. There will be no change in operating efficiency.
6. There will be no change in the general price level.
7. Volume of production is the only factor affecting the cost.
8. Volume of sales and volume of production are equal. Hence there is no unsold stock.
9. There is only one product or in the case of multiple products. Sales mix remains constant.

Merits:

1. Information provided by the Break Even Chart can be understood more easily then those contained in the profit and Loss Account and the cost statement.
2. Break Even Chart discloses the relationship between cost, volume and profit. It reveals how changes in profit. So, it helps management in decision-making.
3. It is very useful for forecasting costs and profits long term planning and growth
4. The chart discloses profits at various levels of production.
5. It serves as a useful tool for cost control.
6. It can also be used to study the comparative plant efficiencies of the industry.
7. Analytical Break-even chart present the different elements, in the costs - direct material, direct labour, fixed and variable overheads.

Demerits:

1. Break-even chart presents only cost volume profits. It ignores other considerations such as capital amount, marketing aspects and effect of government policy etc., which are necessary in decision making.
2. It is assumed that sales, total cost and fixed cost can be represented as straight lines. In actual practice, this may not be so.
3. It assumes that profit is a function of output. This is not always true. The firm may increase the profit without increasing its output.
4. A major draw back of BEC is its inability to handle production and sale of multiple products.
5. It is difficult to handle selling costs such as advertisement and sale promotion in BEC.
6. It ignores economics of scale in production.
7. Fixed costs do not remain constant in the long run.
8. Semi-variable costs are completely ignored.
9. It assumes production is equal to sale. It is not always true because generally there may be opening stock.
10. When production increases variable cost per unit may not remain constant but may reduce on account of bulk buying etc.
11. The assumption of static nature of business and economic activities is a well-known defect of BEC.
    1. Fixed cost
    2. Variable cost
    3. Contribution
    4. Margin of safety
    5. Angle of incidence
    6. Profit volume ratio
    7. Break-Even-Point

Fixed cost: Expenses that do not vary with the volume of production are known as fixed expenses.

Eg. Manager's salary, rent and taxes, insurance etc. It should be noted that fixed changes are fixed only within a certain range of plant capacity. The concept of fixed overhead is most useful in formulating a price fixing policy. Fixed cost per unit is not fixed.

Variable Cost: Expenses that vary almost in direct proportion to the volume of production of sales are called variable expenses. Eg. Electric power and fuel, packing materials consumable stores. It should be noted that variable cost per unit is fixed.

Contribution: Contribution is the difference between sales and variable costs and it contributed towards fixed costs and profit. It helps in sales and pricing policies and measuring the profitability of different proposals. Contribution is a sure test to decide whether a product is worthwhile to be continued among different products.

Contribution = Sales - Variable cost

Contribution = Fixed Cost + Profit.

Margin of safety: Margin of safety is the excess of sales over the break even sales. It can be expressed in absolute sales amount or in percentage. It indicates the extent to which the sales can be reduced without resulting in loss. A large margin of safety indicates the soundness of the business. The formula for the margin of safety is:

$$\text{Present sales} - \text{Break even sales or } \frac{\text{Profit}}{\text{P.V. ratio}}$$

Margin of safety can be improved by taking the following steps.

1. Increasing production
2. Increasing selling price
3. Reducing the fixed or the variable costs or both
4. Substituting unprofitable product with profitable one.

Angle of incidence: This is the angle between sales line and total cost line at the Break-even point. It indicates the profit earning capacity of the concern. Large angle of incidence indicates a high rate of profit; a small angle indicates a low rate of earnings. To improve this angle, contribution should be increased either by raising the selling price and/or by reducing variable cost. It also indicates as to what extent the output and sales price can be changed to attain a desired amount of profit.

Profit Volume Ratio is usually called P. V. ratio. It is one of the most useful ratios for studying the profitability of business. The ratio of contribution to sales is the P/V ratio. It may be expressed in percentage. Therefore, every organization tries to improve the P. V. ratio of each product by reducing the variable cost per unit or by increasing the selling price per unit. The concept of P. V. ratio helps in determining break even-point, a desired amount of profit etc.

The formula is, $\frac{\text{Contribution}}{\textit{Sales}} \times 100$

Break – Even- Point: If we divide the term into three words, then it does not require further explanation.

Break Even Point refers to the point where total cost is equal to total revenue. It is a point of no profit, no loss. This is also a minimum point of no profit, no loss. This is also a minimum point of production where total costs are recovered. If sales go up beyond the Break Even Point, organization makes a profit. If they come down, a loss is incurred.

1. Break Even point (Units) = $\frac{\text{Fixed Expenses}}{\text{Contribution per unit}}$

2. Break Even point (In Rupees) = $\frac{\text{Fixed expenses}}{\text{Contribution}} \times \text{sales}$

7

Introduction to Market and Pricing Strategies

INTRODUCTION

Pricing is an important, if not the most important function of all enterprises. Since every enterprise is engaged in the production of some goods or/and service. Incurring some expenditure, it must set a price for the same to sell it in the market. It is only in extreme cases that the firm has no say in pricing its product; because there is severe or rather perfect competition in the market of the good happens to be of such public significance that its price is decided by the government. In an overwhelmingly large number of cases, the individual producer plays the role in pricing its product. It is said that if a firm were good in setting its product price it would certainly flourish in the market. This is because the price is such a parameter that it exerts a direct influence on the products demand as well as on its supply, leading to firm's turnover (sales) and profit.

Every manager endeavors to find the price, which would best meet with his firm's objective. If the price is set too high the seller may not find enough customers to buy his product. On the other hand, if the price is set too low the seller may not be able to recover his costs. There is a need for the right price further, since demand and supply conditions are variable over time what is a right price today may not be so tomorrow hence, pricing decision must be reviewed and reformulated from time to time.

Price

Price denotes the exchange value of a unit of good expressed in terms of money. Thus the current price of a maruti car around

Rs. 2,00,000, the price of a hair cut is Rs. 25 the price of a economics book is Rs. 150 and so on. Nevertheless, if one gives a little, if one gives a little thought to this subject, one would realize that there is nothing like a unique price for any good. Instead, there are multiple prices.

Price concepts

Price of a well-defined product varies over the types of the buyers, place it is received, credit sale or cash sale, time taken between final production and sale, etc.

It should be obvious to the readers, that the price difference on account of the above four factors are more significant. The multiple prices is more serious in the case of items like cars refrigerators, coal, furniture and bricks and is of little significance for items like shaving blade, soaps, tooth pastes, creams and stationeries. Differences in various prices of any good are due to differences in transport cost, storage cost accessories, interest cost, intermediaries' profits etc. Once can still conceive of a basic price, which would be exclusive of all these items of cost and then rationalize other prices by adding the cost of special items attached to the particular transaction, in what follows we shall explain the determination of this basis price alone and thus resolve the problem of multiple prices.

Price determinants - Demand and supply

The price of a product is determined by the demand for and supply of that product. According to Marshall the role of these two determinants is like that of a pair of scissors in cutting cloth. It is possible that at times, while one pair is held fixed, the other is moving to cut the cloth. Similarly, it is conceivable that there could be situations under which either demand or supply is playing a passive role, and the other, which is active, alone appear to be determining the price. However, just as one pair of scissors alone can never cut a cloth, demand or supply alone is insufficient to determine the price.

Equilibrium Price

The price at which demand and supply of a commodity is equal known as equilibrium price. The demand and supply schedules of a good are shown in the table below.

Demand supply schedule

Price	*Demand*	*Supply*
50	100	200
40	120	180
30	150	150
20	200	110
10	300	50

Of the five possible prices in the above example, price Rs.30 would be the market-clearing price. No other price could prevail in the market. If price is Rs. 50 supply would exceed demand and consequently the producers of this good would not find enough customers for their demand, thereby they would accumulate unwanted inventories of output, which, in turn, would lead to competition among the producers, forcing price to Rs.30. Similarly if price were Rs.10, there would be excess demand, which would give rise to competition among the buyers of good, forcing price to Rs.30. At price Rs.30, demand equals supply and thus both producers and consumers are satisfied. The economist calls such a price as equilibrium price.

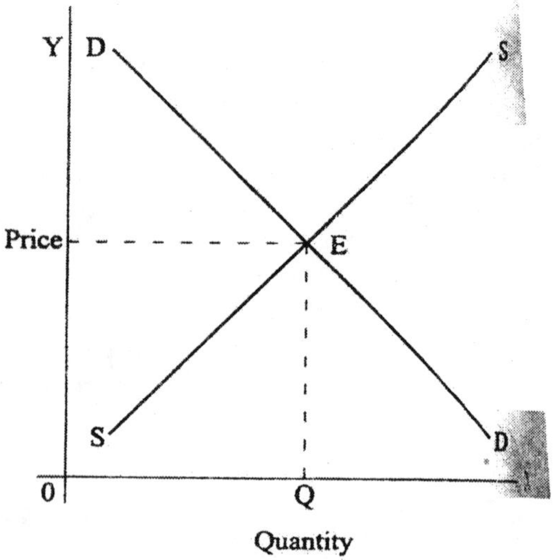

Fig. 6.1

It was seen in unit 1 that the demand for a good depends on, a number of factors and thus, every factor, which influences either demand or supply is in fact a determinant of price. Accordingly, a change in demand or/and supply causes price change.

MARKET

Market is a place where buyer and seller meet, goods and services are offered for the sale and transfer of ownership occurs. A market may be also defined as the demand made by a certain group of potential buyers for a good or service. The former one is a narrow concept and later one, a broader concept. Economists describe a market as a collection of buyers and sellers who transact over a particular product or product class (the housing market, the clothing market, the grain market etc.).

For business purpose we define a market as people or organizations with wants (needs) to satisfy, money to spend, and the willingness to spend it. Broadly, market represents the structure and nature of buyers and sellers for a commodity/service and the process by which the price of the commodity or service is established. In this sense, we are referring to the structure of competition and the process of price determination for a commodity or service. The determination of price for a commodity or service depends upon the structure of the market for that commodity or service (i.e., competitive structure of the market). Hence the understanding on the market structure and the nature of competition are a pre-requisite in price determination.

Different Market Structures

Market structure describes the competitive environment in the market for any good or service. A market consists of all firms and individuals who are willing and able to buy or sell a particular product. This includes firms and individuals currently engaged in buying and selling a particular product, as well as potential entrants.

The determination of price is affected by the competitive structure of the market. This is because the firm operates in a market and not in isolation. In marking decisions concerning economic variables it is affected, as are all institutions in society by its environment.

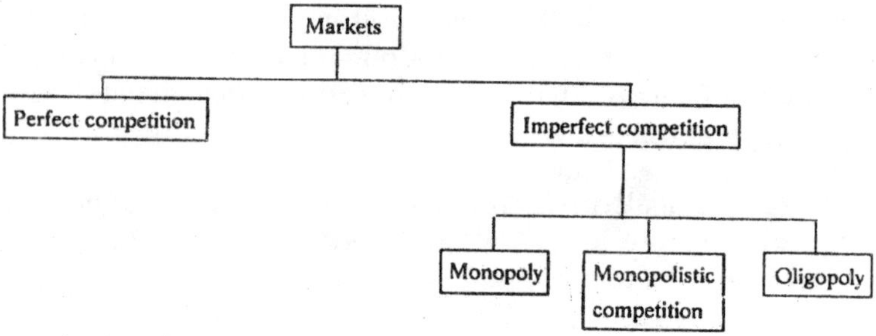

Perfect Competition

Perfect competition refers to a market structure where competition among the sellers and buyers prevails in its most perfect form. In a perfectly competitive market, a single market price prevails for the commodity, which is determined by the forces of total demand and total supply in the market.

Characteristics of Perfect Competition

The following features characterize a perfectly competitive market:

1. A large number of buyers and sellers: The number of buyers and sellers is large and the share of each one of them in the market is so small that none has any influence on the market price.
2. Homogeneous product: The product of each seller is totally undifferentiated from those of the others.
3. Free entry and exit: Any buyer and seller is free to enter or leave the market of the commodity.
4. Perfect knowledge: All buyers and sellers have perfect knowledge about the market for the commodity.
5. Indifference: No buyer has a preference to buy from a particular seller and no seller to sell to a particular buyer.
6. Non-existence of transport costs: Perfectly competitive market also assumes the non-existence of transport costs.
7. Perfect mobility of factors of production: Factors of production must be in a position to move freely into or out of industry and from one firm to the other.

Under such a market no single buyer or seller plays a significant role in price determination. One the other hand all of them jointly determine the price. The price is determined in the industry, which is composed of all the buyers and seller for the commodity. The demand curve facing the industry is the sum of all consumers' demands at various prices. The industry supply curve is the sum of all sellers' supplies at various prices.

Pure competition and perfect competition

The term perfect competition is used in a wider sense. Pure competition has only limited assumptions.

When the assumptions, that large number of buyers and sellers, homogeneous products, free entry and exit are satisfied, there exists pure competition. Competition becomes perfect only when all the assumptions (features) are satisfied. Generally pure competition can be seen in agricultural products.

Equilibrium of a firm and industry under perfect competition

Equilibrium is a position where the firm has no incentive either to expand or contrast its output. The firm is said to be in equilibrium when it earn maximum profit. There are two conditions for attaining equilibrium by a firm. They are:

Marginal cost is an additional cost incurred by a firm for producing and additional unit of output. Marginal revenue is the additional revenue accrued to a firm when it sells one additional unit of output.

A firm increases its output so long as its marginal cost becomes equal to marginal revenue. When marginal cost is more than marginal revenue, the firm reduces output as its costs exceed the revenue. It is only at the point where marginal cost is equal to marginal revenue, and then the firm attains equilibrium. Secondly, the marginal cost curve must cut the marginal revenue curve from below.

If marginal cost curve cuts the marginal revenue curve from above, the firm is having the scope to increase its output as the marginal cost curve slopes downwards. It is only with the upward sloping marginal cost curve, there the firm attains equilibrium. The reason is that the marginal cost curve when rising cuts the marginal revenue curve from below.

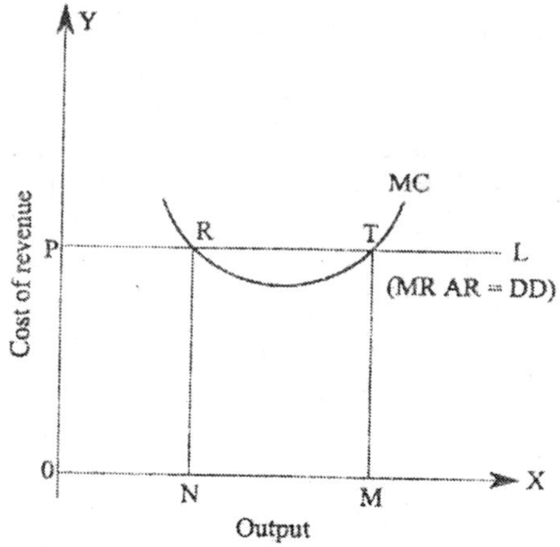

Fig. 6.2

The equilibrium of a perfectly competitive firm may be explained with the help of the fig. 6.2.

In the given fig. PL and MC represent the Price line and Marginal cost curve. PL also represents Marginal revenue, Average revenue and demand. As Marginal revenue, Average revenue and demand are the same in perfect competition, all are equal to the price line. Marginal cost curve is U- shaped curve cutting MR curve at R and T. At point R marginal cost becomes equal to marginal revenue. But MC curve cuts the MR curve fro above. So this is not the equilibrium position. The downward sloping marginal cost curve indicates that the firm can reduce its cost of production by increasing output. As the firm expands its output, it will reach equilibrium at point T. At this point, on price line PL; the two conditions of equilibrium are satisfied. Here the marginal cost and marginal revenue of the firm remain equal. The firm is producing maximum output and is in equilibrium at this stage. If the firm continues its output beyond this stage, its marginal cost exceeds marginal revenue resulting in losses. As the firm has no idea of expanding or contracting its size of out, the firm is said to be in equilibrium at point T.

Pricing under perfect competition

The price or value of a commodity under perfect competition is determined by the demand for and the supply of that commodity.

Under perfect competition there is large number of sellers trading in a homogeneous product. Each firm supplies only very small portion of the market demand. No single buyer or seller is powerful enough to influence the price. The demand of all consumers and the supply of all firms together determine the price. The individual seller is only a price taker and not a price maker. An individual firm has no price policy of it's own. Thus, the main problem of a firm in a perfectly competitive market is not to determine the price of its product but to adjust its output to the given price, So that the profit is maximum. Marshall however gives great importance to the time element for the determination of price. He divided the time periods on the basis of supply and ignored the forces of demand. He classified the time into four periods to determine the price as follows.

1. Very short period or Market period
2. Short period
3. Long period
4. Very long period or secular period.

Very short period: It is the period in which the supply is more or less fixed because the time available to the firm to adjust the supply of the commodity to its changed demand is extremely short; say a single day or a few days. The price determined in this period is known as Market Price.

Short Period: In this period, the time available to firms to adjust the supply of the commodity to its changed demand is, of course, greater than that in the market period. In this period altering the variable factors like raw materials, labour, etc can change supply. During this period new firms cannot enter into the industry.

Long period: In this period, a sufficiently long time is available to the firms to adjust the supply of the commodity fully to the changed demand. In this period not only variable factors of production but also fixed factors of production can be changed. In this period new firms can also enter the industry. The price determined in this period is known as long run normal price.

Secular Period: In this period, a very long time is available to adjust the supply fully to change in demand. This is very long period consisting of a number of decades. As the period is very long it is difficult to lay down principles determining the price.

Price Determination in the market period

The price determined in very short period is known as Market price. Market price is determined by the equilibrium between demand and supply in a market period. The nature of the commodity determines the nature of supply curve in a market period. Under this period goods are classified in to (a) Perishable goods and (b) Non-perishable goods.

Perishable Goods: In the very short period, the supply of perishable goods like fish, milk vegetables etc. cannot be increased. And it cannot be decreased also. As a result the supply curve under very short period will be parallel to the Y-axis or Vertical to X-axis. Supply is perfectly inelastic. The price determination of perishable goods in very short period may be shown with the help of the following fig. 6.5

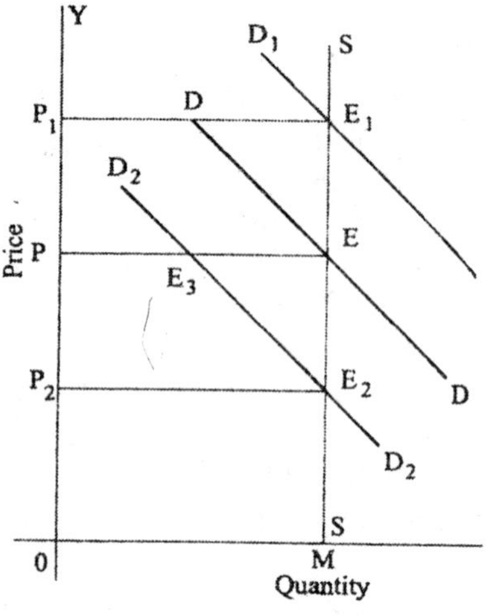

Fig. 6.5

In this figure quantity is represented along X-axis and price is represented along Y-axis. MS is the very short period supply curve of perishable goods. DD is demand curve. It intersects supply curve at E. The price is OP. The quantity exchanged is OM. D1 D1 represents increased demand. This curve cuts the supply curve at E1. Even at the new equilibrium, supply is OM only. But price increases to OP1. So, when demand increases, the price will increase but not the supply. If demand decreases new demand curve will be D2 D2. This curve cuts the supply curve at E2. Even at this new equilibrium, the supply is OM only. But price falls to OP2. Hence in very short period, given the supply, it is the change in demand that influences price. The price determined in a very short period is called Market Price.

Non-perishable goods: In the very short period, the supply of non-perishable goods like cloth, pen, watches etc. cannot be increased.

But if price falls, preserving some stock can decrease their supply. If price falls too much, the whole stock will be held back from the market and carried over to the next market period. The price below, which the seller will refuse to sell, is called Reserve Price.

The Price determination of non-perishable goods in very short period may be shown with the help of the following fig 6.6.

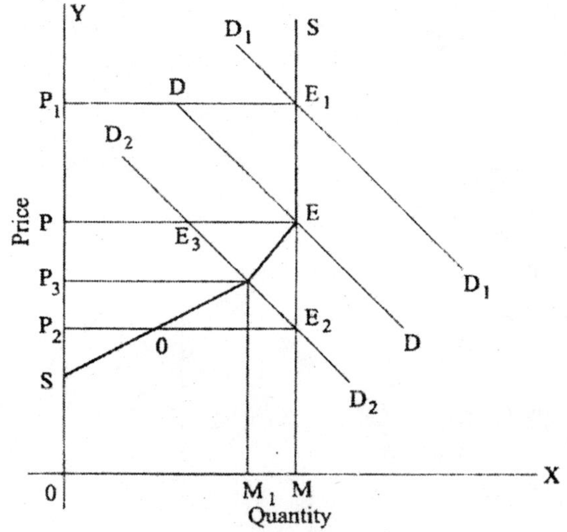

Fig. 6.6

In the given figure quantity is shown on X-axis and the price on Y-axis. SES is the supply curve. It slopes upward up to the point E. From E it becomes a vertical straight line. This is because the quantity existing with sellers is OM, the maximum amount they have is thus OM. Till OM quantity (i.e., point E) the supply curve sloped upward. At the point S, nothing is offered for sale.

It means that the seller with hold the entire stock if the price is OS. OS is thus the reserve price. As the price rises, supply increases up to point E. At OP price (Point E), the entire stock is offered for sale.

Suppose demand increases, the DD curve shift upward. It becomes D1D1 price raises to OP1. If demand decreases, the demand curve becomes D2D2. It intersects the supply curve at E3. The price will fall to OP3. We find that at OS price, supply is zero. It is the reserve price.

Price Determination in the short period

Short period is a period in which supply can be increased by altering the variable factors. In this period fixed costs will remain constant. The supply is increased when price rises and vice versa. So the supply curve slopes upwards from left to right. The price in short period may be explained with the help of a diagram.

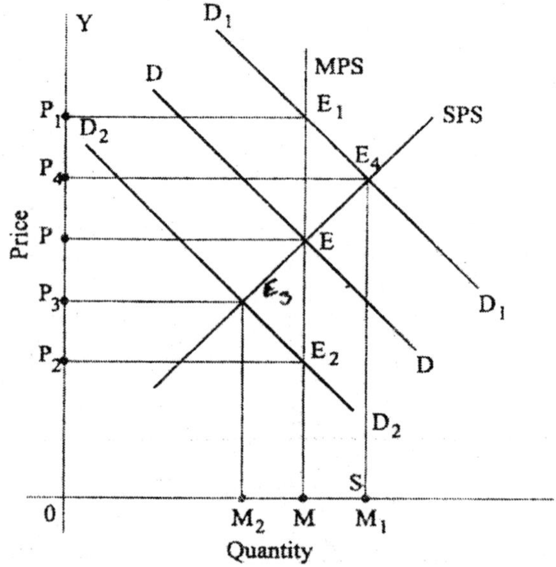

Fig. 6.7

In the given diagram MPS is the market period supply curve. DD is the initial demand curve. It intersects MPS curve at E. The price is OP and out put OM. Suppose demand increases, the demand curve shifts upwards and becomes D1D1. In the very short period, supply remains fixed on OM. The new demand curve D1D1 intersects MPS at E1. The price will rise to OP1. This is what happen in the very short-period. As the price rises from OP to OP1, firms expand output. As firms can vary some factors but not all, the law of variable proportions operates. This results in new short-run supply curve SPS. It interests D1 D1 curve at E4. The price will fall from OP1 to OP4.

It the demand decreases, DD curve shifts downward and becomes D2D2. It interests MPS curve at E2. The price will fall to OP2. This is what happens in market period. In the short period, the supply curve is SPS. D2D2 curve interests SPS curve at E3. The short period price is higher than the market period price.

Price determination in the long period (Normal Price)

Market price may fluctuate due to a sudden change either on the supply side or on the demand side. A big arrival of milk may decrease the price of that production in the market period. Similarly, a sudden cold wave may raise the price of woolen garments. This type of temporary change in supply and demand may cause changes in market price. In the absence of such disturbing causes, the price tends to come back to a certain level. Marshall called this level is normal price level. In the words of Marshall Normal value (Price) of a commodity is that which economics force would tend to bring about in the long period.

In order to describe how long run normal price is determined, it is useful to refer to the market period as short period also. The market period is so short that no adjustment in the output can be made. Here cost of production has no influence on price. A short period is sufficient only to allow the firms to make only limited output adjustment. In the long period, supply conditions are fully sufficient to meet the changes in demand. In the long period, all factors are alterable and the new firms may enter into or old firms leave the; industry.

In the long period all costs are variable costs. So supply will be increased only when price is equal to average cost.

Hence, in long period normal price will be equal to minimum average cost of the industry. Will this price be more or less than the short period normal price? The answer depends on the stage of returns to which the industry is subject. There are three stages of return on the stage of returns to which the industry is subject. There are three stages of returns.

1. Increasing returns or decreasing costs.
2. Constant Returns or Constant costs.
3. Diminishing returns or increasing costs.

Determination of long period normal price in decreasing cost industry

At this stage, average cost falls due to an increase in the output. So, the supply curve at this stage will slope downwards from left to right. The long period Normal price determination at this stage can be explained with the help of a diagram.

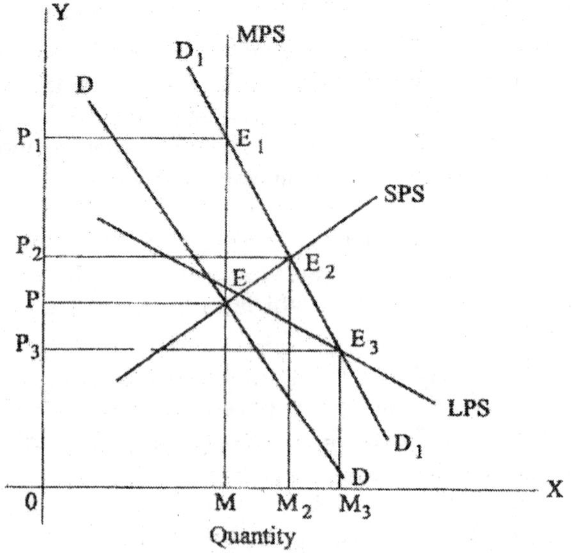

Fig. 6.8

In the diagram, MPS represents market period supply curve. DD is demand curve. DD cuts LPS, SPS and MPS at point E. At point E the supply is OM and the price is OP. If demand increases from DD to D1D1 market price increases to OP1. In the short period it is OP2. In the long period supply increases considerably to OM3. So price has fallen to OP3, which is less than the price of market period.

Determination of Long Period Normal Price in Constant Cost Industry

In this case average cost does not change even though the output increases. Hence long period supply curve is horizontal to X-axis. The determination of long period normal price can be explained with the help of the diagram. In the fig. 6.9, LPS is horizontal to X-axis. MPS represents market period supply curve, and SPS represents short period supply curve. At point 'E' the output is OM and price is OP. If demand increases from DD to D1D1 market price increases to OP1. In the short period, supply increases and hence the price will be OP2. In the long run supply is adjusted fully to meet increased demand. The price remains constant at OP because costs are constant at OP and market is perfect market.

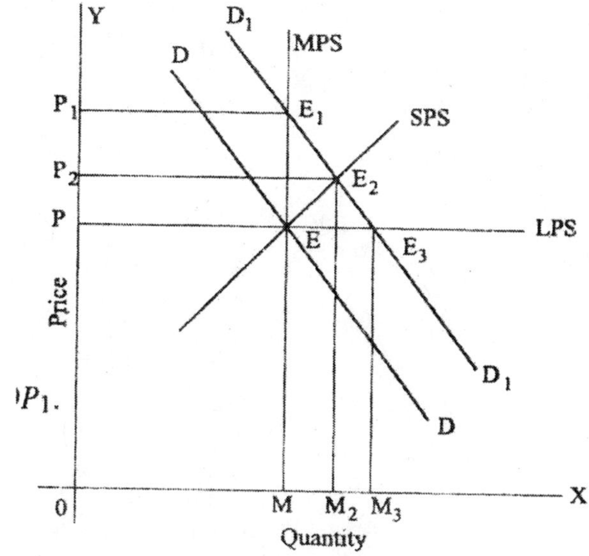

Fig. 6.9

Determination of long period normal price in increase cost industry

If the industry is subject to increasing costs (diminishing returns) the supply curve slopes upwards from left to right like an ordinary supply curve. The determination of long period normal price in increasing cost industry can be explained with the help of the following diagram. In the diagram LPS represents long period supply curve. The industry is subject to diminishing return or increasing costs. So, LPS slopes upwards from left to right. SPS is short period supply curve and MPS is market period supply curve. DD is demand curve. It cuts all the supply curves at E. Here the price is OP and output is OM. If demand increases from DD to D1D1 in the market period, supply will not change but the price increases to OP1. In the short period, price increase but the price increases to OP1. In the short period, price increases to OP2 as the supply increased from OM to OM2. In the long period supply increases to OM3 and price increases to OP3. But this increase in price is less than the price increase in a market period or short period.

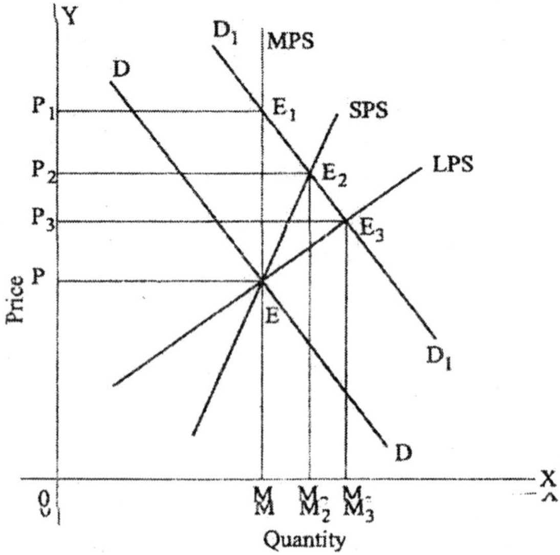

Fig. 6.10

MONOPOLY

The word monopoly is made up of two syllables, Mono and poly. Mono means single while poly implies selling. Thus monopoly is a form of market organization in which there is only one seller of the commodity. There are no close substitutes for the commodity sold by the seller. Pure monopoly is a market situation in which a single firm sells a product for which there is no good substitute.

Features of monopoly

The following are the features of monopoly.

1. Single person or a firm: A single person or a firm controls the total supply of the commodity. There will be no competition for monopoly firm. The monopolist firm is the only firm in the whole industry.
2. No close substitute: The goods sold by the monopolist shall not have closely competition substitutes. Even if price of monopoly product increase people will not go in far substitute. For example: If the price of electric bulb increase slightly, consumer will not go in for kerosene lamp.
3. Large number of Buyers: Under monopoly, there may be a large number of buyers in the market who compete among themselves.
4. Price Maker: Since the monopolist controls the whole supply of a commodity, he is a price-maker, and then he can alter the price.
5. Supply and Price: The monopolist can fix either the supply or the price. He cannot fix both. If he charges a very high price, he can sell a small amount. If he wants to sell more, he has to charge a low price. He cannot sell as much as he wishes for any price he pleases.
6. Downward Sloping Demand Curve: The demand curve (average revenue curve) of monopolist slopes downward from left to right. It means that he can sell more only by lowering price.

Types of Monopoly

Monopoly may be classified into various types. The different types of monopolies are explained below:

1. Legal Monopoly: If monopoly arises on account of legal support or as a matter of legal privilege, it is called Legal Monopoly. Ex. Patent rights, special brands, trade means, copyright etc.
2. Voluntary Monopoly: To get the advantages of monopoly some private firms come together voluntarily to control

the supply of a commodity. These are called voluntary monopolies. Generally, these monopolies arise with industrial combinations. These voluntary monopolies are of three kinds (a) cartel (b) trust (c) holding company. It may be called artificial monopoly.

3. Government Monopoly: Sometimes the government will take the responsibility of supplying a commodity and avoid private interference. Ex. Water, electricity. These monopolies, created to satisfy social wants, are formed on social considerations. These are also called Social Monopolies.
4. Private Monopoly: If the total supply of a good is produced by a single private person or firm, it is called private monopoly. Hindustan Lever Ltd. Is having the monopoly power to produce Lux Soap.
5. Limited Monopoly: if the monopolist is having limited power in fixing the price of his product, it is called as 'Limited Monopoly'. It may be due to the fear of distant substitutes or government intervention or the entry of rivals firms.
6. Unlimited Monopoly: If the monopolist is having unlimited power in fixing the price of his good or service, it is called unlimited monopoly. Ex. A doctor in a village.
7. Single Price Monopoly: When the monopolist charges same price for all units of his product, it is called single price monopoly. Ex. Tata Company charges the same price to all the Tata Indiaca Cars of the same model.
8. Discriminating Monopoly: When a Monopolist charges different prices to different consumers for the same product, it is called discriminating monopoly. A doctor may take Rs.20 from a rich man and only Rs.2 from a poor man for the same treatment.
9. Natural Monopoly: Sometimes monopoly may arise due to scarcity of natural resources. Nature provides raw materials only in some places. The owner of the place will become monopolist. For Ex. Diamond mine in South Africa.

Pricing under Monopoly

Monopoly refers to a market situation where there is only one seller. He has complete control over the supply of a commodity.

He is therefore in a position to fix any price. Under monopoly there is no distinction between a firm and an industry. This is because the entire industry consists of a single firm.

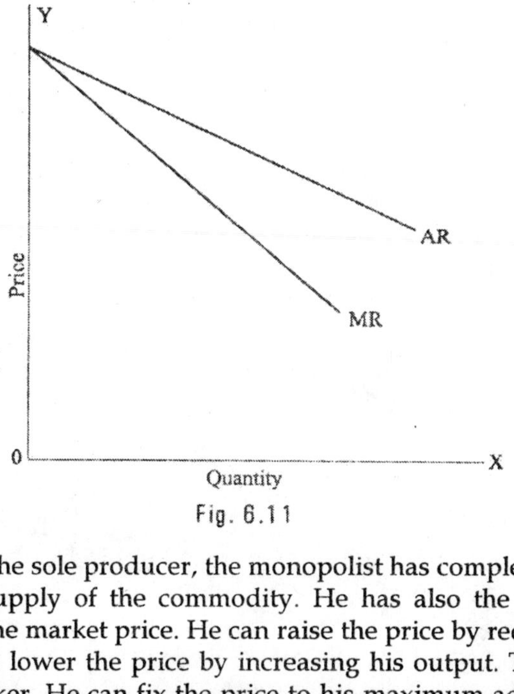

Fig. 6.11

Being the sole producer, the monopolist has complete control over the supply of the commodity. He has also the power to influence the market price. He can raise the price by reducing his output and lower the price by increasing his output. Thus he is a price-maker. He can fix the price to his maximum advantages. But he cannot fix both the supply and the price, simultaneously. He can do one thing at a time. If the fixes the price, his output will be determined by the market demand for his commodity. On the other hand, if he fixes the output to be sold, its market will determine the price for the commodity. Thus his decision to fix either the price or the output is determined by the market demand.

The market demand curve of the monopolist (the average revenue curve) is downward sloping. Its corresponding marginal revenue curve is also downward sloping. But the marginal revenue curve lies below the average revenue curve as shown in the figure. The monopolist faces the down-sloping demand curve because to sell more output, he must reduce the price of his product. The firm's demand curve and industry's demand curve are one and the same. The average cost and marginal cost curve are U shaped curve. Marginal cost falls and rises steeply when compared to average cost.

Price output determination (Equilibrium Point)

The monopolistic firm attains equilibrium when its marginal cost becomes equal to the marginal revenue. The monopolist always desires to make maximum profits. He makes maximum profits when MC=MR. He does not increasing his output if his revenue exceeds his costs. But when the costs exceed the revenue, the monopolist firm incur loses. Hence the monopolist curtails his production. He produces up to that point where additional cost is equal to the additional revenue (MR=MC). Thus point is called equilibrium point. The price output determination under monopoly may be explained with the help of a diagram.

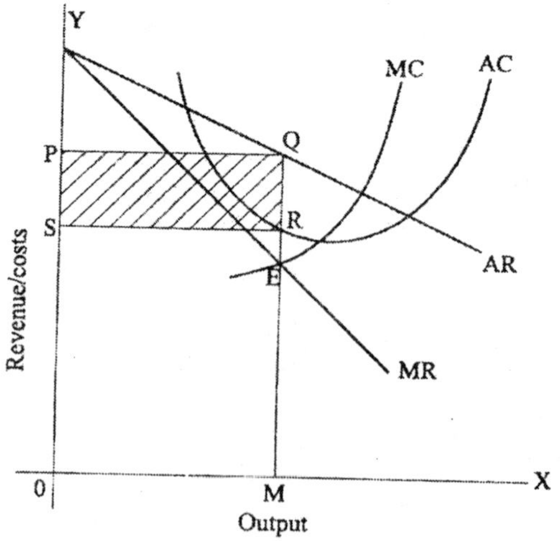

Fig. 6.12

In the diagram 6.12 the quantity supplied or demanded is shown along X-axis. The cost or revenue is shown along Y-axis. AC and MC are the average cost and marginal cost curves respectively. AR and MR curves slope downwards from left to right. AC and MC and U shaped curves. The monopolistic firm attains equilibrium when its marginal cost is equal to marginal revenue (MC=MR). Under monopoly, the MC curve may cut the MR curve from below or from a side. In the diagram, the above condition is satisfied at point E. At point E, MC=MR. The firm is in equilibrium. The equilibrium output is OM.

The above diagram (Average revenue) = MQ or OP

Average cost = MR

Profit per unit = Average Revenue-Average cost=MQ-MR=QR

Total Profit = QRXSR=PQRS

The area PQRS resents the maximum profit earned by the monopoly firm.

But it is not always possible for a monopolist to earn super-normal profits. If the demand and cost situations are not favorable, the monopolist may realize short run losses.

Through the monopolist is a price marker, due to weak demand and high costs; he suffers a loss equal to PABC.

If AR > AC -> Abnormal or super normal profits.

If AR = AC -> Normal Profit

If AR < AC -> Loss

In the long run the firm has time to adjust his plant size or to use existing plant so as to maximize profits.

Monopolistic competition

Perfect competition and pure monopoly are rate phenomena in the real world. Instead, almost every market seems to exhibit characteristics of both perfect competition and monopoly. Hence in the real world it is the state of imperfect competition lying between these two extreme limits that work. Edward. H. Chamberlain developed the theory of monopolistic competition, which presents a more realistic picture of the actual market structure and the nature of competition.

CHARACTERISTICS OF MONOPOLISTIC COMPETITION

The important characteristics of monopolistic competition are:

1. Existence of Many firms: Industry consists of a large number of sellers, each one of whom does not feel dependent upon others. Every firm acts independently without bothering about the reactions of its rivals. The size is so large that an individual firm has only a relatively small part in the total market, so that each firm has very limited control over the price of the product. As the number is relatively

large it is difficult for these firms to determine its price-output policies without considering the possible reactions of the rival forms. A monopolistically competitive firm follows an independent price policy.

2. Product Differentiation: Product differentiation means that products are different in some ways, but not altogether so. The products are not identical but the same time they will not be entirely different from each other. IT really means that there are various monopolist firms competing with each other. An example of monopolistic competition and product differentiation is the toothpaste produced by various firms. The product of each firm is different from that of its rivals in one or more respects. Different toothpastes like Colgate, Close-up, Forehans, Cibaca, etc., provide an example of monopolistic competition. These products are relatively close substitute for each other but not perfect substitutes. Consumers have definite preferences for the particular verities or brands of products offered for sale by various sellers. Advertisement, packing, trademarks, brand names etc. help differentiation of products even if they are physically identical.
3. Large Number of Buyers: There are large number buyers in the market. But the buyers have their own brand preferences. So the sellers are able to exercise a certain degree of monopoly over them. Each seller has to plan various incentive schemes to retain the customers who patronize his products.
4. Free Entry and Exist of Firms: As in the perfect competition, in the monopolistic competition too, there is freedom of entry and exit. That is, there is no barrier as found under monopoly.
5. Selling costs: Since the products are close substitute much effort is needed to retain the existing consumers and to create new demand. So each firm has to spend a lot on selling cost, which includes cost on advertising and other sale promotion activities.
6. Imperfect Knowledge: Imperfect knowledge about the product leads to monopolistic competition. If the buyers are fully aware of the quality of the product they cannot be influenced much by advertisement or other sales

promotion techniques. But in the business world we can see that thought the quality of certain products is the same, effective advertisement and sales promotion techniques make certain brands monopolistic. For examples, effective dealer service backed by advertisement-helped popularization of some brands through the quality of almost all the cement available in the market remains the same.

7. The Group: Under perfect competition the term industry refers to all collection of firms producing a homogenous product. But under monopolistic competition the products of various firms are not identical through they are close substitutes. Prof. Chamberlin called the collection of firms producing close substitute products as a group.

Price - Output Determination under Monopolistic Competition

Since under monopolistic competition different firms produce different varieties of products, different prices for them will be determined in the market depending upon the demand and cost conditions. Each firm will set the price and output of its own product. Here also the profit will be maximized when marginal revenue is equal to marginal cost.

Short-run equilibrium of the firm:

In the short-run the firm is in equilibrium when marginal Revenue = Marginal Cost. In Fig 6.15 AR is the average revenue curve. NMR marginal revenue curve, SMC short-run marginal cost curve, SAC short-run average cost curve, MR and SMC interest at point E where output in OM and price MQ (i.e. OP). Thus the equilibrium output or the maximum profit output is OM and the price MQ or OP. When the price (average revenue) is above average cost a firm will be making supernormal profit. From the figure it can be seen that AR is above AC in the equilibrium point. As AR is above AC, this firm is making abnormal profits in the short-run. The abnormal profit per unit is QR, i.e., the difference between AR and AC at equilibrium point and the total supernormal profit is OR X OM. This total abnormal profits is represented by the rectangle PQRS. As the demand curve here is highly elastic, the excess price over marginal cost is rather low. But in monopoly the demand curve is inelastic. So the gap between price and marginal cost will be rather large.

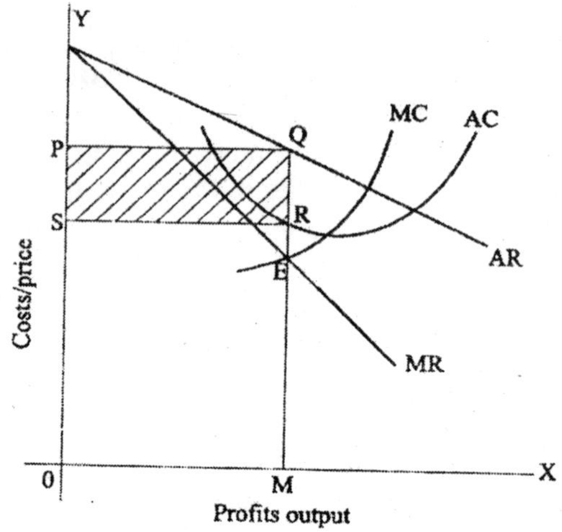

Fig. 6.15

If the demand and cost conditions are less favorable the monopolistically competitive firm may incur loss in the short-run fig 6.16 Illustrates this. A firm incurs loss when the price is less than the average cost of production. MQ is the average cost and OS (i.e. MR) is the price per unit at equilibrium output OM. QR is the loss per unit. The total loss at an output OM is OR X OM. The rectangle PQRS represents the total loses in the short run.

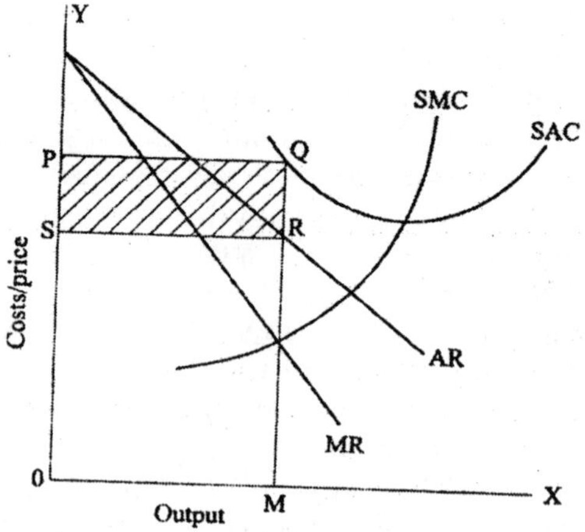

Fig. 6.16

Long - Run Equilibrium of the Firm

A monopolistically competitive firm will be long - run equilibrium at the output level where marginal cost equal to marginal revenue. Monopolistically competitive firm in the long run attains equilibrium where MC=MR and AC=AR Fig 6.17 shows this trend.

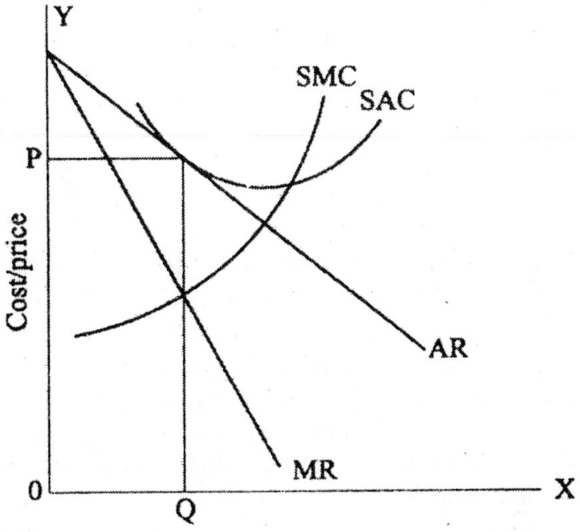

Fig. 6.17

OLIGOPOLY

The term oligopoly is derived from two Greek words, oligos meaning a few, and pollen meaning to sell. Oligopoly is the form of imperfect competition where there are a few firms in the market, producing either a homogeneous product or producing products, which are close but not perfect substitute of each other.

Characteristics of Oligopoly

The main features of oligopoly are:

1. Few Firms: There are only a few firms in the industry. Each firm contributes a sizeable share of the total market. Any decision taken by one firm influence the actions of other firms in the industry. The various firms in the industry compete with each other.

2. Interdependence: As there are only very few firms, any steps taken by one firm to increase sales, by reducing price or by changing product design or by increasing advertisement expenditure will naturally affect the sales of other firms in the industry. An immediate retaliatory action can be anticipated from the other firms in the industry every time when one firm takes such a decision. He has to take this into account when he takes decisions. So the decisions of all the firms in the industry are interdependent.
3. Indeterminate Demand Curve: The interdependence of the firms makes their demand curve indeterminate. When one firm reduces price other firms also will make a cut in their prices. So he firm cannot be certain about the demand for its product. Thus the demand curve facing an oligopolistic firm loses its definiteness and thus is indeterminate as it constantly changes due to the reactions of the rival firms.
4. Advertising and selling costs: Advertising plays a greater role in the oligopoly market when compared to other market systems. According to Prof. William J. Banumol "it is only oligopoly that advertising comes fully into its own". A huge expenditure on advertising and sales promotion techniques is needed both to retain the present market share and to increase it. So Banumol concludes "under oligopoly, advertising can become a life-and-death matter where a firm which fails to keep up with the advertising budget of its competitors may find its customers drifting off to rival products."
5. Price Rigidity: In the oligopoly market price remain rigid. If one firm reduced price it is with the intention of attracting the customers of other firms in the industry. In order to retain their consumers they will also reduce price. Thus the pricing decision of one firm results in a loss to all the firms in the industry. If one firm increases price. Other firms will remain silent there by allowing that firm to lost its customers. Hence, no firm will be ready to change the prevailing price. It causes price rigidity in the oligopoly market.

OTHER MARKET STRUCTURES

Duopoly

Duopoly refers to a market situation in which there are only two sellers. As there are only two sellers any decision taken by one seller will have reaction from the other Eg. Coca-Cola and Pepsi. Usually these two sellers may agree to co-operate each other and share the market equally between them, So that they can avoid harmful competition.

The duopoly price, in the long run, may be a monopoly price or competitive price, or it may settle at any level between the monopoly price and competitive price. In the short period, duopoly price may even fall below the level competitive price with the both the firms earning less than even the normal price.

Monopsony

Mrs. Joan Robinson was the first writer to use the term monopsony to refer to market, which there is a single buyer. Monoposony is a single buyer or a purchasing agency, which buys the show, or nearly whole of a commodity or service produced. It may be created when all consumers of a commodity are organized together and/or when only one consumer requires that commodity which no one else requires.

Bilateral Monopoly

A bilateral monopoly is a market situation in which a single seller (Monopoly) faces a single buyer (Monoposony). It is a market of monopoly-monoposy.

Oligopsony

Oligopsony is a market situation in which there will be a few buyers and many sellers. As the sellers are more and buyers are few, the price of product will be comparatively low but not as low as under monopoly.

Pricing Methods

The micro - economic principle of profit maximization suggests pricing by the marginal analysis. That is by equating MR to MC. However the pricing methods followed by the firms in practice around the world rarely follow this procedure. This is for two reasons; uncertainty with regard to demand and cost function and the deviation from the objective of short run profit maximization.

It was seen that there is no unique theory of firm behavior. While profit certainly on important variable for which every firm cares. Maximization of short – run profit is not a popular objective of a firm today. At the most firms seek maximum profit in the long run. If so the problem is dynamic and its solution requires accurate knowledge of demand and cost conditions over time. Which is impossible to come by?

In view of these problems economic prices are a rare phenomenon. Instead, firms set prices for their products through several alternative means. The important pricing methods followed in practice are shown in the chart.

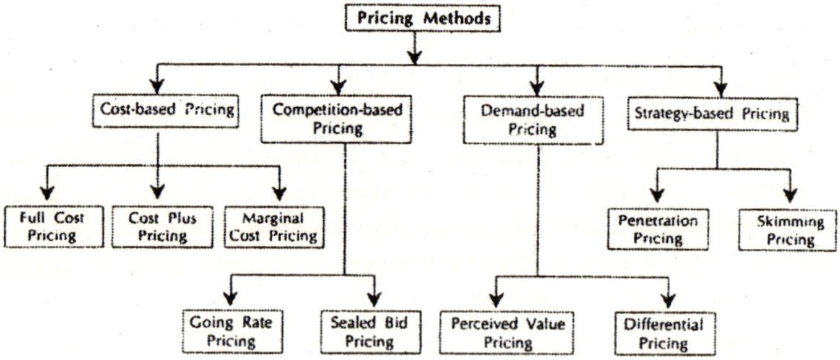

Cost Based Pricing

There are three versions of the cost – based pricing. Full – cost or break even pricing, cost plus pricing and the marginal cost pricing. Under the first version, price just equals the average (total) cost. In the second version, some mark-up is added to the average cost in arriving at the price. In the last version, price is set equal to the marginal cost. While all these methods appear to be easy and straight forward, they are in fact associated with a number of difficulties. Even through difficulties are there, the cost- oriented pricing is quite popular today.

The cost – based pricing has several strengths as well as limitations. The advantages are its simplicity, acceptability and consistency with the target rate of return on investment and the price stability in general. The limitations are difficulties in getting accurate estimates of cost (particularly of the future cost rather than the historic cost) Volatile nature of the variable cost and its ignoring of the demand side of the market etc.

Competition based pricing

Some commodities are priced according to the competition in their markets. Thus we have the going rate method of price and the sealed bid pricing technique. Under the former a firm prices its new product according to the prevailing prices of comparable products in the market. If the product is new in the country, then its import cost – inclusive of the costs of certificates, insurance, and freight and customs duty, is used as the basis for pricing, Incidentally, the price is not necessarily equal to the import cost, but to the firm is either new in the country, or is a close substitute or complimentary to some other products, the prices of hitherto existing bands or/and of the related goods are taken in to a account while deciding its price. Thus, when television was first manufactures in India, its import cost must have been a guiding force in its price determination. Similarly, when maruti car was first manufactured in India, it must have taken into account the prices of existing cars, price of petrol, price of car accessories, etc. Needless to say, the going rate price could be below or above the average cost and it could even be an economic price.

The sealed bid pricing method is quite popular in the case of construction activities and in the disposition of used produces. In this method the prospective seller (buyers) are asked to quote their prices through a sealed cover, all the offers are opened at a preannounce time in the presence of all the competitors, and the one who quoted the least is awarded the contract (purchase/sale deed). As it sound, this method is totally competition based and if the competitors unit by any change, the buyers (seller) may have to pay (receive) an exorbitantly high (too low) price, thus there is a great degree of risk attached to this method of pricing.

Demand Based Pricing

The demand – based pricing and strategy – based pricing are quite related. The seller knows rather well that the demand for its product is a decreasing function of the price its sets for product. Thus if seller wishes to sell more he must reduce the price of his product, and if he wants a good price for his product, he could sell only a limited quantity of his good. Demand oriented pricing rules imply establishment of prices in accordance with consumer preference and perceptions and the intensity of demand.

Two general types demand oriented pricing rules can be identified.

i. Perceived value pricing and

ii. Differential pricing

Perceived value pricing considers the buyer's perception of the value of the product ad the basis of pricing. Here the pricing rule is that the firm must develop procedures for measuring the relative value of the product as perceived by consumers.

Differential pricing is nothing but price discrimination. In involves selling a product or service for different prices in different market segments. Price differentiation depends on geographical location of the consumers, type of consumer, purchasing quantity, season, time of the service etc. E.g. Telephone charges, APSRTC charges.

Strategy based pricing (new product pricing)

A firm which products a new product, if it is also new to industry, can earn very good profits it if handles marketing carefully, because of the uniqueness of the product. The price fixed for the new product must keep the competitors away. Earn good profits for the firm over the life of the product and must help to get the product accepted. The company can select either skimming pricing or penetration pricing.

While there are some firms, which follow the strategy of price penetration, there are some others who opt for price - skimming. Under the former, firms sell their new product at a low price in the beginning in order to catch the attention of consumers, once the product image and credibility is established, the seller slowly starts jacking up the price to reap good profits in future.

Under this strategy, a firm might well sell its product below the cost of production and thus runs into losses to start with but eventually it recovers all its losses and even makes good overall profits.

The Rin washing soap perhaps falls into this category. This soap was sold at a rather low price in the beginning and the firm even distributed free samples. Today, it is quite an expensive brand and yet it is selling very well. Under the price - skimming strategy, the new product is priced high in the beginning, and its price is reduced gradually as it faces a dearth of buyers such a strategy may be beneficial for products, which are fancy, but of poor quality and/or of insignificant use over a period of time.

A prudent producer follows a good mix of the various pricing methods rather than adapting any once of them. This is because no method is perfect and every method has certain good features further a firm might adopt one method at one time and another method at some other accession.

8

Business and New Economic Environment

Imagine you want to do business. Which are you interested in? For example, you want to get into InfoTech industry. What can you do in this industry?

Which one do you choose? The following are the alternatives you have on hand:

- You can bye and sell
- You can set up a small/medium/large industry to manufacture
- You can set up a workshop to repair
- You can develop software
- You can design hardware
- You can be a consultant/trouble-shooter

If you choose any one or more of the above, you have chosen the line of activity. The next step for you is to decide whether.

- You want to be only owner (It means you what to be sole trader) or
- You want to take some more professionals as co-owners along with you (If means you what to from partnership with others as partners) or
- You want to be a global player by mobilizing large resources across the country/world
- You want to bring all like-minded people to share the benefits of the common enterprise (You want to promote a joint stock company) or

- You want to involve government in the IT business (here you want to suggest government to promote a public enterprise!)

To decide this, it is necessary to know how to evaluate each of these alternatives.

FACTORS AFFECTING THE CHOICE OF FORM OF BUSINESS ORGANIZATION

Before we choose a particular form of business organization, let us study what factors affect such a choice? The following are the factors affecting the choice of a business organization:

1. Easy to start and easy to close: The form of business organization should be such that it should be easy to close. There should not be hassles or long procedures in the process of setting up business or closing the same.
2. Division of labour: There should be possibility to divide the work among the available owners.
3. Large amount of resources: Large volume of business requires large volume of resources. Some forms of business organization do not permit to raise larger resources. Select the one which permits to mobilize the large resources.
4. Liability: The liability of the owners should be limited to the extent of money invested in business. It is better if their personal properties are not brought into business to make up the losses of the business.
5. Secrecy: The form of business organization you select should be such that it should permit to take care of the business secrets. We know that century old business units are still surviving only because they could successfully guard their business secrets.
6. Transfer of ownership: There should be simple procedures to transfer the ownership to the next legal heir.
7. Ownership, Management and control: If ownership, management and control are in the hands of one or a small group of persons, communication will be effective and coordination will be easier. Where ownership, management and control are widely distributed, it calls for a high degree of professional's skills to monitor the performance of the business.

8. Continuity: The business should continue forever and ever irrespective of the uncertainties in future.
9. Quick decision-making: Select such a form of business organization, which permits you to take decisions quickly and promptly. Delay in decisions may invalidate the relevance of the decisions.
10. Personal contact with customer: Most of the times, customers give us clues to improve business. So choose such a form, which keeps you close to the customers.
11. Flexibility: In times of rough weather, there should be enough flexibility to shift from one business to the other. The lesser the funds committed in a particular business, the better it is.
12. Taxation: More profit means more tax. Choose such a form, which permits to pay low tax.

These are the parameters against which we can evaluate each of the available forms of business organizations.

SOLE TRADER

The sole trader is the simplest, oldest and natural form of business organization. It is also called sole proprietorship. 'Sole' means one. 'Sole trader' implies that there is only one trader who is the owner of the business.

It is a one-man form of organization wherein the trader assumes all the risk of ownership carrying out the business with his own capital, skill and intelligence. He is the boss for himself. He has total operational freedom. He is the owner, Manager and controller. He has total freedom and flexibility. Full control lies with him. He can take his own decisions. He can choose or drop a particular product or business based on its merits. He need not discuss this with anybody. He is responsible for himself. This form of organization is popular all over the world. Restaurants, Supermarkets, pan shops, medical shops, hosiery shops etc.

Features

- It is easy to start a business under this form and also easy to close.
- He introduces his own capital. Sometimes, he may borrow, if necessary
- He enjoys all the profits and in case of loss, he lone suffers.

- He has unlimited liability which implies that his liability extends to his personal properties in case of loss.
- He has a high degree of flexibility to shift from one business to the other.
- Business secretes can be guarded well
- There is no continuity. The business comes to a close with the death, illness or insanity of the sole trader. Unless, the legal heirs show interest to continue the business, the business cannot be restored.
- He has total operational freedom. He is the owner, manager and controller.
- He can be directly in touch with the customers.
- He can take decisions very fast and implement them promptly.
- Rates of tax, for example, income tax and so on are comparatively very low.

Advantages

The following are the advantages of the sole trader from of business organization:

1. Easy to start and easy to close: Formation of a sole trader from of organization is relatively easy even closing the business is easy.
2. Personal contact with customers directly: Based on the tastes and preferences of the customers the stocks can be maintained.
3. Prompt decision-making: To improve the quality of services to the customers, he can take any decision and implement the same promptly. He is the boss and he is responsible for his business Decisions relating to growth or expansion can be made promptly.
4. High degree of flexibility: Based on the profitability, the trader can decide to continue or change the business, if need be.
5. Secrecy: Business secrets can well be maintained because there is only one trader.
6. Low rate of taxation: The rate of income tax for sole traders is relatively very low.

7. Direct motivation: If there are profits, all the profits belong to the trader himself. In other words. If he works more hard, he will get more profits. This is the direct motivating factor. At the same time, if he does not take active interest, he may stand to lose badly also.
8. Total Control: The ownership, management and control are in the hands of the sole trader and hence it is easy to maintain the hold on business.
9. Minimum interference from government: Except in matters relating to public interest, government does not interfere in the business matters of the sole trader. The sole trader is free to fix price for his products/services if he enjoys monopoly market.
10. Transferability: The legal heirs of the sole trader may take the possession of the business.

Disadvantages

The following are the disadvantages of sole trader form:

1. Unlimited liability: The liability of the sole trader is unlimited. It means that the sole trader has to bring his personal property to clear off the loans of his business. From the legal point of view, he is not different from his business.
2. Limited amounts of capital: The resources a sole trader can mobilize cannot be very large and hence this naturally sets a limit for the scale of operations.
3. No division of labour: All the work related to different functions such as marketing, production, finance, labour and so on has to be taken care of by the sole trader himself. There is nobody else to take his burden. Family members and relatives cannot show as much interest as the trader takes.
4. Uncertainty: There is no continuity in the duration of the business. On the death, insanity of insolvency the business may be come to an end.
5. Inadequate for growth and expansion: This from is suitable for only small size, one-man-show type of organizations. This may not really work out for growing and expanding organizations.

6. Lack of specialization: The services of specialists such as accountants, market researchers, consultants and so on, are not within the reach of most of the sole traders.
7. More competition: Because it is easy to set up a small business, there is a high degree of competition among the small businessmen and a few who are good in taking care of customer requirements along can service.
8. Low bargaining power: The sole trader is the in the receiving end in terms of loans or supply of raw materials. He may have to compromise many times regarding the terms and conditions of purchase of materials or borrowing loans from the finance houses or banks.

PARTNERSHIP

Partnership is an improved from of sole trader in certain respects. Where there are like-minded persons with resources, they can come together to do the business and share the profits/ losses of the business in an agreed ratio. Persons who have entered into such an agreement are individually called 'partners' and collectively called 'firm'. The relationship among partners is called a partnership.

Indian Partnership Act, 1932 defines partnership as the relationship between two or more persons who agree to share the profits of the business carried on by all or any one of them acting for all.

Features

1. Relationship: Partnership is a relationship among persons. It is relationship resulting out of an agreement.
2. Two or more persons: There should be two or more number of persons.
3. There should be a business: Business should be conducted.
4. Agreement: Persons should agree to share the profits/ losses of the business
5. Carried on by all or any one of them acting for all: The business can be carried on by all or any one of the persons acting for all. This means that the business can be carried on by one person who is the agent for all other persons. Every partner is both an agent and a principal. Agent for

other partners and principal for himself. All the partners are agents and the 'partnership' is their principal.

The following are the other features:

(a) Unlimited liability: The liability of the partners is unlimited. The partnership and partners, in the eye of law, and not different but one and the same. Hence, the partners have to bring their personal assets to clear the losses of the firm, if any.

(b) Number of partners: According to the Indian Partnership Act, the minimum number of partners should be two and the maximum number if restricted, as given below:
   - 10 partners is case of banking business
   - 20 in case of non-banking business

(c) Division of labour: Because there are more than two persons, the work can be divided among the partners based on their aptitude.

(d) Personal contact with customers: The partners can continuously be in touch with the customers to monitor their requirements.

(e) Flexibility: All the partners are likeminded persons and hence they can take any decision relating to business.

Partnership Deed

The written agreement among the partners is called 'the partnership deed'. It contains the terms and conditions governing the working of partnership. The following are contents of the partnership deed.

1. Names and addresses of the firm and partners
2. Nature of the business proposed
3. Duration
4. Amount of capital of the partnership and the ratio for contribution by each of the partners.
5. Their profit sharing ration (this is used for sharing losses also)
6. Rate of interest charged on capital contributed, loans taken from the partnership and the amounts drawn, if any, by the partners from their respective capital balances.
7. The amount of salary or commission payable to any partner

8. Procedure to value good will of the firm at the time of admission of a new partner, retirement of death of a partner
9. Allocation of responsibilities of the partners in the firm
10. Procedure for dissolution of the firm
11. Name of the arbitrator to whom the disputes, if any, can be referred to for settlement.
12. Special rights, obligations and liabilities of partners(s), if any.

Kind of partners

The following are the different kinds of partners:

1. Active Partner: Active partner takes active part in the affairs of the partnership. He is also called working partner.
2. Sleeping Partner: Sleeping partner contributes to capital but does not take part in the affairs of the partnership.
3. Nominal Partner: Nominal partner is partner just for namesake. He neither contributes to capital nor takes part in the affairs of business. Normally, the nominal partners are those who have good business connections, and are well places in the society.
4. Partner by Estoppels: Estoppels means behavior or conduct. Partner by estoppels gives an impression to outsiders that he is the partner in the firm. In fact be neither contributes to capital, nor takes any role in the affairs of the partnership.
5. Partner by holding out: If partners declare a particular person (having social status) as partner and this person does not contradict even after he comes to know such declaration, he is called a partner by holding out and he is liable for the claims of third parties. However, the third parties should prove they entered into contract with the firm in the belief that he is the partner of the firm. Such a person is called partner by holding out.
6. Minor Partner: Minor has a special status in the partnership. A minor can be admitted for the benefits of the firm. A minor is entitled to his share of profits of the firm. The liability of a minor partner is limited to the extent of his contribution of the capital of the firm.

RIGHT OF PARTNERS

Every partner has right

(a) To take part in the management of business

(b) To express his opinion

(c) Of access to and inspect and copy and book of accounts of the firm

(d) To share equally the profits of the firm in the absence of any specific agreement to the contrary

(e) To receive interest on capital at an agreed rate of interest from the profits of the firm

(f) To receive interest on loans, if any, extended to the firm.

(g) To be indemnified for any loss incurred by him in the conduct of the business

(h) To receive any money spent by him in the ordinary and proper conduct of the business of the firm.

Advantages

The following are the advantages of the partnership from:

1. Easy to form: Once there is a group of like-minded persons and good business proposal, it is easy to start and register a partnership.
2. Availability of larger amount of capital: More amount of capital can be raised from more number of partners.
3. Division of labour: The different partners come with varied backgrounds and skills. This facilities division of labour.
4. Flexibility: The partners are free to change their decisions, add or drop a particular product or start a new business or close the present one and so on.
5. Personal contact with customers: There is scope to keep close monitoring with customers requirements by keeping one of the partners in charge of sales and marketing. Necessary changes can be initiated based on the merits of the proposals from the customers.
6. Quick decisions and prompt action: If there is consensus among partners, it is enough to implement any decision and initiate prompt action. Sometimes, it may more time for the partners on strategic issues to reach consensus.

7. The positive impact of unlimited liability: Every partner is always alert about his impending danger of unlimited liability. Hence he tries to do his best to bring profits for the partnership firm by making good use of all his contacts.

Disadvantages

The following are the disadvantages of partnership:

1. Formation of partnership is difficult: Only like-minded persons can start a partnership. It is sarcastically said,' it is easy to find a life partner, but not a business partner'.
2. Liability: The partners have joint and several liabilities beside unlimited liability. Joint and several liability puts additional burden on the partners, which means that even the personal properties of the partner or partners can be attached. Even when all but one partner become insolvent, the solvent partner has to bear the entire burden of business loss.
3. Lack of harmony or cohesiveness: It is likely that partners may not, most often work as a group with cohesiveness. This result in mutual conflicts, an attitude of suspicion and crisis of confidence. Lack of harmony results in delay in decisions and paralyses the entire operations.
4. Limited growth: The resources when compared to sole trader, a partnership may raise little more. But when compare to the other forms such as a company, resources raised in this form of organization are limited. Added to this, there is a restriction on the maximum number of partners.
5. Instability: The partnership form is known for its instability. The firm may be dissolved on death, insolvency or insanity of any of the partners.
6. Lack of Public confidence: Public and even the financial institutions look at the unregistered firm with a suspicious eye. Though registration of the firm under the Indian Partnership Act is a solution of such problem, this cannot revive public confidence into this form of organization overnight. The partnership can create confidence in other only with their performance.

JOINT STOCK COMPANY

The joint stock company emerges from the limitations of partnership such as joint and several liability, unlimited liability, limited resources and uncertain duration and so on. Normally, to take part in a business, it may need large money and we cannot foretell the fate of business. It is not literally possible to get into business with little money. Against this background, it is interesting to study the functioning of a joint stock company. The main principle of the joint stock company from is to provide opportunity to take part in business with a low investment as possible say Rs.1000. Joint Stock Company has been a boon for investors with moderate funds to invest.

The word ' company' has a Latin origin, com means ' come together', pany means ' bread', joint stock company means, people come together to earn their livelihood by investing in the stock of company jointly.

Company Defined

Lord justice Lindley explained the concept of the joint stock company from of organization as 'an association of many persons who contribute money or money's worth to a common stock and employ it for a common purpose.

Features

This definition brings out the following features of the company:

1. Artificial person: The Company has no form or shape. It is an artificial person created by law. It is intangible, invisible and existing only, in the eyes of law.
2. Separate legal existence: it has an independence existence, it separate from its members. It can acquire the assets. It can borrow for the company. It can sue other if they are in default in payment of dues, breach of contract with it, if any. Similarly, outsiders for any claim can sue it. A shareholder is not liable for the acts of the company. Similarly, the shareholders cannot bind the company by their acts.
3. Voluntary association of persons: The Company is an association of voluntary association of persons who want

to carry on business for profit. To carry on business, they need capital. So they invest in the share capital of the company.

4. Limited Liability: The shareholders have limited liability i.e., liability limited to the face value of the shares held by him. In other words, the liability of a shareholder is restricted to the extent of his contribution to the share capital of the company. The shareholder need not pay anything, even in times of loss for the company, other than his contribution to the share capital.
5. Capital is divided into shares: The total capital is divided into a certain number of units. Each unit is called a share. The price of each share is priced so low that every investor would like to invest in the company. The companies promoted by promoters of good standing (i.e., known for their reputation in terms of reliability character and dynamism) are likely to attract huge resources.
6. Transferability of shares: In the company form of organization, the shares can be transferred from one person to the other. A shareholder of a public company can cell sell his holding of shares at his will. However, the shares of a private company cannot be transferred. A private company restricts the transferability of the shares.
7. Common Seal: As the company is an artificial person created by law has no physical form, it cannot sign its name on a paper; so, it has a common seal on which its name is engraved. The common seal should affix every document or contract; otherwise the company is not bound by such a document or contract.
8. Perpetual succession: 'Members may comes and members may go, but the company continues for ever and ever' A. company has uninterrupted existence because of the right given to the shareholders to transfer the shares.
9. Ownership and Management separated: The shareholders are spread over the length and breadth of the country, and sometimes, they are from different parts of the world. To facilitate administration, the shareholders elect some among themselves or the promoters of the company as directors to a Board, which looks after the management of the

business. The Board recruits the managers and employees at different levels in the management. Thus the management is separated from the owners.

10. Winding up: Winding up refers to the putting an end to the company. Because law creates it, only law can put an end to it in special circumstances such as representation from creditors of financial institutions, or shareholders against the company that their interests are not safeguarded. The company is not affected by the death or insolvency of any of its members.
11. The name of the company ends with 'limited': it is necessary that the name of the company ends with limited (Ltd.) to give an indication to the outsiders that they are dealing with the company with limited liability and they should be careful about the liability aspect of their transactions with the company.

FORMATION OF JOINT STOCK COMPANY

There are two stages in the formation of a joint stock company. They are:

(a) To obtain Certificates of Incorporation

(b) To obtain certificate of commencement of Business

Certificate of Incorporation: The certificate of Incorporation is just like a 'date of birth' certificate. It certifies that a company with such and such a name is born on a particular day.

Certificate of commencement of Business: A private company need not obtain the certificate of commencement of business. It can start its commercial operations immediately after obtaining the certificate of Incorporation.

The persons who conceive the idea of starting a company and who organize the necessary initial resources are called promoters. The vision of the promoters forms the backbone for the company in the future to reckon with.

The promoters have to file the following documents, along with necessary fee, with a registrar of joint stock companies to obtain certificate of incorporation:

(a) Memorandum of Association: The Memorandum of Association is also called the charter of the company. It outlines the relations of the company with the outsiders.

If furnishes all its details in six clause such as (ii) Name clause (II) situation clause (iii) objects clause (iv) Capital clause and (vi) subscription clause duly executed by its subscribers.

(b) Articles of association: Articles of Association furnishes the byelaws or internal rules government the internal conduct of the company.

(c) The list of names and address of the proposed directors and their willingness, in writing to act as such, in case of registration of a public company.

(d) A statutory declaration that all the legal requirements have been fulfilled. The declaration has to be duly signed by any one of the following: Company secretary in whole practice, the proposed director, legal solicitor, chartered accountant in whole time practice or advocate of High court.

The registrar of joint stock companies peruses and verifies whether all these documents are in order or not. If he is satisfied with the information furnished, he will register the documents and then issue a certificate of incorporation, if it is private company, it can start its business operation immediately after obtaining certificate of incorporation.

Advantages

The following are the advantages of a joint Stock Company

1. Mobilization of larger resources: A joint stock company provides opportunity for the investors to invest, even small sums, in the capital of large companies. The facilities rising of larger resources.
2. Separate legal entity: The Company has separate legal entity. It is registered under Indian Companies Act, 1956.
3. Limited liability: The shareholder has limited liability in respect of the shares held by him. In no case, does his liability exceed more than the face value of the shares allotted to him.
4. Transferability of shares: The shares can be transferred to others. However, the private company shares cannot be transferred.

5. Liquidity of investments: By providing the transferability of shares, shares can be converted into cash.
6. Inculcates the habit of savings and investments: Because the share face value is very low, this promotes the habit of saving among the common man and mobilizes the same towards investments in the company.
7. Democracy in management: the shareholders elect the directors in a democratic way in the general body meetings. The shareholders are free to make any proposals, question the practice of the management, suggest the possible remedial measures, as they perceive, The directors respond to the issue raised by the shareholders and have to justify their actions.
8. Economics of large scale production: Since the production is in the scale with large funds at
9. Continued existence: The Company has perpetual succession. It has no natural end. It continues forever and ever unless law put an end to it.
10. Institutional confidence: Financial Institutions prefer to deal with companies in view of their professionalism and financial strengths.
11. Professional management: With the larger funds at its disposal, the Board of Directors recruits competent and professional managers to handle the affairs of the company in a professional manner.
12. Growth and Expansion: With large resources and professional management, the company can earn good returns on its operations, build good amount of reserves and further consider the proposals for growth and expansion.

All that shines is not gold. The company from of organization is not without any disadvantages. The following are the disadvantages of joint stock companies.

Disadvantages

1. Formation of company is a long drawn procedure: Promoting a joint stock company involves a long drawn procedure. It is expensive and involves large number of legal formalities.

2. High degree of government interference: The government brings out a number of rules and regulations governing the internal conduct of the operations of a company such as meetings, voting, audit and so on, and any violation of these rules results into statutory lapses, punishable under the companies act.
3. Inordinate delays in decision-making: As the size of the organization grows, the number of levels in organization also increases in the name of specialization. The more the number of levels, the more is the delay in decision-making. Sometimes, so-called professionals do not respond to the urgencies as required. It promotes delay in administration, which is referred to 'red tape and bureaucracy'.
4. Lack or initiative: In most of the cases, the employees of the company at different levels show slack in their personal initiative with the result, the opportunities once missed do not recur and the company loses the revenue.
5. Lack of responsibility and commitment: In some cases, the managers at different levels are afraid to take risk and more worried about their jobs rather than the huge funds invested in the capital of the company lose the revenue.
6. Lack of responsibility and commitment: In some cases, the managers at different levels are afraid to take risk and more worried about their jobs rather than the huge funds invested in the capital of the company. Where managers do not show up willingness to take responsibility, they cannot be considered as committed. They will not be able to handle the business risks.

PUBLIC ENTERPRISES

Public enterprises occupy an important position in the Indian economy. Today, public enterprises provide the substance and heart of the economy. Its investment of over Rs.10,000 crore is in heavy and basic industry, and infrastructure like power, transport and communications. The concept of public enterprise in Indian dates back to the era of pre-independence.

Genesis of Public Enterprises

In consequence to declaration of its goal as socialistic pattern of society in 1954, the Government of India realized that it is through progressive extension of public enterprises only, the following aims of our five years plans can be fulfilled.

- Higher production
- Greater employment
- Economic equality, and
- Dispersal of economic power.

The government found it necessary to revise its industrial policy in 1956 to give it a socialistic bent.

Need for Public Enterprises

The Industrial Policy Resolution 1956 states the need for promoting public enterprises as follows:

- To accelerate the rate of economic growth by planned development
- To speed up industrialization, particularly development of heavy industries and to expand public sector and to build up a large and growing cooperative sector.
- To increase infrastructure facilities
- To disperse the industries over different geographical areas for balanced regional development
- To increase the opportunities of gainful employment
- To help in raising the standards of living
- To reducing disparities in income and wealth (By preventing private monopolies and curbing concentration of economic power and vast industries in the hands of a small number of individuals)

Achievements of public Enterprises

The achievements of public enterprise are vast and varied. They are:

1. Setting up a number of public enterprises in basic and key industries
2. Generating considerably large employment opportunities in skilled, unskilled, supervisory and managerial cadres.
3. Creating internal resources and contributing towards national exchequer for funds for development and welfare.
4. Bringing about development activities in backward regions, through locations in different areas of the country.

5. Assisting in the field of export promotion and conservation of foreign exchange.
6. Creating viable infrastructure and bringing about rapid industrialization (ancillary industries developed around the public sector as its nucleus).
7. Restricting the growth of private monopolies
8. Stimulating diversified growth in private sector
9. Taking over sick industrial units and putting them, in most of the vases, in order,
10. Creating financial systems, through a powerful networking of financial institutions, development and promotional institutions, which has resulted in social control and social orientation of investment, credit and capital management systems.
11. Benefiting the rural areas, priority sectors, small business in the fields of industry, finance, credit, services, trade, transport, consultancy and so on.

Let us see the different forms of public enterprise and their features now.

FORMS OF PUBLIC ENTERPRISES

Public enterprises can be classified into three forms:

(a) Departmental undertaking

(b) Public corporation

(c) Government company

These are explained below:

Departmental Undertaking

This is the earliest from of public enterprise. Under this form, the affairs of the public enterprise are carried out under the overall control of one of the departments of the government. The government department appoints a managing director (normally a civil servant) for the departmental undertaking. He will be given the executive authority to take necessary decisions. The departmental undertaking does not have a budget of its own. As and when it wants, it draws money from the government exchequer and when it has surplus money, it deposits it in the government exchequer. However, it is subject to budget, accounting and audit controls.

Examples for departmental undertakings are Railways, Department of Posts, All India Radio, Doordarshan, Defence undertakings like DRDL, DLRL, ordinance factories, and such.

Features

1. Under the control of a government department: The departmental undertaking is not an independent organization. It has no separate existence. It is designed to work under close control of a government department. It is subject to direct ministerial control.
2. More financial freedom: The departmental undertaking can draw funds from government account as per the needs and deposit back when convenient.
3. Like any other government department: The departmental undertaking is almost similar to any other government department
4. Budget, accounting and audit controls: The departmental undertaking has to follow guidelines (as applicable to the other government departments) underlying the budget preparation, maintenance of accounts, and getting the accounts audited internally and by external auditors.
5. More a government organization, less a business organization. The set up of a departmental undertaking is more rigid, less flexible, slow in responding to market needs.

Advantages

1. Effective control: Control is likely to be effective because it is directly under the Ministry.
2. Responsible Executives: Normally the administration is entrusted to a senior civil servant. The administration will be organized and effective.
3. Less scope for mystification of funds: Departmental undertaking does not draw any money more than is needed, that too subject to ministerial sanction and other controls. So chances for mis-utilisation are low.
4. Adds to Government revenue: The revenue of the government is on the rise when the revenue of the departmental undertaking is deposited in the government account.

Disadvantages

1. Decisions delayed: Control is centralized. This results in lower degree of flexibility. Officials in the lower levels cannot take initiative. Decisions cannot be fast and actions cannot be prompt.
2. No incentive to maximize earnings: The departmental undertaking does not retain any surplus with it. So there is no inventive for maximizing the efficiency or earnings.
3. Slow response to market conditions: Since there is no competition, there is no profit motive; there is no incentive to move swiftly to market needs.
4. Redtapism and bureaucracy: The departmental undertakings are in the control of a civil servant and under the immediate supervision of a government department. Administration gets delayed substantially.
5. Incidence of more taxes: At times, in case of losses, these are made up by the government funds only. To make up these, there may be a need for fresh taxes, which is undesirable.

Any business organization to be more successful needs to be more dynamic, flexible, and responsive to market conditions, fast in decision marking and prompt in actions.

None of these qualities figure in the features of a departmental undertaking. It is true that departmental undertaking operates as a extension to the government. With the result, the government may miss certain business opportunities. So as not to miss business opportunities, the government has thought of another form of public enterprise, that is, Public corporation.

PUBLIC CORPORATION

Having released that the routing government administration would not be able to cope up with the demand of its business enterprises, the Government of India, in 1948, decided to organize some of its enterprises as statutory corporations. In pursuance of this, Industrial Finance Corporation, Employees' State Insurance Corporation was set up in 1948.

Public corporation is a 'right mix of public ownership, public accountability and business management for public ends'. The public corporation provides machinery, which is flexible, while at the same time retaining public control.

Definition

A public corporation is defined as a 'body corporate create by an Act of Parliament or Legislature and notified by the name in the official gazette of the central or state government. It is a corporate entity having perpetual succession, and common seal with power to acquire, hold, dispose off property, sue and be sued by its name".

Examples of a public corporation are Life Insurance Corporation of India, Unit Trust of India, Industrial Finance Corporation of India, Damodar Valley Corporation and others.

Features

1. A body corporate: It has a separate legal existence. It is a separate company by itself. If can raise resources, buy and sell properties, by name sue and be sued.
2. More freedom and day-to-day affairs: It is relatively free from any type of political interference. It enjoys administrative autonomy.
3. Freedom regarding personnel: The employees of public corporation are not government civil servants. The corporation has absolute freedom to formulate its own personnel policies and procedures, and these are applicable to all the employees including directors.
4. Perpetual succession: A statute in parliament or state legislature creates it. It continues forever and till a statue is passed to wind it up.
5. Financial autonomy: Through the public corporation is fully owned government organization, and the initial finance are provided by the Government, it enjoys total financial autonomy, Its income and expenditure are not shown in the annual budget of the government, it enjoys total financial autonomy. Its income and expenditure are not shown in the annual budget of the government. However, for its freedom it is restricted regarding capital expenditure beyond the laid down limits, and raising the capital through capital market.

6. Commercial audit: Except in the case of banks and other financial institutions where chartered accountants are auditors, in all corporations, the audit is entrusted to the comptroller and auditor general of India.
7. Run on commercial principles: As far as the discharge of functions, the corporation shall act as far as possible on sound business principles.

Advantages

1. Independence, initiative and flexibility: The corporation has an autonomous set up. So it is independent, take necessary initiative to realize its goals, and it can be flexible in its decisions as required.
2. Scope for Redtapism and bureaucracy minimized: The Corporation has its own policies and procedures. If necessary they can be simplified to eliminate redtapism and bureaucracy, if any.
3. Public interest protected: The corporation can protect the public interest by making its policies more public friendly, Public interests are protected because every policy of the corporation is subject to ministerial directives and board parliamentary control.
4. Employee friendly work environment: Corporation can design its own work culture and train its employees accordingly. It can provide better amenities and better terms of service to the employees and thereby secure greater productivity.
5. Competitive prices: the corporation is a government organization and hence can afford with minimum margins of profit, It can offer its products and services at competitive prices.
6. Economics of scale: By increasing the size of its operations, it can achieve economics of large-scale production.
7. Public accountability: It is accountable to the Parliament or legislature; it has to submit its annual report on its working results.

Disadvantages

1. Continued political interference: the autonomy is on paper only and in reality, the continued.

2. Misuse of Power: In some cases, the greater autonomy leads to misuse of power. It takes time to unearth the impact of such misuse on the resources of the corporation. Cases of misuse of power defeat the very purpose of the public corporation.
3. Burden for the government: Where the public corporation ignores the commercial principles and suffers losses, it is burdensome for the government to provide subsidies to make up the losses.

GOVERNMENT COMPANY

Section 617 of the Indian Companies Act defines a government company as "any company in which not less than 51 percent of the paid up share capital" is held by the Central Government or by any State Government or Governments or partly by Central Government and partly by one or more of the state Governments and includes and company which is subsidiary of government company as thus defined".

A government company is the right combination of operating flexibility of privately organized companies with the advantages of state regulation and control in public interest.

Government companies differ in the degree of control and their motive also.

Some government companies are promoted as

- industrial undertakings (such as Hindustan Machine Tools, Indian Telephone Industries, and so on)
- Promotional agencies (such as National Industrial Development Corporation, National Small Industries Corporation, and so on) to prepare feasibility reports for promoters who want to set up public or private companies.
- Agency to promote trade or commerce. For example, state trading corporation, Export Credit Guarantee Corporation and so such like.
- A company to take over the existing sick companies under private management (E.g. Hindustan Shipyard)
- A company established as a totally state enterprise to safeguard national interests such as Hindustan Aeronautics Ltd. And so on.

- Mixed ownership company in collaboration with a private consult to obtain technical know how and guidance for the management of its enterprises, e.g. Hindustan Cables)

Features

The following are the features of a government company:

1. Like any other registered company: It is incorporated as a registered company under the Indian companies Act. 1956. Like any other company, the government company has separate legal existence. Common seal, perpetual succession, limited liability, and so on. The provisions of the Indian Companies Act apply for all matters relating to formation, administration and winding up. However, the government has a right to exempt the application of any provisions of the government companies.
2. Shareholding: The majority of the share are held by the Government, Central or State, partly by the Central and State Government(s), in the name of the President of India, It is also common that the collaborators and allotted some shares for providing the transfer of technology.
3. Directors are nominated: As the government is the owner of the entire or majority of the share capital of the company, it has freedom to nominate the directors to the Board. Government may consider the requirements of the company in terms of necessary specialization and appoints the directors accordingly.
4. Administrative autonomy and financial freedom: A government company functions independently with full discretion and in the normal administration of affairs of the undertaking.
5. Subject to ministerial control: Concerned minister may act as the immediate boss. It is because it is the government that nominates the directors, the minister issue directions for a company and he can call for information related to the progress and affairs of the company any time.

Advantages

1. Formation is easy: There is no need for an Act in legislature or parliament to promote a government company. A Government company can be promoted as per the provisions of the companies Act. Which is relatively easier?

2. Separate legal entity: It retains the advantages of public corporation such as autonomy, legal entity.
3. Ability to compete: It is free from the rigid rules and regulations. It can smoothly function with all the necessary initiative and drive necessary to complete with any other private organization. It retains its independence in respect of large financial resources, recruitment of personnel, management of its affairs, and so on.
4. Flexibility: A Government company is more flexible than a departmental undertaking or public corporation. Necessary changes can be initiated, which the framework of the company law. Government can, if necessary, change the provisions of the Companies Act. If found restricting the freedom of the government company. The form of Government Company is so flexible that it can be used for taking over sick units promoting strategic industries in the context of national security and interest.
5. Quick decision and prompt actions: In view of the autonomy, the government company take decision quickly and ensure that the actions and initiated promptly.
6. Private participation facilitated: Government company is the only from providing scope for private participation in the ownership. The facilities to take the best, necessary to conduct the affairs of business, from the private sector and also from the public sector.

Disadvantages

1. Continued political and government interference: Government seldom leaves the government company to function on its own. Government is the major shareholder and it dictates its decisions to the Board. The Board of Directors gets these approved in the general body. There were a number of cases where the operational polices were influenced by the whims and fancies of the civil servants and the ministers.
2. Higher degree of government control: The degree of government control is so high that the government company is reduced to mere adjuncts to the ministry and is, in majority of the cases, not treated better than the subordinate organization or offices of the government.

3. Evades constitutional responsibility· A government company is creating by executive action of the government without the specific approval of the parliament or Legislature.
4. Poor sense of attachment or commitment: The members of the Board of Management of government companies and from the ministerial departments in their ex-officio capacity. The lack the sense of attachment and do not reflect any degree of commitment to lead the company in a competitive environment.
5. Divided loyalties: The employees are mostly drawn from the regular government departments for a defined period. After this period, they go back to their government departments and hence their divided loyalty dilutes their interest towards their job in the government company.
6. Flexibility on paper: The powers of the directors are to be approved by the concerned Ministry, particularly the power relating to borrowing, increase in the capital, appointment of top officials, entering into contracts for large orders and restrictions on capital expenditure. The government companies are rarely allowed to exercise their flexibility and independence.

9

Capital and Capital Budgeting

INTRODUCTION

Finance is the prerequisite to commence and vary on business. It is rightly said to be the lifeblood of the business. No growth and expansion of business can take place without sufficient finance. It shows that no business activity is possible without finance. This is why; every business has to make plans regarding acquisition and utilization of funds. However efficient a firm may be in terms of production as well as marketing if it ignores the proper management of flow of funds it certainly lands in financial crunch and the very survival of the firm would be at a stake.

FUNCTION OF FINANCE

According to B. O. Wheeler, Financial Management is concerned with the acquisition and utiliasation of capital funds in meeting the financial needs and overall objectives of a business enterprise. Thus the primary function of finance is to acquire capital funds and put them for proper utilization, with which the firm's objectives are fulfilled. The firm should be able to procure sufficient funds on reasonable terms and conditions and should exercise proper control in applying them in order to earn a good rate of return, which in turn allows the firm to reward the sources of funds reasonably, and leaves the firm with good surplus to grow further. These activities viz. financing, investing and dividend payment are not sequential they are performed simultaneously and continuously. Thus, the Financial Management can be broken down in to three major decisions or functions of finance. They are: (i) the investment decision, (ii) the financing decision and (iii) the dividend policy decision.

Investment Decision

The investment decision relates to the selection of assets in which funds will be invested by a firm. The assets as per their duration of benefits, can be categorized into two groups: (i) long-term assets which yield a return over a period of time in future (ii) short-term or current assents which in the normal course of business are convertible into cash usually with in a year. Accordingly, the asset selection decision of a firm is of two types. The investment in long-term assets is popularly known as capital budgeting and in short-term assets, working capital management.

Capital budgeting: Capital budgeting - the long - term investment decision – is probably the most crucial financial decision of a firm. It relates to the selection of an assent or investment proposal or course of action that benefits are likely to be available in future over the lifetime of the project.

The long-term investment may relate to acquisition of new asset or replacement of old assets. Whether an asset will be accepted or not will depend upon the relative benefits and returns associated with it. The measurement of the worth of the investment proposals is, therefore, a major element in the capital budgeting exercise. The second element of the capital budgeting decision is the analysis of risk and uncertainty as the benefits from the investment proposals pertain the future, which is uncertain. They have to be estimated under various assumptions and thus there is an element of risk involved in the exercise. The return from the capital budgeting decision should, therefore, be evaluated in relation to the risk associated with it.

The third and final element is the ascertainment of a certain norm or standard against which the benefits are to be judged. The norm is known by different names such as cut-off rate, hurdle rate, required rate, minimum rate of return and so on. This standard is broadly expressed in terms of the cost of capital is, thus, another major aspect of the capital; budgeting decision. In brief, the main elements of the capital budgeting decision are: (i) The total assets and their composition (ii) The business risk complexion of the firm, and (iii) concept and measurement of the cost of capital.

Working Capital Management: Working capital management is concerned with the management of the current assets. As we know, the short-term survival is a pre-requisite to long-term success.

The major thrust of working capital management is the trade-off between profitability and risk (liquidity), which are inversely related to each other. If a firm does not have adequate working capital it may not have the ability to meet its current obligations and thus invite the risk of bankrupt. One the other hand if the current assets are too large the firm will be loosing the opportunity of making a good return and thus may not serve the requirements of suppliers of funds. Thus, the profitability and liquidity are the two major dimensions of working capital management. In addition, the individual current assets should be efficiently managed so that neither inadequate nor unnecessary funds are locked up.

Finance Decision

The second major decision involved in financial management is the financing decision, which is concerned with the financing - mix or capital structure of leverage. The term capital structure refers to the combination of debt (fixed interest sources of financing) and equity capital (variable - dividend securities/source of funds). The financing decision of a firm relates to the choice of the proportion of these sources to finance the investment requirements. A higher proportion of debt implies a higher return to the shareholders and also the higher financial risk and vice versa. A proper balance between debt and equity is a must to ensure a trade - off between risk and return to the shareholders. A capital structure with a reasonable proportion of debt and equity capital is called the optimum capital structure.

The second aspect of the financing decision is the determination of an appropriate capital structure, which will result, is maximum return to the shareholders and in turn maximizes the worth of the firm. Thus, the financing decision covers two inter-related aspects: (a) capital structure theory, and (b) capital structure decision.

Dividend Policy decision

The third major decision of financial management is relating to dividend policy. The firm has two alternatives with regard to management of profits of a firm. They can be either distributed to the shareholder in the form of dividends or they can be retained in the business or even distribute some portion and retain the remaining. The course of action to be followed is a significant element in the dividend decision. The dividend pay out ratio i.

e. the proportion of net profits to be paid out to the shareholders should be in tune with the investment opportunities available within the firm. The second major aspect of the dividend decision is the study of factors determining dividend policy of a firm in practice.

Working capital analysis

Finance is required for two purpose viz. for it establishment and to carry out the day-to-day operations of a business. Funds are required to purchase the fixed assets such as plant, machinery, land, building, furniture, etc, on long-term basis. Investments in these assets represent that part of firm's capital, which is blocked on a permanent of fixed basis and is called fixed capital. Funds are also needed for short-term purposes such as the purchase of raw materials, payment of wages and other day-to-day expenses, etc. and these funds are known as working capital. In simple words working capital refers that part of the firm's capital, which is required for financing short term or current assets such as cash, marketable securities, debtors and inventories. The investment in these current assets keeps revolving and being constantly converted into cash and which in turn financed to acquire current assets. Thus the working capital is also known as revolving or circulating capital or short-term capital.

CONCEPT OF WORKING CAPITAL

There are two concepts of working capital:

1. Gross working capital
2. Net working capital

Gross working capital

In the broader sense, the term working capital refers to the gross working capital. The notion of the gross working capital refers to the capital invested in total current assets of the enterprise. Current assets are those assets, which in the ordinary course of business, can be converted into cash within a short period, normally one accounting year.

Examples of current assets:

1. Cash in hand and bank balance
2. Bills receivables or Accounts Receivables
3. Sundry Debtors (less provision for bad debts)

4. Short-term loans and advances.
5. Inventories of stocks, such as:
   (a) Raw materials
   (b) Work - in process
   (c) Stores and spares
   (d) Finished goods
6. Temporary Investments of surplus funds.
7. Prepaid Expenses
8. Accrued Incomes etc.

Net working capital

In a narrow sense, the term working capital refers to the net working capital. Networking capital represents the excess of current assets over current liabilities.

Current liabilities are those liabilities, which are intend to be paid in the ordinary course of business within a short period, normally one accounting year out of the current assets or the income of the business. Net working capital may be positive or negative. When the current assets exceed the current liabilities net working capital is positive and the negative net working capital results when the liabilities are more then the current assets.

Examples of current liabilities:

1. Bills payable
2. Sundry Creditors or Accounts Payable.
3. Accrued or Outstanding Expanses.
4. Short term loans, advances and deposits.
5. Dividends payable
6. Bank overdraft
7. Provision for taxation etc.

CLASSIFICATION OR KINDS OF WORKING CAPITAL

Working capital may be classified in two ways:

a. On the basis of concept.
b. On the basis of time permanency

On the basis of concept, working capital is classified as gross working capital and net working capital is discussed earlier. This classification is important from the point of view of the financial manager. On the basis of time, working capital may be classified as:

1. Permanent or fixed working capital
2. Temporary of variable working capital

Permanent or fixed working capital: There is always a minimum level of current assets, which is continuously required by the enterprise to carry out its normal business operations and this minimum is known as permanent of fixed working capital. For example, every firm has to maintain a minimum level of raw materials, work in process; finished goods and cash balance to run the business operations smoothly and profitably.

This minimum level of current assets is permanently blocked in current assets. As the business grows, the requirement of permanent working capital also increases due to the increases in current assets.

The permanent working capital can further be classified into regular working capital and reserve working capital. Regular working capital is the minimum amount of working capital required to ensure circulation of current assets from cash to inventories, from inventories to receivables and from receivable to cash and so on.

Reserve working capital is the excess amount over the requirement for regular working capital which may be provided for contingencies that may arise at unstated period such as strikes, rise in prices, depression etc.

Temporary or variable working capital: Temporary or variable working capital is the amount of working capital, which is required to meet the seasonal demands and some special exigencies. Thus the variable working capital can be further classified into seasonal working capital and special working capital. While seasonal working capital is required to meet certain seasonal demands, the special working capital is that part of working capital which is required to meet special exigencies such as launching of extensive marketing campaigns, for conducting research etc.

Temporary working capital differs from permanent working capital in the sense that it is required for short periods and cannot be permanently employed gainfully in the business. Figures given below illustrate the different between permanent and temporary working capital.

IMPORTANCE OF WORKING CAPITAL

Working capital is refereed to be the lifeblood and nerve center of a business. Working capital is as essential to maintain the smooth functioning of a business as blood circulation in a human body. No business can run successfully with out an adequate amount of working capital. The main advantages of maintaining adequate amount of working capital are as follows:

1. Solvency of the business: Adequate working capital helps in maintaining solvency of the business by providing uninterrupted flow of production.
2. Good will: Sufficient working capital enables a business concern to make prompt payment and hence helps in creating and maintaining good will.
3. Easy loans: A concern having adequate working capital, high solvency and good credit standing can arrange loans from banks and others on easy and favorable terms.
4. Cash Discounts: Adequate working capital also enables a concern to avail cash discounts on the purchases and hence it reduces costs.
5. Regular supply of raw materials: Sufficient working capital ensures regular supply of raw materials and continuous production.
6. Regular payments of salaries wages and other day to day commitments: A company which has ample working capital can make regular payment of salaries, wages and other day to day commitments which raises the morale of its employees, increases their efficiency, reduces wastage and cost and enhances production and profits.
7. Exploitation of favorable market conditions: The concerns with adequate working capital only can exploit favorable market conditions such as purchasing its requirements in bulk when the prices are lower.
8. Ability to face crisis: Adequate working capital enables a concern to face business crisis in emergencies.
9. Quick and regular return on Investments: Every investor wants a quick and regular return on his investment. Sufficiency of working capital enables a concern to pay quick and regular dividends to its investors, as there may

not be much pressure to plough back profits. This gains the confidence of its investors and creates a favorable market to raise additional funds in the future.

10. High morale: Adequacy of working capital creates an environment of security, confidence, and high morale and creates overall efficiency in a business. Every business concern should have adequate working capital to run its business operations. It should have neither redundant excess working capital nor inadequate shortage of working capital. Both, excess as well as short working capital positions are bad for any business. However, out of the two, it is the inadequacy of working capital which is more dangerous from the point of view of the firm.

THE NEED OR OBJECTIVES OF WORKING CAPITAL

The need for working capital arises mainly due to the time gap between production and realization of cash. The process of production and sale cannot be done instantaneously and hence the firm needs to hold the current assets to fill-up the time gaps. There are time gaps in purchase of raw materials and production; production and sales: and sales and realization of cash. The working capital is needed mainly for the following purposes:

1. For the purchase of raw materials.
2. To pay wages, salaries and other day-to-day expenses and overhead cost such as fuel, power and office expenses, etc.
3. To meet the selling expenses such as packing, advertising, etc.
4. To provide credit facilities to the customers and
5. To maintain the inventories of raw materials, work-in-progress, stores and spares and finishes stock etc.

Generally, the level of working capital needed depends upon the time gap (known as operating cycle) and the size of operations. Greater the size of the business unit generally, larger will be the requirements of working capital. The amount of working capital needed also goes on increasing with the growth and expansion of business. Similarly, the larger the operating cycle, the larger the requirement for working capital. There are many other factors, which influence the need of working capital in a business, and these are discussed below in the following pages.

FACTORS DETERMINING THE WORKING CAPITAL REQUIREMENTS

There are a large number of factors such as the nature and size of business, the character of their operations, the length of production cycle, the rate of stock turnover and the state of economic situation etc. that decode requirement of working capital. These factors have different importance and influence on firm differently. In general following factors generally influence the working capital requirements.

1. Nature or character of business: The working capital requirements of a firm basically depend upon the nature of its business. Public utility undertakings like electricity, water supply and railways need very limited working capital as their sales are on cash and are engaged in provision of services only. On the other hand, trading firms require more investment in inventories, receivables and cash and such they need large amount of working capital. The manufacturing undertakings also require sizable working capital.
2. Size of business or scale of operations: The working capital requirements of a concern are directly influenced by the size of its business, which may be measured in terms of scale of operations. Greater the size of a business unit, generally, larger will be the requirements of working capital. However, in some cases, even a smaller concern may need more working capital due to high overhead charges, inefficient use of available resources and other economic disadvantages of small size.
3. Production policy: If the demand for a given product is subject to wide fluctuations due to seasonal variations, the requirements of working capital, in such cases, depend upon the production policy. The production could be kept either steady by accumulating inventories during stack periods with a view to meet high demand during the peck season or the production could be curtailed during the slack season and increased during the peak season. If the policy is to keep the production steady by accumulating inventories it will require higher working capital.
4. Manufacturing process/Length of production cycle: In manufacturing business, the requirements of working

capital will be in direct proportion to the length of manufacturing process. Longer the process period of manufacture, larger is the amount of working capital required, as the raw materials and other supplies have to be carried for a longer period.

5. Seasonal variations: If the raw material availability is seasonal, they have to be bought in bulk during the season to ensure an uninterrupted material for the production. A huge amount is, thus, blocked in the form of material, inventories during such season, which give rise to more working capital requirements. Generally, during the busy season, a firm requires larger working capital then in the slack season.
6. Working capital cycle: In a manufacturing concern, the working capital cycle starts with the purchase of raw material and ends with the realization of cash from the sale of finished products. This cycle involves purchase of raw materials and stores, its conversion into stocks of finished goods through work–in progress with progressive increment of labour and service costs, conversion of finished stock into sales, debtors and receivables and ultimately realization of cash. This cycle continues again from cash to purchase of raw materials and so on. In general the longer the operating cycle, the larger the requirement of working capital.
7. Credit policy: The credit policy of a concern in its dealings with debtors and creditors influences considerably the requirements of working capital. A concern that purchases its requirements on credit requires lesser amount of working capital compared to the firm, which buys on cash. On the other hand, a concern allowing credit to its customers shall need larger amount of working capital compared to a firm selling only on cash.
8. Business cycles: Business cycle refers to alternate expansion and contraction in general business activity. In a period of boom, i.e., when the business is prosperous, there is a need for larger amount of working capital due to increase in sales. On the contrary, in the times of depression, i.e., when there is a down swing of the cycle, the business contracts, sales decline, difficulties are faced in collection

from debtors and firms may have to hold large amount of working capital.

9. Rate of growth of business: The working capital requirements of a concern increase with the growth and expansion of its business activities. The retained profits may provide for a part of working capital but the fast growing concerns need larger amount of working capital than the amount of undistributed profits.

SOURCE OF FINANCE

Incase of proprietorship business, the individual proprietor generally invests his own savings to start with, and may borrow money on his personal security or the security of his assets from others. Similarly, the capital of a partnership from consists partly of funds contributed by the partners and partly of borrowed funds. But the company from of organization enables the promoters to raise necessary funds from the public who may contribute capital and become members (share holders) of the company. In course of its business, the company can raise loans directly from banks and financial institutions or by issue of securities (debentures) to the public. Besides, profits earned may also be reinvested instead of being distributed as dividend to the shareholders.

Thus for any business enterprise, there are two sources of finance, viz, funds contributed by owners and funds available from loans and credits. In other words the financial resources of a business may be own funds and borrowed funds.

Owner funds or ownership capital

The ownership capital is also known as 'risk capital' because every business runs the risk of loss or low profits, and it is the owner who bears this risk. In the event of low profits they do not have adequate return on their investment. If losses continue the owners may be unable to recover even their original investment. However, in times of prosperity and in the case of a flourishing business the high level of profits earned accrues entirely to the owners of the business. Thus, after paying interest on loans at a fixed rate, the owners may enjoy a much higher rate of return on their investment. Owners contribute risk capital also in the hope that the value of the firm will appreciate as a result of higher earnings and growth in the size of the firm.

The second characteristic of this source of finance is that ownership capital remains permanently invested in the business. It is not refundable like loans or borrowed capital. Hence a large part of it is generally used for a acquiring long – lived fixed assets and to finance a part of the working capital which is permanently required to hold a minimum level of stock of raw materials, a minimum amount of cash, etc.

Another characteristic of ownership capital related to the management of business. It is on the basis of their contribution to equity capital that owners can exercise their right of control over the management of the firm. Managers cannot ignore the owners in the conduct of business affairs. The sole proprietor directly controls his own business. In a partnership firm, the active partner will take part in the management of business. A company is managed by directors who are elected by the members (shareholders).

Merits

Arising out of its characteristics, the advantages of ownership capital may be briefly stated as follows:

1. It provides risk capital
2. It is a source of permanent capital
3. It is the basis on which owners 'acquire their right of control over management
4. It does not require security of assets to be offered to raise ownership capital

Limitations

There are also certain limitations of ownership capital as a source of finance. These are:

The amount of capital, which may be raised as owners fund depends on the number of persons, prepared to take the risks involved. In a partnership confer, a few persons cannot provide ownership capital beyond a certain limit and this limitation is more so in case of proprietary form of organization.

A joint stock company can raise large amount by issuing shares to the public. Bus it leads to an increased number of people having ownership interest and right of control over management. This may reduce the original investors' power of control over management. Being a permanent source of capital, ownership funds are not refundable as long as the company is in existence, even when the funds remain idle.

A company may find it difficult to raise additional ownership capital unless it has high profit-earning capacity or growth prospects. Issue of additional shares is also subject to so many legal and procedural restrictions.

Borrowed funds and borrowed capital: It includes all funds available by way of loans or credit. Business firms raise loans for specified periods at fixed rates of interest. Thus borrowed funds may serve the purpose of long-term, medium-term or short-term finance. The borrowing is generally at against the security of assets from banks and financial institutions. A company to borrow the funds can also issue various types of debentures.

Interest on such borrowed funds is payable at half yearly or yearly but the principal amount is being repaid only at the end of the period of loan. These interest and principal payments have to be met even if the earnings are low or there is loss. Lenders and creditors do not have any right of control over the management of the borrowing firm. But they can sue the firm in a law court if there is default in payment, interest or principal back.

Merits

From the business point of view, borrowed capital has several merits.

1. It does not affect the owner's control over management.
2. Interest is treated as an expense, so it can be charged against income and amount of tax payable thereby reduced.
3. The amount of borrowing and its timing can be adjusted according to convenience and needs, and
4. It involves a fixed rate of interest to be paid even when profits are very high, thus owners may enjoy a much higher rate of return on investment then the lenders.

Limitations

There are certain limitations, too in case of borrowed capacity. Payment of interest and repayment of loans cannot be avoided even if there is a loss. Default in meeting these obligations may create problems for the business and result in decline of its credit worthiness. Continuing default may even lead to insolvency of firm.

Secondly, it requires adequate security to be offered against loans. Moreover, high rates of interest may be charged if the firm's ability to repay the loan in uncertain.

SOURCE OF COMPANY FINANCE

Based upon the time, the financial resources may be classified into (1) sources of long term (2) sources of short – term finance. Some of these sources also serve the purpose of medium – term finance.

I. The source of long – term finance are:

1. Issue of shares
2. Issue debentures
3. Loan from financial institutions
4. Retained profits and
5. Public deposits

II. Sources of Short-term Finance are:

1. Trade credit
2. Bank loans and advances and
3. Short-term loans from finance companies.

Sources of Long Term Finance

1. Issue of Shares: The amount of capital decided to be raised from members of the public is divided into units of equal value. These units are known as share and the aggregate values of shares are known as share capital of the company. Those who subscribe to the share capital become members of the company and are called shareholders. They are the owners of the company. Hence shares are also described as ownership securities.
2. Issue of Preference Shares: Preference share have three distinct characteristics. Preference shareholders have the right to claim dividend at a fixed rate, which is decided according to the terms of issue of shares. Moreover, the preference dividend is to be paid first out of the net profit. The balance, it any, can be distributed among other shareholders that is, equity shareholders. However,

payment of dividend is not legally compulsory. Only when dividend is declared, preference shareholders have a prior claim over equity shareholders.

Preference shareholders also have the preferential right of claiming repayment of capital in the event of winding up of the company. Preference capital has to be repaid out of assets after meeting the loan obligations and claims of creditors but before any amount is repaid to equity shareholders.

Holders of preference shares enjoy certain privileges, which cannot be claimed by the equity shareholders. That is why; they cannot directly take part in matters, which may be discussed at the general meeting of shareholders, or in the election of directors.

Depending upon the terms of conditions of issue, different types of preference shares may be issued by a company to raises funds. Preference shares may be issued as:

1. Cumulative or Non-cumulative
2. Participating or Non-participating
3. Redeemable or Non-redeemable, or as
4. Convertible or non-convertible preference shares.

In the case of cumulative preference shares, the dividend unpaid if any in previous years gets accumulated until that is paid. No cumulative preference shares have any such provision.

Participatory shareholders are entitled to a further share in the surplus profits after a reasonable divided has been paid to equity shareholders. Non-participating preference shares do not enjoy such right.

Redeemable preference shares are those, which are repaid after a specified period, where as the irredeemable preference shares are not repaid. However, the company can also redeem these shares after a specified period by giving notice as per the terms of issue. Convertible preference shows are those, which are entitled to be converted into equity shares after a specified period.

Merits

Many companies due to the following reasons prefer issue of preference shares as a source of finance.

1. It helps to enlarge the sources of funds.

2. Some financial institutions and individuals prefer to invest in preference shares due to the assurance of a fixed return.
3. Dividend is payable only when there are profits.
4. If does not affect the equity shareholders' control over management

Limitations

The limitations of preference shares relates to some of its main features:

1. Dividend paid cannot be charged to the company's income as an expense; hence there is no tax saving as in the case of interest on loans.
2. Even through payment of dividend is not legally compulsory, if it is not paid or arrears accumulate there is an adverse effect on the company's credit.
3. Issue of preference share does not attract many investors, as the return is generally limited and not exceed the rates of interest on loan. On the other than, there is a risk of no dividend being paid in the event of falling income.

Issue of Equity Shares: The most important source of raising long-term capital for a company is the issue of equity shares. In the case of equity shares there is no promise to shareholders a fixed dividend. But if the company is successful and the level profits are high, equity shareholders enjoy very high returns on their investment. This feature is very attractive to many investors even through they run the risk of having no return if the profits are inadequate or there is loss. They have the right of control over the management of the company and their liability is limited to the value of shares held by them.

From the above it can be said that equity shares have three distinct characteristics:

1. The holders of equity shares are the primary risk bearers. It is the issue of equity shares that mainly provides 'risk capital', unlike borrowed capital. Even compared with preference capital, equity shareholders are to bear ultimate risk.
2. Equity shares enable much higher return sot be earned by shareholders during prosperity because after meeting the preference dividend and interest on borrowed capital at

a fixed rate, the entire surplus of profit goes to equity shareholders only.

3. Holders of equity shares have the right of control over the company. Directors are elected on the vote of equity shareholders.

Merits

From the company' point of view; there are several merits of issuing equity shares to raise long-term finance.

1. It is a source of permanent capital without any commitment of a fixed return to the shareholders. The return on capital depends ultimately on the profitability of business.
2. It facilities a higher rate of return to be earned with the help borrowed funds. This is possible due to two reasons. Loans carry a relatively lower rate of interest than the average rate of return on total capital. Secondly, there is tax saving as interest paid can be charged to income as a expense before tax calculation.
3. Assets are not required to give as security for raising equity capital. Thus additional funds can be raised as loan against the security of assets.

Limitations

Although there are several advantages of issuing equity shares to raise long-term capital.

1. The risks of fluctuating returns due to changes in the level of earnings of the company do not attract many people to subscribe to equity capital.
2. The value of shares in the market also fluctuate with changes in business conditions, this is another risk, which many investors want to avoid.

Issue of Debentures

When a company decides to raise loans from the public, the amount of loan is dividend into units of equal. These units are known as debentures. A debenture is the instrument or certificate issued by a company to acknowledge its debt. Those who invest money in debentures are known as 'debenture holders'. They are creditors of the company. Debentures are therefore called 'creditor ship' securities. The value of each debentures is generally fixed in multiplies of 10 like Rs. 100 or Rs. 500, or Rs. 1000.

Debentures carry a fixed rate of interest, and generally are repayable after a certain period, which is specified at the time of issue. Depending upon the terms and conditions of issue there are different types of debentures. There are:

a. Secured or unsecured Debentures and

b. Convertible of Non convertible Debentures.

It debentures are issued on the security of all or some specific assets of the company, they are known as secured debentures. The assets are mortgaged in favor of the debenture holders. Debentures, which are not secured by a charge or mortgage of any assets, are called unsecured debentures. The holders of these debentures are treated as ordinary creditors.

Sometimes under the terms of issue debenture holders are given an option to covert their debentures into equity shares after a specified period. Or the terms of issue may lay down that the whole or part of the debentures will be automatically converted into equity shares of a specified price after a certain period. Such debentures are known as convertible debentures. If there is no mention of conversion at the time of issue, the debentures are regarded as non-convertible debentures.

Merits

Debentures issue is a widely used method of raising long-term finance by companies, due to the following reasons.

1. Interest payable on Debentures can be fixed at low rates than rate of return on equity shares. Thus Debentures issue is a cheaper source of finance.
2. Interest paid can be deducted from income tax purpose; there by the amount of tax payable is reduced.
3. Funds raised for the issue of debentures may be used in business to earn a much higher rate of return then the rate of interest. As a result the equity shareholders earn more.
4. Another advantage of debenture issue is that funds are available from investors who are not entitled to have any control over the management of the company.
5. Companies often find it convenient to raise debenture

capital from financial institutions, which prefer to invest in debentures rather than in shares. This is due to the assurance of a fixed return and repayment after a specified period.

Limitations

Debenture issue as a source of finance has certain limitations too.

1. It involves a fixed commitment to pay interest regularly even when the company has low earnings or incurring losses.
2. Debentures issue may not be possible beyond a certain limit due to the inadequacy of assets to be offered as security.

Methods of Issuing Securities: The firm after deciding the amount to be raised and the type of securities to be issued, must adopt suitable methods to offer the securities to potential investors. There are for common methods followed by companies for the purpose.

When securities are offered to the general public a document known as Prospectus, or a notice, circular or advertisement is issued inviting the public to subscribe to the securities offered thereby all particulars about the company and the securities offered are made to the public. Brokers are appointed and one or more banks are authorized to collect subscription.

Some times the entire issue is subscribed by an organization known as Issue House, which in turn sells the securities to the public at a suitable time.

The company may negotiate with large investors of financial institutions who agree to take over the securities. This is known as 'Private Placement' of securities.

When an exiting company decides to raise funds by issue of equity shares, it is required under law to offer the new shares to the existing shareholders. This is described as right issue of equity shares. But if the existing shareholders decline, the new shares can be offered to the public.

Loans from financial Institutions

Government with the main object of promoting industrial

development has set up a number of financial institutions. These institutions play an important role as sources of company finance. Besides they also assist companies to raise funds from other sources.

These institutions provide medium and long-term finance to industrial enterprises at a reason able rate of interest. Thus companies may obtain direct loan from the financial institutions for expansion or modernization of existing manufacturing units or for starting a new unit.

Often, the financial institutions subscribe to the industrial debenture issue of companies some of the institutions (ICICI) and (IDBI) also subscribe to the share issued by companies.

All such institutions also underwrite the public issue of shares and debentures by companies. Underwriting is an agreement to take over the securities to the extent there is no public response to the issue. They may guarantee loans, which may be raised by companies from other sources.

Loans in foreign currency may also be granted for the import of machinery and equipment wherever necessary from these institutions, which stand guarantee for re-payments. Apart from the national level institutions mentioned above, there are a number of similar institutions set up in different states of India. The state-level financial institutions are known as State Financial Corporation, State Industrial Development Corporations, State Industrial Investment Corporation and the like. The objectives of these institutions are similar to those of the national-level institutions. But they are mainly concerned with the development of medium and small-scale industrial units. Thus, smaller companies depend on state level institutions as a source of medium and long-term finance for the expansion and modernization of their enterprise.

Retained Profits

Successful companies do not distribute the whole of their profits as dividend to shareholders but reinvest a part of the profits. The amount of profit reinvested in the business of a company is known as retained profit. It is shown as reserve in the accounts. The surplus profits retained and reinvested may be regarded as an internal source of finance. Hence, this method of financing is known as self-financing. It is also called sloughing back of profits.

Since profits belong to the shareholders, the amount of retained profit is treated as ownership fund. It serves the purpose of medium and long-term finance. The total amount of ownership capital of a company can be determined by adding the share capital and accumulated reserves.

Merits

This source of finance is considered to be better than other sources for the following reasons.

1. As an internal source, it is more dependable than external sources. It is not necessary to consider investor's preference.
2. Use of retained profit does not involve any cost to be incurred for raising the funds. Expenses on prospectus, advertising, etc, can be avoided.
3. There is no fixed commitment to pay dividend on the profits reinvested. It is a part of risk capital like equity share capital.
4. Control over the management of the company remains unaffected, as there is no addition to the number of shareholder.
5. It does not require the security of assets, which can be used for raising additional funds in the form of loan.

Limitations

However, there are certain limitations on the part of retained profit.

1. Only well established companies can be avail of this sources of finance. Even for such companies retained profits cannot be used to an unlimited extent.
2. Accumulation of reserves often attract competition in the market,
3. With the increased earnings, shareholders expect a high rate of dividend to be paid.
4. Growth of companies through internal financing may attract government restrictions as it leads to concentration of economic power.

Public Deposits

An important source of medium – term finance which

companies make use of is public deposits. This requires advertisement to be issued inviting the general public of deposits. This requires advertisement to be issued inviting the general public to deposit their savings with the company. The period of deposit may extend up to three yeas. The rate of interest offered is generally higher than the interest on bank deposits. Against the deposit, the company mentioning the amount, rate of interest, time of repayment and such other information issues a receipt.

Since the public deposits are unsecured loans, profitable companies enjoying public confidence only can be able to attract public deposits. Even for such companies there are rules prescribed by government limited its use.

SOURCES OF SHORT TERM FINANCE

The major sources of short-term finance are discussed below:

Trade credit: Trade credit is a common source of short-term finance available to all companies. It refers to the amount payable to the suppliers of raw materials, goods etc. after an agreed period, which is generally less than a year. It is customary for all business firms to allow credit facility to their customers in trade business. Thus, it is an automatic source of finance. With the increase in production and corresponding purchases, the amount due to the creditors also increases. Thereby part of the funds required for increased production is financed by the creditors. The more important advantages of trade credit as a source of short-term finance are the following: It is readily available according to the prevailing customs. There are no special efforts to be made to avail of it. Trade credit is a flexible source of finance. It can be easily adjusted to the changing needs for purchases.

Where there is an open account for any creditor failure to pay the amounts on time due to temporary difficulties does not involve any serious consequence Creditors often adjust the time of payment in view of continued dealings. It is an economical source of finance.

However, the liability on account of trade credit cannot be neglected. Payment has to be made regularly. If the company is required to accept a bill of exchange or to issue a promissory note against the credit, payment must be made on the maturity of the bill or note. It is a legal commitment and must be honored; otherwise legal action will follow to recover the dues.

Bank loans and advances: Money advanced or granted as loan by commercial banks is known as bank credit. Companies generally secure bank credit to meet their current operating expenses. The most common forms are cash credit and overdraft facilities. Under the cash credit arrangement the maximum limit of credit is fixed in advance on the security of goods and materials in stock or against the personal security of directors. The total amount drawn is not to exceed the limit fixed. Interest is charged on the amount actually drawn and outstanding. During the period of credit, the company can draw, repay and again draw amounts with in the maximum limit. In the case of overdraft, the company is allowed to overdraw its current account up to the sanctioned limit. This facility is also allowed either against personal security or the security of assets. Interest is charged on the amount actually overdrawn, not on the sanctioned limit.

The advantage of bank credit as a source of short-term finance is that the amount can be adjusted according to the changing needs of finance. The rate of interest on bank credit is fairly high. But the burden is no excessive because it is used for short periods and is compensated by profitable use of the funds.

Commercial banks also advance money by discounting bills of exchange. A company having sold goods on credit may draw bills of exchange on the customers for their acceptance. A bill is an order in writing requiring the customer to pay the specified amount after a certain period (say 60 days or 90 days). After acceptance of the bill, the company can drawn the amount as an advance from many commercial banks on payment of a discount. The amount of discount, which is equal to the interest for the period of the bill, and the balance, is available to the company. Bill discounting is thus another source of short-term finance available from the commercial banks.

Short term loans from finance companies: Short-term funds may be available from finance companies on the security of assets. Some finance companies also provide funds according to the value of bills receivable or amount due from the customers of the borrowing company, which they take over.

CAPITAL BUDGETING

Capital Budgeting: Capital budgeting is the process of making investment decision in long-term assets or courses of action. Capital expenditure incurred today is expected to bring its benefits over a period of time. These expenditures are related to the acquisition & improvement of fixes assets.

Capital budgeting is the planning of expenditure and the benefit, which spread over a number of years. It is the process of deciding whether or not to invest in a particular project, as the investment possibilities may not be rewarding.

The manager has to choose a project, which gives a rate of return, which is more than the cost of financing the project. For this the manager has to evaluate the worth of the projects in-terms of cost and benefits. The benefits are the expected cash inflows from the project, which are discounted against a standard, generally the cost of capital.

Capital Budgeting Process:

The capital budgeting process involves generation of investment, proposal estimation of cash-flows for the proposals, evaluation of cash-flows, selection of projects based on acceptance criterion and finally the continues revaluation of investment after their acceptance the steps involved in capital budgeting process are as follows.

1. Project generation
2. Project evaluation
3. Project selection
4. Project execution

Project generation: In the project generation, the company has to identify the proposal to be undertaken depending upon its future plans of activity. After identification of the proposals they can be grouped according to the following categories:

a. Replacement of equipment: In this case the existing outdated equipment and machinery may be replaced by purchasing new and modern equipment.

b. Expansion: The Company can go for increasing additional capacity in the existing product line by purchasing additional equipment.

c. Diversification: The Company can diversify its product line by way of producing various products and entering into different markets. For this purpose, It has to acquire the fixed assets to enable producing new products.

d. Research and Development: Where the company can go for installation of research and development suing by incurring heavy expenditure with a view to innovate new methods of production new products etc.,

Project evaluation: In involves two steps.

a. Estimation of benefits and costs: These must be measured in terms of cash flows. Benefits to be received are measured in terms of cash flows. Benefits to be received are measured in terms of cash in flows, and costs to be incurred are measured in terms of cash flows.

b. Selection of an appropriate criterion to judge the desirability of the project.

Project selection: There is no standard administrative procedure for approving the investment decisions. The screening and selection procedure would differ from firm to firm. Due to lot of importance of capital budgeting decision, the final approval of the project may generally rest on the top management of the company. However the proposals are scrutinized at multiple levels. Some times top management may delegate authority to approve certain types of investment proposals. The top management may do so by limiting the amount of cash out lay. Prescribing the selection criteria and holding the lower management levels accountable for the results.

Project Execution: In the project execution the top management or the project execution committee is responsible for effective utilization of funds allocated for the projects. It must see that the funds are spent in accordance with the appropriation made in the capital budgeting plan. The funds for the purpose of the project execution must be spent only after obtaining the approval of the finance controller. Further to have an effective cont. It is necessary to prepare monthly budget reports to show clearly the total amount appropriated, amount spent and to amount unspent.

CAPITAL BUDGETING TECHNIQUES:

The capital budgeting appraisal methods are techniques of evaluation of investment proposal will help the company to decide upon the desirability of an investment proposal depending upon their; relative income generating capacity and rank them in order of their desirability. These methods provide the company a set of norms on the basis of which either it has to accept or reject the investment proposal. The most widely accepted techniques used in estimating the cost-returns of investment projects can be grouped under two categories.

Traditional methods

These methods are based on the principles to determine the desirability of an investment project on the basis of its useful life and expected returns. These methods depend upon the accounting information available from the books of accounts of the company. These will not take into account the concept of 'time value of money', which is a significant factor to determine the desirability of a project in terms of present value.

A. Pay-back period method: It is the most popular and widely recognized traditional method of evaluating the investment proposals. It can be defined, as 'the number of years required to recover the original cash out lay invested in a project'.

According to Weston & Brigham, "The pay back period is the number of years it takes the firm to recover its original investment by net returns before depreciation, but after taxes".

According to James. C. Vanhorne, "The payback period is the number of years required to recover initial cash investment.

The pay back period is also called payout or payoff period. This period is calculated by dividing the cost of the project by the annual earnings after tax but before depreciation under this method the projects are ranked on the basis of the length of the payback period.

A project with the shortest payback period will be given the highest rank and taken as the best investment. The shorter the payback period, the less risky the investment is the formula for payback period is

$$\text{Pay-back period} = \frac{\text{Cash outlay (or) original cost of project}}{\text{Annual cash inflow}}$$

Merits:

1. It is one of the earliest methods of evaluating the investment projects.
2. It is simple to understand and to compute.

3. It dose not involve any cost for computation of the payback period
4. It is one of the widely used methods in small scale industry sector
5. It can be computed on the basis of accounting information available from the books.

Demerits

1. This method fails to take into account the cash flows received by the company after the pay back period.
2. It doesn't take into account the interest factor involved in an investment outlay.
3. It doesn't take into account the interest factor involved in an investment outlay.
4. It is not consistent with the objective of maximizing the market value of the company's share.
5. It fails to consider the pattern of cash inflows i. e., the magnitude and timing of cash in flows.

Accounting (or) Average rate of return method (ARR)

It is an accounting method, which uses the accounting information repeated by the financial statements to measure the probability of an investment proposal. It can be determine by dividing the average income after taxes by the average investment i.e., the average book value after depreciation.

On the basis of this method, the company can select all those projects who's ARR is higher than the minimum rate established by the company. It can reject the projects with an ARR lower than the expected rate of return.

This method can also help the management to rank the proposal on the basis of ARR. A highest rank will be given to a project with highest ARR, where as a lowest rank to a project with lowest ARR.

Merits

1. It is very simple to understand and calculate.
2. It can be readily computed with the help of the available accounting data.
3. It uses the entire stream of earning to calculate the ARR.

Demerits

1. It is not based on cash flows generated by a project.
2. This method does not consider the objective of wealth maximization
3. IT ignores the length of the projects useful life.
4. It does not take into account the fact that the profits can be re-invested.

DISCOUNTED CASH FLOW METHODS:

The traditional method does not take into consideration the time value of money. They give equal weight age to the present and future flow of incomes. The DCF methods are based on the concept that a rupee earned today is more worth than a rupee earned tomorrow. These methods take into consideration the profitability and also time value of money.

A. Net present value method (NPV)

The NPV takes into consideration the time value of money. The cash flows of different years and valued differently and made comparable in terms of present values for this the net cash inflows of various period are discounted using required rate of return which is predetermined.

According to Ezra Solomon, "It is a present value of future returns, discounted at the required rate of return minus the present value of the cost of the investment."

NPV is the difference between the present value of cash inflows of a project and the initial cost of the project.

According the NPV technique, only one project will be selected whose NPV is positive or above zero. If a project(s) NPV is less than 'Zero'. It gives negative NPV hence. It must be rejected. If there are more than one project with positive NPV's the project is selected whose NPV is the highest.

Merits

1. It recognizes the time value of money.
2. It is based on the entire cash flows generated during the useful life of the asset.
3. It is consistent with the objective of maximization of wealth of the owners.

4. The ranking of projects is independent of the discount rate used for determining the present value.

Demerits

1. It is different to understand and use.
2. The NPV is calculated by using the cost of capital as a discount rate. But the concept of cost of capital. If self is difficult to understood and determine.
3. It does not give solutions when the comparable projects are involved in different amounts of investment.
4. It does not give correct answer to a question whether alternative projects or limited funds are available with unequal lines.

INTERNAL RATE OF RETURN METHOD (IRR)

The IRR for an investment proposal is that discount rate which equates the present value of cash inflows with the present value of cash out flows of an investment. The IRR is also known as cutoff or handle rate. It is usually the concern's cost of capital.

According to Weston and Brigham "The internal rate is the interest rate that equates the present value of the expected future receipts to the cost of the investment outlay.

When compared the IRR with the required rate of return (RRR), if the IRR is more than RRR then the project is accepted else rejected. In case of more than one project with IRR more than RRR, the one, which gives the highest IRR, is selected.

The IRR is not a predetermine rate, rather it is to be trial and error method. It implies that one has to start with a discounting rate to calculate the present value of cash inflows. If the obtained present value is higher than the initial cost of the project one has to try with a higher rate. Like wise if the present value of expected cash inflows obtained is lower than the present value of cash flow. Lower rate is to be taken up. The process is continued till the net present value becomes Zero. As this discount rate is determined internally, this method is called internal rate of return method.

$$IRR = L + \frac{P1 - Q}{P1 - P2} \times D$$

L- Lower discount rate

P1 - Present value of cash inflows at lower rate.

P2 - Present value of cash inflows at higher rate.

Q- Actual investment

D- Difference in Discount rates.

Merits:

1. It consider the time value of money
2. It takes into account the cash flows over the entire useful life of the asset.
3. It has a psychological appear to the user because when the highest rate of return projects are selected, it satisfies the investors in terms of the rate of return an capital
4. It always suggests accepting to projects with maximum rate of return.
5. It is inconformity with the firm's objective of maximum owner's welfare.

Demerits:

1. It is very difficult to understand and use.
2. It involves a very complicated computational work.
3. It may not give unique answer in all situations.

Probability Index Method (PI)

The method is also called benefit cost ration. This method is obtained cloth a slight modification of the NPV method. In case of NPV the present value of cash out flows are profitability index (PI), the present value of cash inflows are divide by the present value of cash out flows, while NPV is a absolute measure, the PI is a relative measure.

It the PI is more than one (>1), the proposal is accepted else rejected. If there are more than one investment proposal with the more than one PI the one with the highest PI will be selected. This method is more useful incase of projects with different cash outlays cash outlays and hence is superior to the NPV method.

The formula for PI is

$$\text{Probability index} = \frac{\text{Present Value of Future Cash Inflow}}{\text{Investment}}$$

Merits:

1. It requires less computational work then IRR method
2. It helps to accept/reject investment proposal on the basis of value of the index.
3. It is useful to rank the proposals on the basis of the highest/lowest value of the index.
4. It is useful to tank the proposals on the basis of the highest/lowest value of the index.
5. It takes into consideration the entire stream of cash flows generated during the useful life of the asset.

Demerits:

1. It is some what difficult to understand
2. Some people may feel no limitation for index number due to several limitation involved in their competitions
3. It is very difficult to understand the analytical part of the decision on the basis of probability index.

10

Financial Accounting

INTRODUCITON

As you are aware, every trader generally starts business for purpose of earning profit. While establishing business, he brings own capital, borrows money from relatives, friends, outsiders or financial institutions. Then he purchases machinery, plant , furniture, raw materials and other assets. He starts buying and selling of goods, paying for salaries, rent and other expenses, depositing and withdrawing cash from bank. Like this he undertakes innumerable transactions in business. Observe the following transactions of small trader for one week during the month of July, 1998.

1998		Rs.
July 24	Purchase of goods from Sree Ram	12,000
July 25	Goods sold for cash	5,000
July 25	Sold gods to Syam on credit	8,000
July 26	Advertising expenses	5,200
July 27	Stationary expenses	600
July 27	Withdrawal for personal use	2,500
July 28	Rent paid through cheque	1,000
July 31	Salaries paid	9,000
July 31	Received cash from Syam	5,000

The number of transactions in an organization depends upon the size of the organization. In small organizations, the transactions generally will be in thousand and in big organizations they may be in lakhs. As such it is humanly impossible to remember all these transactions. Further, it may not by possible to find out the final result of the business without recording and analyzing these transactions.

Accounting came into practice as an aid to human memory by maintaining a systematic record of business transactions.

History of Accounting

Accounting is as old as civilization itself. From the ancient relics of Babylon, it can be will proved that accounting did exist as long as 2600 B.C.

However, in modern form accounting based on the principles of Double Entry System came into existence in 17th Century. Fra Luka Paciolo, a Fransiscan monk and mathematician published a book *De computic et scripturies* in 1494 at Venice in Italyl. This book was translated into English in 1543. In this book he covered a brief section on 'book-keeping'.

Origin of Accounting in India

Accounting was practiced in India thousand years ago and there is a clear evidence for this. In his famous book *Arthashastra* Kautilya dealt with not only politics and economics but also the art of proper keeping of accounts. However, the accounting on modern lines was introduced in India after 1850 with the formation joint stock companies in India.

Accounting in India is now a fast developing discipline. The two premier Accounting Institutes in India viz., chartered Accountants of India and the Institute of Cost and Works Accountants of India are making continuous and substantial contributions. The international Accounts Standards Committee (IASC) was established as on 29th June. In India the 'Accounting Standards Board (ASB) is formulating 'Accounting Standards' on the lines of standards framed by International Accounting Standards Committee.

BOOK-KEEPING AND ACCOUNTING

According to G.A. Lee the accounting system has two stages.

1. The making of routine records in the prescribed from and according to set rules of all events with affect the financial state of the organization; and
2. The summarization from time to time of the information contained in the records, its presentation in a significant

form to interested parties and its interpretation as an aid to decision making by these parties.

First stage is called Book-Keeping and the second one is Accounting.

Book - Keeping: Book - Keeping involves the chronological recording of financial transactions in a set of books in a systematic manner.

Accounting: Accounting is concerned with the maintenance of accounts giving stress to the design of the system of records, the preparation of reports based on the recorded date and the interpretation of the reports.

Distinction between Book - Keeping and Accountancy

Thus, the terms, book-keeping and accounting are very closely related, through there is a subtle difference as mentioned below.

1. Object : The object of book-keeping is to prepare original books of Accounts. It is restricted to journal, subsidiary book and ledge accounts only. On the other hand, the main object of accounting is to record analyse and interpret the business transactions.
2. Level of Work: Book-keeping is restricted to level of work. Clerical work is mainly involved in it. Accountancy on the other hand, is concerned with all level of management.
3. Principles of Accountancy: In Book-keeping Accounting concepts and conventions will be followed by all without any difference. On the other hand, various firms follow various methods of reporting and interpretation in accounting.
3. Final Result: In Book-Keeping it is not possible to know the final result of business every year,

Meaning of Accounting

Thus, book-keeping is an art of recording the business transactions in the books of original entry and the ledges. Accountancy begins where Book-keeping ends. Accountancy means the compiliation of accounts in such a way that one is in a position to know the state of affairs of the business. The work of an accountant is to analyse, interpret and review the accounts and draw conclusion with a view to guide the management in chalking out the future policy of the business.

Definition of Accounting:

Smith and Ashburne: "Accounting is a means of measuring and reporting the results of economic activities."

R.N. Anthony: "Accounting system is a means of collecting summarizing, analyzing and reporting in monetary terms, the information about the business.

American Institute of Certified Public Accountants (AICPA): "The art of recording, classifying and summarizing in a significant manner and in terms of money transactions and events, which are in part at least, of a financial character and interpreting the results thereof."

Thus, accounting is an art of identifying, recording, summarizing and interpreting business transactions of financial nature. Hence accounting is the Language of Business.

Branches of Accounting:

The important branches of accounting are:

1. Financial Accounting: The purpose of Accounting is to ascertain the financial results i.e. profit or loass in the operations during a specific period. It is also aimed at knowing the financial position, i.e. assets, liabilities and equity position at the end of the period. It also provides other relevant information to the management as a basic for decision-making for planning and controlling the operations of the business.
2. Cost Accounting: The purpose of this branch of accounting is to ascertain the cost of a product/operation/project and the costs incurred for carrying out various activities. It also assist the management in controlling the costs. The necessary data and information are gatherr4ed form financial and other sources.
3. Management Accounting : Its aim to assist the management in taking correct policy decision and to evaluate the impact of its decisions and actions. The data required for this purpose are drawn accounting and cost-accounting.
4. Inflation Accounting : It is concerned with the adjustment in the values of assest and of profit in light of changes in the price level. In a way it is concerned with the overcoming

of limitations that arise in financial statements on account of the cost assumption (i.e recording of the assets at their historical or original cost) and the assumption of stable monetary unit.

5. Human Resource Accounting : It is a branch of accounting which seeks to report and emphasize the importance of human resources in a company's earning process and total assets. It is concerned with the process of identifying and measuring data about human resources and communicating this information to interested parties. In simple words, it is accounting for people as organizational resources.

FUNCTIONS OF AN ACCOUNTANT

The job of an accountant involves the following types of accounting works :

1. Designing Work : It includes the designing of the accounting system, basis for identification and classification of financial transactions and events, forms, methods, procedures, etc.
2. Recording Work : The financial transactions are identified, classified and recorded in appropriate books of accounts according to principles. This is "Book Keeping". The recording of transactions tends to be mechanical and repetitive.
3. Summarizing Work : The recorded transactions are summarized into significant form according to generally accepted accounting principles. The work includes the preparation of profit and loss account, balance sheet. This phase is called 'preparation of final accounts'
4. Analysis and Interpretation Work: The financial statements are analysed by using ratio analysis, break-even analysis, funds flow and cash flow analysis.
5. Reporting Work: The summarized statements along with analysis and interpretation are communicated to the interested parties or whoever has the right to receive them. For Ex. Share holders. In addition, the accou8nting departments has to prepare and send regular reports so as to assist the management in decision making. This is 'Reporting'.

6. Preparation of Budget : The management must be able to reasonably estimate the future requirements and opportunities. As an aid to this process, the accountant has to prepare budgets, like cash budget, capital budget, purchase budget, sales budget etc. this is 'Budgeting'.
7. Taxation Work : The accountant has to prepare various statements and returns pertaining to income-tax, sales-tax, excise or customs duties etc., and file the returns with the authorities concerned.
8. Auditing : It involves a critical review and verification of the books of accounts statements and reports with a view to verifying their accuracy. This is 'Auditing'

This is what the accountant or the accounting department does. A person may be placed in any part of Accounting Department or MIS (Management Information System) Department or in small organization, the same person may have to attend to all this work.

USERS OF ACCOUNTING INFORMATION

Different categories of users need different kinds of information for making decisions. The users of accounting can be divided in two board groups (1). Internal users and (2). External users.

Internal Users:

Managers : These are the persons who manage the business, i.e. management at he top, middle and lower levels. Their requirements of information are different because they make different types of decisions.

Accounting reports are important to managers for evaluating the results of their decisions. In additions to external financial statements, managers need detailed internal reports either branch division or department or product-wise. Accounting reports for managers are prepared much more frequently than external reports.

Accounting information also helps the managers in appraising the performance of subordinates. As such Accounting is termed as " the eyes and ears of management."

External Users :

1. Investors : Those who are interested in buying the shares of company are naturally interested in the financial

statements to know how safe the investment already made is and how safe the proposed investments will be.

2. Creditors : Lenders are interested to know whether their load, principal and interest, will be paid when due. Suppliers and other creditors are also interested to know the ability of the firm to pay their dues in time.
3. Workers : In our country, workers are entitled to payment of bonus which depends on the size of profit earned. Hence, they would like to be satisfied that he bonus being paid to them is correct. This knowledge also helps them in conducting negotiations for wages.
4. Customers : They are also concerned with the stability and profitability of the enterprise. They may be interested in knowing the financial strength of the company to rent it for further decisions relating to purchase of goods.
5. Government: Governments all over the world are using financial statements for compiling statistics concerning business which, in turn, helps in compiling national accounts. The financial statements are useful for tax authorities for calculating taxes.
6. Public : The public at large interested in the functioning of the enterprises because it may make a substantial contribution to the local economy in many ways including the number of people employed and their patronage to local suppliers.
7. Researchers: The financial statements, being a mirror of business conditions, is of great interest to scholars undertaking research in accounting theory as well as business affairs and practices.

ADVANTAGES FROM ACCOUNTING

The role of accounting has changed from that of a mere record keeping during the 1st decade of 20th century of the present stage, which it is accepted as information system and decision making activity. The following are the advantages of accounting.

1. Provides for systematic records: Since all the financial transactions are recorded in the books, one need not rely on memory. Any information required is readily available from these records.

2. Facilitates the preparation of financial statements: Profit and loss accountant and balance sheet can be easily prepared with the help of the information in the records. This enables the trader to know the net result of business operations (i.e. profit/loss) during the accounting period and the financial position of the business at the end of the accounting period.
3. Provides control over assets: Book-keeping provides information regarding cash in had, cash at bank, stock of goods, accounts receivables from various parties and the amounts invested in various other assets. As the trader knows the values of the assets he will have control over them.
4. Provides the required information: Interested parties such as owners, lenders, creditors etc., get necessary information at frequent intervals.
5. Comparative study: One can compare the present performance of the organization with that of its past. This enables the managers to draw useful conclusion and make proper decisions.
6. Less Scope for fraud or theft: It is difficult to conceal fraud or theft etc., because of the balancing of the books of accounts periodically. As the work is divided among many persons, there will be check and counter check.
7. Tax matters: Properly maintained book-keeping records will help in the settlement of all tax matters with the tax authorities.
8. Ascertaining Value of Business: The accounting records will help in ascertaining the correct value of the business. This helps in the event of sale or purchase of a business.
9. Documentary evidence: Accounting records can also be used as an evidence in the court to substantiate the claim of the business. These records are based on documentary proof. Every entry is supported by authentic vouchers. As such, Courts accept these records as evidence.
10. Helpful to management: Accounting is useful to the management in various ways. It enables the management to asses the achievement of its performance. The weakness of the business can be identified and corrective measures can be applied to remove them with the helps accounting.

LIMITATIONS OF ACCOUNTING

The following are the limitations of accounting.

1. Does not record all events: Only the transactions of a financial character will be recorded under book-keeping. So it does not reveal a complete picture about the quality of human resources, locational advantage, business contacts etc.
2. Does not reflect current values: The data available under book-keeping is historical in nature. So they do not reflect current values. For instance, we record the value of stock at cost price or market price, which ever is less. In case of, building, machinery etc., we adopt historical cost as the basis. Infact, the current values of buildings, plant and machinery may be much more than what is recorded in the balance sheet.
3. Estimates based on Personal Judgment: The estimate used for determining the values of various items may not be correct. For example, debtor are estimated in terms of collectibility, inventories are based on marketability, and fixed assets are based on useful working life. These estimates are based on personal judgment and hence sometimes may not be correct.
4. Inadequate information on costs and Profits: Book-keeping only provides information about the overall profitability of the business. No information is given about the cost and profitability of different activities of products or divisions.

BASIC ACCOUNTING CONCEPTS

Accounting has been evolved over a period of several centuries. During this period, certain rules and conventions have been adopted. They serve as guidelines in identifying the events and transactions to be accounted for measuring, recording, summarizing and reporting them to the interested parties. These rules and conventions are termed as Generally Accepted Accounting Principles.

These principles are also referred as standards, assumptions, concepts, conventions doctrines, etc. Thus, the accounting concepts are the fundamental ideas or basic assumptions underlying the theory and practice of financial accounting. They are the broad working rules for all accounting activities developed and accepted by the accounting profession.

Basic accounting concepts may be classified into two broad categories.

1. Concept to be observed at the time of recording transactions.(Recording Stage).
2. Concept to be observed at the time of preparing the financial accounts (Reporting Stage)

11

Final Accounts

INTRODUCTION

The main object of any Business is to make profit. Every trader generally starts business for the purpose of earning profit. While establishing Business, he brings his own capital, borrows money from relatives, friends, outsiders or financial institutions, then purchases machinery, plant, furniture, raw materials and other assets. He starts buying and selling of goods, paying for salaries, rent and other expenses, depositing and withdrawing cash from Bank. Like this he undertakes innumerable transactions in Business.

The number of Business transactions in an organization depends up on the size of the organization. In small organizations the transactions generally will be in thousands and in big organizations they may be in lacks. As such it is humanly impossible to remember all these transactions. Further it may not be possible to find out the final result of the Business with out recording and analyzing these transactions.

Accounting came in practice as an aid to human memory by maintaining a systematic record of Business transactions.

BOOK KEEPING AND ACCOUNTING:

According to G.A.Lee the Accounting system has two stages. First stage is Book keeping and the second stage is accounting.

Book keeping

Book keeping involves the chronological recording of financial transactions in a set of books in a systematic manner

"Book keeping is the system of recording Business transactions for the purpose of providing reliable information to the owners and managers about the state and prospect of the Business concepts".

Thus Book keeping is an art of recording business transactions in the books of original entry and the ledges.

ACCOUNTING: Accounting begins where the Bookkeeping ends

1. *SMITH AND ASHBUNNE*: Accounting means "measuring and reporting the results of economic activities".
2. *R.N ANTHONY*: Accounting is a system of "collecting, summarizing, Analyzing and reporting in monster terms, the information about the Business".
3. *ICPA:* Recording, classifying and summarizing is a significant manner and in terms of money transactions and events, which are in part at least, of a financial character and interpreting the results there.

Thus accounting is an art of recording, classifying, summarizing and interpreting business transactions of financial nature. Hence accounting is the "Language of Business".

ADVANTAGE OF ACCOUNTING

The following are the advantages of Accounting...........

1. *PROVIDES FOR SYSTEMATIC RECORDS*: Since all the financial transactions are recorded in the books, one need not rely on memory. Any information required is readily available from these records.
2. *FACILITATES THE PRPARATION OF FINANCIAL STATEMENTS*: Profit and Loss account and balance sheet can be easily prepared with the help of the information in the records. This enables the trader to know the net result of Business operations (i.e. profit/loss) during the accounting period and the financial position of the business at the end of the accounting period.
3. *PROVIDES CONTROL OVER ASSETS*: Book keeping provides information regarding cash in hand, cash at hand, stack of goods, accounts receivable from various parties and the amounts invested in various other assets. As the trader knows the values of the assets he will have control over them.

4. *PROVIES THE REQUIRED INFORMATION*: Interested parties such as owners, lenders, creditors etc, get necessary information at frequent intervals.
5. *COMPARITIVE STUDY*: One can compare present performance of the organization with that of its past. This enables the managers to draw useful conclusions and make proper decisions.
6. *LESS SCOPE FOR FRAUD OR THEFT*: It is difficult to conceal fraud or theft etc. because of the balancing of the books of accounts periodically. As the work is divided among many persons, there will be check and counter check.
7. TAX MALTERS: Properly maintained Book keeping records will help in the settlement of all tax matters with the tax authorities.
8. *ASCERTAINING VALUE OF BUSINESS*: The accounting records will help in ascertaining the correct value of the Business. This helps in the event of sale or purchase of a business.
9. *DOCUMENTARY EVIDENCE*: Accounting records can also be used as evidence in the court of substantial the claim of the Business. Thus records are based on documentary proof. Authentic vouchers support every entry. As such, courts accept these records as evidence.
10. *HELPFUL TO MANAGEMENT*: Accounting is useful to the management in various ways. It enables the management to assess the achievement of its performance. The weaknesses of the business can be identified and corrective measures can be applied to remove them with the help of accounting.

LIMITATIONS OF ACCOUNTING

The following are the limitations of accounting.............

DOES NOT RECORD ALL EVENTS: Only the transactions of a financial character will be recorded under book keeping. So it does not reveal a complete picture about the quality of human resources, locational advantages, business contacts etc.

DOES NOT REFLECT CURRENT VLAUES: The data available under book keeping is historical in nature. So they do not reflect current values. For instance we record the values of stock at cost price or market price, which ever is less. In case of building, machinery etc., we adapt historical case as the basis. Infact, the current values of Buildings, plant and machinery may be much more than what is recorded in the balance sheet.

ESTIMATES BASED ON PERSONAL JUDGEMENT: The estimates used for determining the values of various items may not be correct. For example, debtors are estimated in terms of collectibles, inventories are based on marketability and fixed assets are based on useful working life. These estimates are based on personal judgment and hence sometimes may not be correct.

INADEQUATE INFORMATION ON COSTS AND PROFITS: Book keeping only provides information about over all profitability of the business. No information is given about the cost and profitability of different activities of products or divisions.

BASIC ACCOUNTING CONCEPTS

Accounting is a system evolved to achieve a set of objectives. In order to achieve the goals, we need a set of rules or guidelines. These guidelines are termed here as "BASIC ACCOUNTING ONCEPTS". The term concept means an idea or thought. Basic accounting concepts are the fundamental ideas or basic assumptions underlying the theory and profit of FINANCIAL ACCOUNTING. These concepts help in bringing about uniformity in the practice of accounting. In accountancy following concepts are quite popular.

BUSINESS ENTITY CONEPT: In this concept "Business is treated as separate from the proprietor". All the

Transactions recorded in the book of Business and not in the books of proprietor. The proprietor is also treated as a creditor for the Business.

GOING CONCERN CONCEPT: This concept relates with the long life of Business. The assumption is that business will continue to exist for unlimited period unless it is dissolved due to some reasons or the other.

MONEY MEASUREMENT CONCEPT: In this concept "Only those transactions are recorded in accounting which can be expressed in terms of money, those transactions which can not be expressed in terms of money are not recorded in the books of accounting".

COST CONCEPT: Accounting to this concept, can asset is recorded at its cost in the books of account. i.e., the price, which is paid at the time of acquiring it. In balance sheet, these assets appear not at cost price every year, but depreciation is deducted and they appear at the amount, which is cost, less classification.

ACCOUNTING PERIOD CONCEPT: every Businessman wants to know the result of his investment and efforts after a certain period. Usually one-year period is regarded as an ideal for this purpose. This period is called Accounting Period. It depends on the nature of the business and object of the proprietor of business.

DUAL ASCEPT CONCEPT: According to this concept "Every business transactions has two aspects", one is the receiving benefit aspect another one is giving benefit aspect. The receiving benefit aspect is termed as

"DEBIT", where as the giving benefit aspect is termed as "CREDIT". Therefore, for every debit, there will be corresponding credit.

MATCHING COST CONCEPT: According to this concept "The expenses incurred during an accounting period, e.g., if revenue is recognized on all goods sold during a period, cost of those good sole should also

Be charged to that period.

REALISATION CONCEPT: According to this concept revenue is recognized when a sale is made. Sale is

Considered to be made at the point when the property in goods posses to the buyer and he becomes legally liable to pay.

ACCOUNTING CONVENTIONS

Accounting is based on some customs or usages. Naturally accountants here to adopt that usage or custom.

They are termed as convert conventions in accounting. The following are some of the important accounting conventions.

FULL DISCLOSURE: According to this convention accounting reports should disclose fully and fairly the information. They purport to represent. They should be prepared honestly and sufficiently disclose information which is if material interest to proprietors, present and potential creditors and investors. The companies ACT, 1956 makes it compulsory to provide all the information in the prescribed form.

MATERIALITY: Under this convention the trader records important factor about the commercial activities. In the form of financial statements if any unimportant information is to be given for the sake of clarity it will be given as footnotes.

CONSISTENCY: It means that accounting method adopted should not be changed from year to year. It means that there should be consistent in the methods or principles followed. Or else the results of a year

Cannot be conveniently compared with that of another.

CONSERVATISM: This convention warns the trader not to take unrealized income in to account. That is why the practice of valuing stock at cost or market price, which ever is lower is in vague. This is the policy of "playing safe"; it takes in to consideration all prospective losses but leaves all prospective profits.

KEY WORDS IN BOOK-KEEPING

TRANSACTIONS: Any sale or purchase of goods of services is called the transaction.

Transactions are two types.

[a]. cash transaction: cash transaction is one where cash receipt or payment is involved in the exchange.

[b]. Credit transaction: Credit transaction will not have cash, either received or paid, for something given or received respectively.

GOODS: Fill those things which a firm purchases for resale are called goods.

PURCHASES: Purchases means purchase of goods, unless it is stated otherwise it also represents the Goods purchased.

SALES: Sales means sale of goods, unless it is stated otherwise it also represents these goods sold.

EXPENSES: Payments for the purchase of goods as services are known as expenses.

REVENUE: Revenue is the amount realized or receivable from the sale of goods or services.

ASSETS: The valuable things owned by the business are known as assets. These are the properties Owned by the business.

LIABILITIES: Liabilities are the obligations or debts payable by the enterprise in future in the term Of money or goods.

DEBTORS: Debtors means a person who owes money to the trader.

CREDITORS: A creditor is a person to whom something is owned by the business.

DRAWINGS: cash or goods withdrawn by the proprietor from the Business for his personal or Household is termed to as "drawing".

RESERVE: An amount set aside out of profits or other surplus and designed to meet contingencies.

ACCOUNT: A summarized statements of transactions relating to a particular person, thing, Expense or income.

DISCOUNT: There are two types of discounts..

a. cash discount: An allowable made to encourage frame payment or before the expiration of the period allowed for credit.

b. Trade discount: A deduction from the gross or catalogue price allowed to traders who buys them for resale.

CLASSIFICATION OF BUSINESS TRANSACTIONS

All business transactions are classified into three categories:

1. Those relating to persons
2. Those relating to property(Assets)
3. Those relating to income & expenses

Thus, three classes of accounts are maintained for recording all business transactions. They are:

1. Personal accounts
2. Real accounts
3. Nominal accounts

Personal Accounts :Accounts which are transactions with persons are called "Personal Accounts".

A separate account is kept on the name of each person for recording the benefits received from ,or given to the person in the course of dealings with him.

E.g.: Krishna's A/C, Gopal's A/C, SBI A/C, Nagarjuna Finanace Ltd.A/C, ObulReddy & Sons A/C , HMT Ltd. A/C, Capital A/C, Drawings A/C etc.

Real Accounts: The accounts relating to properties or assets are known as "Real Accounts".Every business needs assets such as machinery , furniture etc, for running its activities.A separate account is maintained for each asset owned by the business.

E.g.: cash A/C, furniture A/C, building A/C, machinery A/C etc.

NominalAccounts:Accounts relating to expenses, losses, incomes and gains are known as "Nominal Accounts". A separate account is maintained for each item of expenses, losses, income or gain.

E.g.: Salaries A/C, stationery A/C, wages A/C, postage A/C, commission A/C, interest A/C, purchases A/C, rent A/C, discount A/C, commission received A/C, interest received A/C, rent received A/C, discount received A/C.

Before recording a transaction, it is necessary to find out which of the accounts is to be debited and which is to be credited. The following three different rules have been laid down for the three classes of accounts....

Personal Accounts: The account of the person receiving benefit (receiver) is to be debited and the account of the person giving the benefit (given) is to be credited.

Rule: "Debit – –The Receiver

Credit–The Giver"

Real Accounts: When an asset is coming into the business, account of that asset is to be debited.When an asset is going out of the business, the account of that asset is to be credited.

Rule: "Debit– –What comes in

Credit–What goes out"

Nominal Accounts: When an expense is incurred or loss encountered, the account representing the expense or loss is to be debited. When any income is earned or gain made, the account representing the income of gain is to be credited.

Rule: "Debit– –All expenses and losses

Credit–All incomes and gains"

JOURNAL

The first step in accounting therefore is the record of all the transactions in the books of original entry viz., Journal and then posting into ledges.

JOURNAL: The word Journal is derived from the Latin word 'journ' which means a day. Therefore, journal means a 'day Book' in day-to-day business transactions are recorded in chronological order. Journal is treated as the book of original entry or first entry or prime entry. All the business transactions are recorded in this book before they are posted in the ledges. The journal is a complete and chronological(in order of dates) record of business transactions. It is recorded in a systematic manner. The process of recording a transaction in the journal is called "JOURNALISING". The entries made in the book are called "Journal Entries".

LEDGER

All the transactions in a journal are recorded in a chronological order. After a certain period, if we want to know whether a particular account is showing a debit or credit balance it becomes very difficult. So, the ledger is designed to accommodate the various accounts maintained the trader. It contains the final or permanent record of all the transactions in duly classified form. "A ledger is a book which contains various accounts." The process of transferring entries from journal to ledger is called "POSTING".

Posting is the process of entering in the ledger the entries given in the journal. Posting into ledger is done periodically, may be weekly or fortnightly as per the convenience of the business. The following are the guidelines for posting transactions in the ledger.

1. After the completion of Journal entries only posting is to be made in the ledger.
2. For each item in the Journal a separate account is to be opened. Further, for each new item a new account is to be opened.
3. Depending upon the number of transactions space for each account is to be determined in the ledger.
4. For each account there must be a name. This should be written in the top of the table. At the end of the name, the word "Account" is to be added.
5. The debit side of the Journal entry is to be posted on the debit side of the account, by starting with "TO".
6. The credit side of the Journal entry is to be posted on the debit side of the account, by starting with "BY".

TRAIL BALANCE

The first step in the preparation of final accounts is the preparation of trail balance. In the double entry system of book keeping, there will be credit for every debit and there will not be any debit without credit. When this principle is followed in writing journal entries, the total amount of all debits is equal to the total amount all credits.

A trail balance is a statement of debit and credit balances. It is prepared on a particular date with the object of checking the accuracy of the books of accounts. It indicates that all the transactions for a particular period have been duly entered in the book, properly posted and balanced. The trail balance doesn't include stock in hand at the end of the period. All adjustments required to be done at the end of the period including closing stock are generally given under the trail balance.

*DEFINITIONS: SPICER AND POGLAR :*A trail balance is a list of all the balances standing on the ledger accounts and cash book of a concern at any given date.

J.R.BATLIBOI: A trail balance is a statement of debit and credit balances extracted from the ledger with a view to test the arithmetical accuracy of the books.

Thus a trail balance is a list of balances of the ledger accounts' and cash book of a business concern at any given date.

Trail Balance

Specimen of trial balance

1	Capital	Credit	Loan
2	Opening stock	Debit	Asset
3	Purchases	Debit	Expense
4	Sales	Credit	Gain
5	Returns inwards	Debit	Loss
6	Returns outwards	Debit	Gain
7	Wages	Debit	Expense
8	Freight	Debit	Expense
9	Transport expenses	Debit	Expense
10	Royalities on production	Debit	Expense
11	Gas, fuel	Debit	Expense
12	Discount received	Credit	Revenue

13	Discount allowed	Debit	Loss
14	Bas debts	Debit	Loss
15	Dab debts reserve	Credit	Gain
16	Commission received	Credit	Revenue
17	Repairs	Debit	Expense
18	Rent	Debit	Expense
19	Salaries	Debit	Expense
20	Loan Taken	Credit	Loan
21	Interest received	Credit	Revenue
22	Interest paid	Debit	Expense
23	Insurance	Debit	Expense
24	Carriage outwards	Debit	Expense
25	Advertisements	Debit	Expense
26	Petty expenses	Debit	Expense
27	Trade expenses	Debit	Expense
28	Petty receipts	Credit	Pevenue
29	Income tax	Debit	Drawings
30	Office expenses	Debit	Expense
31	Customs duty	Debit	Expense
32	Sales tax	Debit	Expense
33	Provision for discount on debtors	Debit	Liability
34	Provision for discount on creditors	Debit	Asset
35	Debtors	Debit	Asset
36	Creditors	Credit	Liability
37	Goodwill	Debit	Asset
38	Plant, machinery	Debit	Asset
39	Land, buildings	Debit	Asset
40	Furniture, fittings	Debit	Asset
41	Investments	Debit	Asset
42	Cash in hand	Debit	Asset
43	Cash at bank	Debit	Asset
44	Reserve fund	Credit	Liability
45	Loan advances	Debit	Asset
46	Horse, carts	Debit	Asset
47	Excise duty	Debit	Expense
48	General reserve	Credit	Liability
49	Provision for depreciation	Credit	Liability
50	Bills receivable	Debit	Asset

51	Bills payable	Credit	Liability
52	Depreciation	Debit	Loss
53	Bank overdraft	Credit	Liability
54	Outstanding salaries	Credit	Liability
55	Prepaid insurance	Debit	Asset
56	Bad debt reserve	Credit	Revenue
57	Patents & Trademarks	Debit	Asset
58	Motor vehicle	Debit	Asset
59	Outstanding rent	Credit	Revenue

FINAL ACCOUNTS

In every business, the business man is interested in knowing whether the business has resulted in profit or loss and what the financial position of the business is at a given time. In brief, he wants to know (i)The profitability of the business and (ii) The soundness of the business.

The trader can ascertain this by preparing the final accounts. The final accounts are prepared from the trial balance. Hence the trial balance is said to be the link between the ledger accounts and the final accounts. The final accounts of a firm can be divided into two stages. The first stage is preparing the trading and profit and loss account and the second stage is preparing the balance sheet.

FINAL ACCOUNTS – ADJUSTMENTS

We know that business is a going concern. It has to be carried on indefinitely. At the end of every accounting year. The trader prepares the trading and profit and loss account and balance sheet. While preparing these financial statements, sometimes the trader may come across certain problems.The expenses of the current year may be still payable or the expenses of the next year have been prepaid during the current year. In the same way, the income of the current year still receivable and the income of the next year have been received during the current year. Without these adjustments, the profit figures arrived at or the financial position of the concern may not be correct. As such these adjustments are to be made while preparing the final accounts.

The adjustments to be made to final accounts will be given under the Trial Balance. While making the adjustment in the final accounts, the student should remember that "every adjustment is to be made in the final accounts twice i.e. once in trading, profit and loss account and later in balance sheet generally". The following are some of the important adjustments to be made at the time of preparing of final accounts:-

CLOSING STOCK :-

(i) *If closing stock is given in Trail Balance*: It should be shown only in the balance sheet "Assets Side".

(ii) *If closing stock is given as adjustment* :

1. First, it should be posted at the credit side of "Trading Account".
2. Next, shown at the asset side of the "Balance Sheet".

OUTSTANDING EXPENSES :-

(i) *If outstanding expenses given in Trail Balance*: It should be only on the liability side of Balance Sheet.

(ii) *If outstanding expenses given as adjustment* :

1. First, it should be added to the concerned expense at the debit side of profit and loss account or Trading Account.
2. Next, it should be added at the liabilities side of the Balance Sheet.

PREAPID EXPENSES :-

(i) *If prepaid expenses given in Trial Balance*: It should be shown only in assets side of the Balance Sheet.

(ii) *If prepaid expense given as adjustment* :

1. First, it should be deducted from the concerned expenses at the debit side of profit and loss account or Trading Account.
2. Next, it should be shown at the assets side of the Balance Sheet.

INCOME EARNED BUT NOT RECEIVED [OR] OUTSTANDING INCOME [OR] ACCURED INCOME :-

(i) *If incomes given in Trial Balance*: It should be shown only on the assets side of the Balance Sheet.

(ii) *If incomes outstanding given as adjustment*:

1. First, it should be added to the concerned income at the credit side of profit and loss account.

2. Next, it should be shown at the assets side of the Balance sheet.

INCOME RECEIVED IN ADVANCE: UNEARNED INCOME:-

(i) *If unearned incomes given in Trail Balance* : It should be shown only on the liabilities side of the Balance Sheet.

(ii) *If unearned income given as adjustment* :

1. First, it should be deducted from the concerned income in the credit side of the profit and loss account.
2. Secondly, it should be shown in the liabilities side of the Balance Sheet.

DEPRECIATION:-

(i) *If Depreciation given in Trail Balance*: It should be shown only on the debit side of the profit and loss account.

(ii) *If Depreciation given as adjustment*

1. First, it should be shown on the debit side of the profit and loss account.
2. Secondly, it should be deduced from the concerned asset in the Balance sheet assets side.

INTEREST ON LOAN [OR] CAPITAL :-

(i) *If interest on loan (or) capital given in Trail balance* :It should be shown only on debit side of the profit and loss account.

(ii) *If interest on loan (or)capital given as adjustment* :

1. First, it should be shown on debit side of the profit and loss account.
2. Secondly, it should added to the loan or capital inthe liabilities side of the Balance Sheet.

BAD DEBTS:-

(i) *If bad debts given in Trail balance* :It should be shown on the debit side of the profit and loss account.

(ii) *If bad debts given as adjustment*:

1. First, it should be shown on the debit side of the profit and loss account.
2. Secondly, it should be deducted from debtors in the assets side of the Balance Sheet.

INTEREST ON DRAWINGS :-

(i) *If interest on drawings given in Trail balance*: It should be shown on the credit side of the profit and loss account.

(ii) *If interest on drawings given as adjustments* :

1. First, it should be shown on the credit side of the profit and loss account.
2. Secondly, it should be deducted from capital on liabilities side of the Balance Sheet.

INTEREST ON INVESTMENTS :-

(i) *If interest on the investments given in Trail balance* :It should be shown on the credit side of the profit and loss account.

(ii) *If interest on investments given as adjustments* :

1. First, it should be shown on the credit side of the profit and loss account.
2. Secondly, it should be added to the investments on assets side of the Balance Sheet.

Note: Problems to be solved on final accounts

SUBSIDIARY BOOKS

In a small business concern, the numbers of transactions are limited. These transactions are first recorded in the journal as and when they take place. Subsequently, these transactions are posted in the appropriate accounts of the ledger. Therefore, the journal is known as "Book Of Original Entry" or "Book of Prime Entry" while the ledger is known as main book of accounts.

On the other hand, the transactions in big concern are numerous and sometimes even run into thousands and lakhs. It is inconvenient and time wasting process if all the transactions are going to be managed with a journal.

Therefore, a convenient device is made. Smaller account books known as subsidiary books or subsidiary journals are disturbed to various sections of the business house. As and when transactions take place, they are recorded in these subsidiary books simultaneously without delay. The original journal (which is known as Journal Proper) is used only occasionally to record those transactions which cannot be recorded in any of the subsidiary books.

TYPES OF SUBSIDIARY BOOKS:– Subsidiary books are divided into eight types. They are,

1. Purchases Book
2. Sales Book

3. Purchase Returns Book
4. Sales Returns Book
5. Cash Book
6. Bills Receivable Book
7. Bills Payable Book
8. Journal Proper

PURCHASES BOOK :- This book records all credit purchases only. Purchase of goods for cash and purchase of assets for cash. Credit will not be recorded in this book. Purchases book is otherwise called Purchases Day Book, Purchases Journal or Purchases Register.

SALES BOOK :-This book is used to record credit sales only. Goods are sold for cash and sale of assets for cash or credit will not be recorded in this book. This book is otherwise called Sales Day Book, Sales Journal or Sales Register.

PURCHASE RETURNS BOOK :- This book is used to record the particulars of goods returned to the suppliers.This book is otherwise called Returns Outward Book.

SALES RETURNS BOOK :- This book is used to record the particulars of goods returned by the customers. This book is otherwise called Returns Inward Book.

CASH BOOK :- All cash transactions , receipts and payments are recorded in this book. Cash includes cheques, money orders etc.

BILLS REECEIVABLE BOOK :- This book is used to record all the bills and promissory notes are received from the customers.

BILLS PAYABLE BOOK :- This book is used to record all the bills or promissory notes accepted to the suppliers.

JOURNAL PROPER :- This is used to record all the transactions that cannot be recorded in any of the above mentioned subsidiary books.

CASH BOOK

Cash book plays an important role in accounting. Whether transactions made are in the form of cash or credit, final statement will be in the form of receipt or payment of cash. So, every transaction finds place in the cash book finally.

Cash book is a principal book as well as the subsidiary book. It is a book of original entry since the transactions are recorded for the first time from the source of documents.

It is a ledger in a sense it is designed in the form of cash account and records cash receipts on the debit side and the cash payments on the credit side. Thus, a cash book fulfils the functions of both a ledger account and a journal.

Cash book is divided into two sides. Receipt side (debit side) and payment side (credit side). The method of recording cash sample is very simple. All cash receipts will be posted on the debit side and all the payments will be recorded on the credit side.

Types of cash book: cash book may be of the following types according to the needs of the business.

- Simple cash book
- Double column or two column cash book
- Three column cash book
- Petty cash book

SINGLE COLUMN CASH BOOK: The simple cash book is a record of only cash transactions. The model of the cash book is given below.

TWO COLUMN CASH BOOK: This book has two columns on each side one for discount and the other for cash. Discount column on debit side represents loss being discount allowed to customers. Similarly, discount column on credit side represents gain being discount received.

Discount may be two types.

(i) Trade discount

(ii) cash discount

TRADE DISCOUNT: when a retailer purchases goods from the wholesaler, he allows some discount on the catalogue price. This discount is called as Trade discount.

Trade discount is adjusted in the invoice and the net amount is recorded in the purchase book. As such it will not appear in the book of accounts.

CASH DISCOUNT: When the goods are purchased on credit, payment will be made in the future as agreed by the parties. If the amount is paid early as promptly a discount by a way of incentive will be allowed by the seller to the buyer. This discount is called as cash discount.

So cash discount is the discount allowed by the seller to encourage prompt payment from the buyer. Cash discount is entered in the discount column of the cash book. The discount recorded in the debit side of the cash book is discount allowed. The discount recorded in the credit side of the cash book is discount received.

12

Financial Analysis through Ratios

RATIO ANALYSIS

Absolute figures are valuable but they standing alone convey no meaning unless compared with another. Accounting ratio show inter-relationships which exist among various accounting data. When relationships among various accounting data supplied by financial statements are worked out, they are known as accounting ratios.

Accounting ratios can be expressed in various ways such as:

1. a pure ratio says ratio of current assets to current liabilities is 2:1 or
2. a rate say current assets are two times of current liabilities or
3. a percentage say current assets are 200% of current liabilities.

Each method of expression has a distinct advantage over the other the analyst will selected that mode which will best suit his convenience and purpose.

USES OR ADVANTAGES OR IMPORTANCE OF RATIO ANALYSIS

Ratio Analysis stands for the process of determining and presenting the relationship of items and groups of items in the financial statements. It is an important technique of financial analysis. It is a way by which financial stability and health of a concern can be judged. The following are the main uses of Ratio analysis:

(a) Useful in financial position analysis: Accounting reveals the financial position of the concern. This helps banks, insurance companies and other financial institution in lending and making investment decisions.

(ii) Useful in simplifying accounting figures: Accounting ratios simplify, summaries and systematic the accounting figures in order to make them more understandable and in lucid form.

(iii) Useful in assessing the operational efficiency: Accounting ratios helps to have an idea of the working of a concern. The efficiency of the firm becomes evident when analysis is based on accounting ratio. This helps the management to assess financial requirements and the capabilities of various business units.

(iv) Useful in forecasting purposes: If accounting ratios are calculated for number of years, then a trend is established. This trend helps in setting up future plans and forecasting.

(v) Useful in locating the weak spots of the business: Accounting ratios are of great assistance in locating the weak spots in the business even through the overall performance may be efficient.

(vi) Useful in comparison of performance: Managers are usually interested to know which department performance is good and for that he compare one department with the another department of the same firm. Ratios also help him to make any change in the organisation structure.

Limitations of Ratio Analysis: These limitations should be kept in mind while making use of ratio analyses for interpreting the financial statements. The following are the main limitations of ratio analysis.

1. False results if based on incorrect accounting data: Accounting ratios can be correct only if the data (on which they are based) is correct. Sometimes, the information given in the financial statements is affected by window dressing, i. e. showing position better than what actually is.
2. No idea of probable happenings in future: Ratios are an attempt to make an analysis of the past financial statements; so they are historical documents. Now-a-days keeping in view the complexities of the business, it is important to have an idea of the probable happenings in future.

3. Variation in accounting methods: The two firms' results are comparable with the help of accounting ratios only if they follow the some accounting methods or bases. Comparison will become difficult if the two concerns follow the different methods of providing depreciation or valuing stock.
4. Price level change: Change in price levels make comparison for various years difficult.
5. Only one method of analysis: Ratio analysis is only a beginning and gives just a fraction of information needed for decision-making so, to have a comprehensive analysis of financial statements, ratios should be used along with other methods of analysis.
6. No common standards: It is very difficult to by down a common standard for comparison because circumstances differ from concern to concern and the nature of each industry is different.
7. Different meanings assigned to the some term: Different firms, in order to calculate ratio may assign different meanings. This may affect the calculation of ratio in different firms and such ratio when used for comparison may lead to wrong conclusions.
8. Ignores qualitative factors: Accounting ratios are tools of quantitative analysis only. But sometimes qualitative factors may surmount the quantitative aspects. The calculations derived from the ratio analysis under such circumstances may get distorted.
9. No use if ratios are worked out for insignificant and unrelated figure: Accounting ratios should be calculated on the basis of cause and effect relationship. One should be clear as to what cause is and what effect is before calculating a ratio between two figures.

Ratio Analysis: Ratio is an expression of one number is relation to another. It is one of the methods of analyzing financial statement. Ratio analysis facilities the presentation of the information of the financial statements in simplified and summarized from. Ratio is a measuring of two numerical positions. It expresses the relation between two numeric figures. It can be found by dividing one figure by another ratios are expressed in three ways.

13

Theoretical Models

A modern economy is a very complicated place. Thousands of firms engage in pro-ducing millions of different goods. Millions of individuals work in all sorts of occu-pations and make decisions about which of these goods to buy. Take peanuts, for example. They must be harvested at the right time and shipped to processors who turn them into peanut butter, peanut oil, peanut brittle, and numerous other peanut delicacies. These processors, in turn, must make certain that their products arrive at thousands of retail outlets in the proper quantities to meet demand.

Because it would be impossible to describe the features of just these peanut mar-kets in complete detail, economists have chosen to abstract from the complexities of the real world and to develop rather simple models that capture the "essentials." Just as a road map is helpful even though it does not record every house or every blade of grass, economic models of, say, the market for peanuts are also very useful even though they do not record every minute feature of the peanut economy. In this book we shall be studying the most widely used economic models. We shall see that, even though they make heroic abstractions from the true complexities of the real world, they nonetheless capture many essential features that are common to all economic activities.

The use of models is widespread in both the physical and social sciences. In physics, the notion of a "perfect" vacuum or an "ideal" gas is an abstraction that per-mits scientists to study real-world phenomena in simplified settings. In chemistry, the idea of an atom or a molecule is in actuality a very simplified model of the struc-ture of matter. Architects use mock-up models to plan buildings. Television repair-ers refer to wiring diagrams to locate problems. So too, economists have developed their models as aids to understanding economic issues. These portray the way indi-viduals make decisions, the way firms behave, and the way in which these two groups interact to establish markets.

VERIFICATION OF ECONOMIC MODELS

Of course, not all models prove to be "good." For example, the earth-centered model of planetary motion devised by Ptolemy was eventually disregarded because it proved incapable of explaining accurately how the planets move around the sun. An important purpose of scientific investigation is to sort out the "bad" models from the "good." Two general methods have been used for verifying economic models: (1) a direct approach, which seeks to establish the validity of the basic as-sumptions on which a model is based; and (2) an indirect approach, which at-tempts to confirm validity by showing that a simplified model correctly predicts real-world events. To illustrate the basic differences in the two approaches, let's briefly examine a model that we will use extensively in later chapters of this book— the model of a firm that seeks to maximize profits.

THE PROFIT-MAXIMIZATION MODEL

The model of a firm seeking to maximize profits is obviously a simplification of re-ality. It ignores the personal motivations of a firm's managers and does not consider personal conflicts among them. It assumes that profits are the only relevant goal of a firm; other possible goals, such as obtaining power or prestige, are treated as unimportant. The model also assumes that a firm has sufficient information about its costs and the nature of the market to which it sells to discover what its profit-maximizing options actually are. Most real-world firms, of course, do not have this information readily available. Yet, such shortcomings in the model are not neces-sarily serious. No model can describe reality exactly. The real question is whether this simple model has any claim to being a good one.

Testing Assumptions

One test of the model of a profit-maximizing firm investigates its basic assumption: Do firms really seek maximum profits? Some economists have examined this ques-tion by sending questionnaires to executives asking them to specify what goals they pursue. The results of such studies have been varied. Businesspeople often mention goals other than profits or claim they only do "the best they can" given their limited information. On the other hand, most respondents also mention a strong "interest" in profits and express the view that profit maximization is an appropriate goal. Test-ing the profit-maximizing model by testing its assumptions has therefore provided inconclusive results.

Testing Predictions

Some economists, most notably Milton Friedman, deny that a model can be tested by inquiring into the "reality" of its assumptions.[1] They argue that all theoretical models are based on "unrealistic" assumptions; the very nature of theorizing de-mands that we make certain abstractions. These economists conclude that the only way to determine the validity of a model is to see whether it is capable of explain-ing and predicting real-world events. The ultimate test of an economic model comes when it is confronted with data from the economy itself.

Friedman provides an important illustration of that principle. He asks what kind of a theory one should use to explain the shots expert pool players will make. He argues that the laws of velocity, momentum, and angles from theoretical classi-cal physics would be a suitable model. Pool players shoot shots *as* z/they followed these laws. But if we ask players whether they understand the physical principles be-hind the game of pool, most will undoubtedly answer that they do not. Nonethe-less, Friedman argues, the physical laws provide very accurate predictions and therefore should be accepted as appropriate theoretical models of how pool is played by experts.

A test of the profit-maximization model, then, would be provided by predicting the behavior of real-world firms by assuming that these firms behave *as* z/they were maximizing profits. If these predictions are reasonably in accord with reality, we may accept the profit-maximization hypothesis. The fact that firms respond to ques-tionnaires by disclaiming any precise attempt at profit maximization is no more damaging to the validity of the basic hypothesis than are pool players' disclaimers

'See M. Friedman, *Essays in Positive Economics* (Chicago: University of Chicago Press, 1953), chap. 1. For an alternative view stressing the importance of using "realistic" assumptions, see H. A. Simon, "Rational Decision Making in Business Organizations,"

American Economic Review 69, no. 4 (September 1979): 493-513. of knowledge of the laws of physics. Rather, the ultimate test of either theory is its ability to predict *real-world events.*

IMPORTANCE OF EMPIRICAL ANALYSIS

The primary concern of this book is the construction of theoretical models. But the ultimate goal of such models is to learn something about the real world. Although the inclusion of a lengthy set of applied examples would needlessly expand an al-ready bulky book,[2] the Extensions included at the end of many chapters are in-tended to provide a transition between the theory presented here and the ways in which that theory is actually applied.

General Features of Economic Models

The number of economic models in current use is, of course, very large. Specific assumptions used and the degree of detail provided vary greatly depending on the problem being addressed. The types of models employed to explain the overall level of economic activity in the United States, for example, must be considerably more aggregated and complex than those that seek to interpret the pricing of Arizona strawberries. Despite this variety, however, practically all economic models incorporate three common elements: (1) the *ceteris paribus* (other things the same) assumption; (2) the supposition that economic decision-makers seek to optimize something; and (3) a careful distinction between "positive" and "normative" ques-tions. Because we will encounter these elements throughout this book, it may be helpful at the outset to describe briefly the philosophy behind each of them.

The *Ceteris Paribus* Assumption

As is the case in most sciences, models used in economics attempt to portray rela-tively simple relationships. A model of the market for wheat, for example, might seek to explain wheat prices with a small number of quantifiable variables, such as wages of farmworkers, rainfall, and consumer incomes. This parsimony in model specification permits the study of wheat pricing in a simplified setting in which it is possible to understand how the specific forces operate. Although any researcher will recognize that many "outside" forces (presence of wheat diseases, changes in the prices of fertilizers or of tractors, or shifts in consumer attitudes about eating bread) affect the price of wheat, these other forces are held constant in the con-struction of the model. It is important to recognize that economists are *not* assum-ing that other factors do not affect wheat prices, but rather, such other variables are assumed to be unchanged during the period of study. In this way the effect of only a few forces can be studied in a simplified setting. Such *ceteris paribus* (other things equal) assumptions are used in all economic modeling.

Use of the *ceteris paribus* assumption does pose some difficulties for the empir-ical verification of economic models from real-world data. In other sciences such problems may not be so severe because of the ability to conduct controlled experi-ments. For example, a physicist who wishes to test a model of the force of gravity would probably not do so by dropping objects from the Empire State Building. Ex-periments conducted in that way would be subject to too many extraneous forces (wind currents, particles in the air, variations in temperature, and so forth) to per-mit a precise test of the theory. Rather, the physicist would conduct experiments in a laboratory, using a partial vacuum in which most other forces could be controlled or eliminated. In this way the theory could be verified in a simple setting, without needing to consider all the other forces that affect falling bodies in the real world. With a few notable exceptions, economists have not been able to conduct con-trolled experiments to test their models. Instead, economists have been forced to rely on various statistical methods to control for other forces when testing their theories. Although these statistical methods are in principle as valid as the con-trolled experiment methods used by other scientists, in practice they raise a num-ber of thorny issues. For that reason, the limitations and precise meaning of the *ceteris paribus* assumption in economics are subject to somewhat greater controversy than in the laboratory sciences.

Optimization Assumptions

Many economic models start from the assumption that the economic actors being studied are rationally pursuing some goal. We briefly discussed such an assumption previously when investigating the notion of firms maximizing profits. Other exam-ples we will encounter in this book include consumers maximizing their own well-being (utility), firms minimizing costs, and government regulators attempting to maximize public welfare.

Although, as we will show, all of these assumptions are somewhat controversial, all have won widespread acceptance as good starting places for developing economic models. There seem to be two reasons for this acceptance. First, the optimization assumptions are very useful for generating precise, solvable models. A primary reason for this is that such models can draw on a variety of math-ematical techniques suitable for optimization problems. Many of these techniques, together with the logic behind them, are reviewed in Chapter 2. A second reason for the popularity of optimization models concerns their apparent empirical valid-ity. As some of our Extensions show, such models seem to be fairly good at ex-plaining reality. In all, then, optimization models have come to occupy a prominent position in modern economic theory.

Positive-Normative Distinction

A final feature of most economic models is the attempt to differentiate carefully be-tween "positive" and "normative" questions. So far we have been concerned prima-rily with *positive* economic theories. Such "scientific" theories take the real world as an object to be studied, attempting to explain those economic phenomena that are observed. Positive economics seeks to determine how resources are *in fact* allocated in an economy. A somewhat different use of economic theory is *normative,* taking a definite stance about what *should be* done. Under the heading of normative analy-sis, economists have a great deal to say about how resources *should be* allocated. For example, an economist engaged in positive analysis might investigate why and how the American health care industry uses the quantities of capital, labor, and land that are currently devoted to providing medical services. The economist might also choose to measure the costs and benefits of devoting even more resources to health care. But when economists advocate that more resources *should* be allocated to health, they have implicitly moved into normative analysis.

Some economists believe that the only proper economic analysis is positive analysis. Drawing an analogy with the physical sciences, they argue that "scien-tific" economics should concern itself only with the description (and possibly pre-diction) of real-world events. To take moral positions and to plead for special interests are considered to be outside the competence of an economist acting as an economist. Other economists, however, believe strict application of the posi-tive-normative distinction to economic matters is inappropriate. They believe that the study of economics necessarily involves the researchers' own views about ethics, morality, and fairness. According to these economists, searching for scien-tific "objectivity" in such circumstances is hopeless. Despite this ambiguity, this book adopts a mainly positivist tone, leaving normative concerns to you to decide for yourself.

DEVELOPMENT OF THE ECONOMIC THEORY OF VALUE

Although economic activity has been a central feature of all societies, it is surpris-ing that these activities were not studied in any detail until fairly recently. For the most part, economic phenomena were treated as a basic aspect of human behavior that was not sufficiently interesting to deserve specific attention. It is, of course, true that individuals have always studied economic activities with a view toward making some kind of personal gain. Roman traders were certainly not above making prof-its on their transactions. But investigations into the basic nature of these activities did not begin in any depth until the eighteenth century.[3] Since this book is about economic theory as it stands today, not about the history of economic thought, our discussion of the evolution of economic theory will be brief. Only one area of eco-nomic study will be examined in its historical setting: the *theory of value.*

Early Economic Thought

The theory of value, not surprisingly, concerns the determinants of the "value" of a commodity. The study of this subject is at the center of modern microeconomic the-ory and is closely intertwined with the subject of the allocation of scarce resources for alternative ends. The logical place to start is with a definition of the word *value.* Unfortunately, the meaning of this term has not been consistent throughout the de-velopment of the subject. Today we regard "value" as being synonymous with the "price" of a commodity.[4] Earlier philosopher-economists, however, made a distinc-tion between the market price of a commodity and its value. The term "value" was then thought of as being in some sense synonymous with "importance," "essentiality,"

Tor a detailed treatment of early economic thought, see the classic work by J. A. Schumpeter, *History of Economic Analysis*

(New York: Oxford University Press, 1954), pt. II, chaps. 1, 2, and 3. or (at times) "godliness." Since "price" and "value" were separate concepts, they could differ, and most early economic discussions centered on these divergences.

For example, St. Thomas Aquinas believed value to be divinely determined. Since prices were set by humans, it was possible for the price of a commodity to differ from its value. A person accused of charging a price in excess of a good's value was guilty of charging an "unjust" price.

For example, St. Thomas believed the "just" rate of interest to be zero. Any lender who demanded a payment for the use of money was charging an unjust price and could be—and often was—prosecuted by church officials.

The Founding of Modern Economics

During the latter part of the eighteenth century, philosophers began to take a more "scientific" approach to economic questions. The publication of *The Wealth of Nations* by Adam Smith (1723-1790) in the eventful year 1776 is generally consid-ered the beginning of modern economics. In his vast, all-encompassing work, Smith laid the foundation for thinking about market forces in an ordered and systematic way. Still, Smith and his immediate successors, such as David Ricardo (1772-1823), continued to distinguish between value and price. To Smith, for example, the value of a commodity meant its "value in use," whereas the price represented its "value in exchange."

The distinction between these two concepts was illustrated by the fa-mous water-diamond paradox. Water, which obviously has great value in use, has little value in exchange (it has a low price); diamonds are of little practical use but have a great value in exchange. The paradox with which early economists struggled derives from the observation that some very "useful" items have low prices whereas certain "nonessential" items have high prices.

Labor Theory of Exchange Value

Neither Smith nor Ricardo ever satisfactorily resolved the water-diamond paradox. The concept of value in use was left for philosophers to debate, while economists turned their attention to explaining the determinants of value in exchange (that is, to explaining relative prices). One obvious possible explanation is that exchange values of goods are determined by what it costs to produce them. Costs of produc-tion are primariiy influenced by labor costs—at least this was so in the time of Smith and Ricardo—and therefore it was a short step to embrace a labor theory of value. For example, to paraphrase an example from Smith, if catching a deer takes twice the number of labor-hours as catching a beaver, then one deer should exchange for two beavers. In other words, the price of a deer should be twice that of a beaver. Similarly, diamonds are relatively costly because their production requires substan-tial labor input.

To students with even a passing knowledge of what we now call the *law of supply and demand,* Smith's and Ricardo's explanation must seem a bit strange. Didn't they recognize the effects of demand on price? The answer to this question is both "yes" and "no."

They did observe periods of rapidly rising and rapidly falling prices and attributed such changes to demand shifts. However, they regarded these changes as abnormalities that produced only a temporary divergence of market price from labor value. Because they had not really solved the paradox of value in use, they were unwilling to assign demand any more than a transient role in determining exchange value. Rather, long-run exchange values were determined solely by labor costs of production.

THE MARGINALIST REVOLUTION

Between 1850 and 1880, economists became increasingly aware that to construct an adequate alternative to the labor theory of value, they had to come to grips with the paradox of value in use. During the 1870s several economists proposed that it is not the total usefulness of a commodity that helps to determine its exchange value, but rather the usefulness of the *last unit consumed.* For example, water is certainly very useful—it is necessary for all life. But, because water is relatively plentiful, consum-ing one more pint *(ceteris paribus)* has a relatively low value to people.

These "mar-ginalists" redefined the concept of value in use from an idea of overall usefulness to one of marginal, or incremental, usefulness—the usefulness of an *additional unit of a commodity*. The concept of the demand for an incremental unit of output was now contrasted to Smith's and Ricardo's analysis of production costs to derive a comprehensive picture of price determination.[5]

Marshallian Supply-Demand Synthesis

The clearest statement of these marginal principles was presented by the English economist Alfred Marshall (1842-1924) in his *Principles of Economics,* published in 1890. Marshall showed that demand and supply *simultaneously* operate to deter-mine price. As Marshall noted, just as you cannot tell which blade of a scissors does the cutting, so too you cannot say that either demand or supply alone de-termines price. That analysis is illustrated by the famous Marshallian cross shown in Figure 1.1. In the diagram the quantity of a good purchased per period is shown on the horizontal axis, and its price appears on the vertical axis. The curve *DD* represents the quantity of the good demanded per period at each possible price. The curve is negatively sloped to reflect the marginalist principle that as quantity increases, people are willing to pay less and less for the last unit pur-chased. It is the value of this last unit that sets the price for all units purchased. The curve *SS* shows how (marginal) production costs rise as more output is pro-duced. This reflects the increasing cost of producing one more unit as total out-put expands. In other words, the upward slope of the *SS* curve reflects increasing marginal costs, just as the downward slope of the *DD* curve reflects decreasing marginal value. The two curves intersect at P^*, Q^*. This is an *equilibrium* point— both buyers and sellers are content with the quantity being traded and the price at which it is traded. If one of the curves should shift, the equilibrium point would shift to a new location. Thus price and quantity are simultaneously determined by the joint operation of supply and demand.

14

Meaning of International Finance

International Finance is a subject of financing of the International Economic and commercial relations as between countries. It encompasses the International trade in merchandise and services, autonomous flows of funds, capital flows for direct investments and portfolio management, borrowings and repayments of funds for working capital and project finance on capital account, flows of multilateral assistance, bilateral assistance, government to government credit on behalf of international transactions, trade credits, IMF credits and a host of capital account transactions of the balance of payment.

It is related to the International financial relations, political systems of system, International capital and money markets, Government to Government the countries, legal and accounting systems of trading countries. Thus it is the financing of receipts and payments as between countries through various currencies which emerge out of external economic and commercial transactions in the International currency market and Foreign exchange market.

"The finance manager of the new century cannot afford to remain ignorant about international financial markets & instruments and their relevance for the treasury function. The financial markets around the world are fast integrating and evolving a whole new range of products & instruments. As national economies are becoming closely knit through cross-border trade & investment, the global financial system must innovate to cater to the ever changing needs of the real economy. The job of finance manager will become increasingly more challenging, demanding & exciting." Apte-IIM, B

In a nut shell International finance is the branch of economics that studies the dynamics of exchange rates, foreign investment, and how these affect international trade. It also studies international projects, international investments and capital flows, and trade deficits. It includes the study of futures, options and currency swaps. Together with international trade theory, international finance is also a branch of international economics.

Some of the theories which are important in international finance include the Mundell-Fleming model, the optimum currency area (OCA) theory, as well as the purchasing power parity (PPP) theory. Moreover, whereas international trade theory makes use of mostly microeconomic methods and theories, international finance theory makes use of predominantly intermediate and advanced macroeconomic methods and concepts.

INTERNATIONAL FINANCE- SCOPE AND METHODOLOGY

The economics of international finance do not differ in principle from the economics of international trade but there are significant differences of emphasis. The practice of international finance tends to involve greater uncertainties and risks because the assets that are traded are claims to flows of returns that often extend many years into the future. Markets in financial assets tend to be more volatile than markets in goods and services because decisions are more often revised and more rapidly put into effect. There is the same presumption that a transaction that is freely undertaken will benefit both parties, but there is a much greater danger that it will be harmful to others. *For example, mismanagement of mortgage lending in the United States led in 2008 to banking failures and credit shortages in other developed countries, and sudden reversals of international flows of capital have often led to damaging financial crises in developing countries.* And, because of the incidence of rapid change, the methodology of *comparative statics* has fewer applications than in the theory of international trade, and *empirical analysis* is more widely employed. Also, the consensus among economists concerning its principle issues is narrower and more open to controversy than is the consensus about international trade.

International Financial Stability

From the time of the Great Depression onwards, regulators and their economic advisors have been aware that economic and financial crises can spread rapidly from country to country, and that financial crises can have serious economic consequences.

For many decades, that awareness led governments to impose strict controls over the activities and conduct of banks and other credit agencies, but in the 1980s many governments pursued a policy of deregulation in the belief that the resulting efficiency gains would outweigh any *systemic risks*. The extensive financial innovations that and one of their effects has been, greatly to increase the international inter-connectedness of the financial markets and to create an international financial system with the characteristics known in control theory as "complex-interactive". The stability of such a system is difficult to analyze because there are many possible failure sequences.

The internationally-systemic crises that followed included the Equity Crash of October 1987, the Japanese Asset Price Collapse of the 1990s[1]the Asian Financial Crisis of 1997 the Russian Government Default of 1998(which brought down the Long-Term Capital Management hedge fund) and the 2007-2008 Sub-prime Mortgages Crisis. The symptoms have generally included collapses in asset prices, increases in risk premiums, and general reductions in liquidity. Measures designed to reduce the vulnerability of the international financial system have been put forward by several international institutions. The Bank for International Settlements made two successive recommendations (Basel I and Basel II) concerning the regulation of banks, and a coordinating group of regulating authorities, and the Financial Stability Forum, that was set up in 1999 to identify and address the weaknesses in the system, has put forward some proposals in an interim report..

Why study International Finance?

- Enormous growth in the volume of International Trade.
- Share of exports in GDP has increased significantly.
- All quantitative restrictions on trade were abolished.(lowering of tariff barriers, greater access to foreign capital)
- FDI grown enormously.
- Massive LPG provides endless speculative opportunities for creative financial management.
- Differences in Currencies & the changes in rates of exchange.

- Immobility of factors of production between two different countries
- Differences in national & international policies and politics.
- Differences in price level and Market & financial structures.
- Differences in positions of Balance Of Payment
- Deregulation on two fronts:
  * By eliminating the segmentation of the markets for financial services with specialized institutions
  * By permitting Foreign Financial Institutions to enter the national markets and compete on equal footing with the domestic institutions in offering financial services to borrowers and investors.

ISSUES INVOLVED IN INTERNATIONAL FINANCE

Macro Issues:

- Trying to have Favorable BOP
- Building up Foreign Exchange Reserves
- Strive for efficient foreign exchange market
- Rising marginal propensity to import
- Debt swapping
- Sterilization operations(deficit financing/buying foreign currencies from the open market) for exchange rate stability
- Localization vs. privatization
- Tariff and non- tariff barriers to trade and payments
- Issues on behalf of factor endowments, socio-economic factors, legal & regulatory framework governments, consumer preferences, quality concerns, waste management and Green issues, TQM, conservation of scarce resources, and issues on Forex reserves.

Micro Issues

- Exporting for maximum profit (David Hume's theory)
- Steady positive returns on FDI
- Risk management issues [(i) to get the insurable risks insured; (ii) to avert risks; (iii) to bear the risks]
- No idle balances
- Banks not to speculate
- Speculation, Hedging & Arbitrage issues

RECENT CHANGES IN GLOBAL FINANCIAL MARKETS

The decades of 80's and 90's were characterised by unprecedented pace of environmental changes for most Indian firms. Political uncertainties at home and abroad, economic liberalisation at home, greater exposure to international markets, marked increase in volatility of critical economic and financial variables such as exchange rates & interest rates, increased competition, threats of hostile takeovers are among the factors that have forced many firms to thoroughly rethink their strategic posture. The start of 21st century was marked by even greater acceleration of environmental changes and significant increase in uncertainties facing the firm. WTO deadlines pertaining to removal of Trade Barriers resulted in facing greater competition by companies in India and abroad. During 2004 & early 2005, the rupee has shown an upward trend against the US Dollar putting a squeeze on margin of exporting industries.

But the picture changes by 2008 with the Global Financial Crisis. By 2008, annual inflation, measured by the wholesale Price Index, accelerated to 12.01 in the week ended July 26 (the highest since April 1995). "The side-effects of the year long global financial market upheaval have hit harvest in the countries that had binged on easy credit - first in US, then in Britain and Spain." - The Hindu Business Line, August 8, 2008. "In Asia, Europe and Latin America, while the pace differs, growth is slowly virtually everywhere" - said Morgan Stanley

The spillovers from US slow down, higher inflation, reduced energy subsidies, tighter monetary policies and tighter financial conditions is seen everywhere. One year after market seized upon concerns over failing sub-prime mortgages, foreign banks have incurred some $400 billion in losses & write-downs. "The main problem especially in US and UK is due to faulty financial system. The financial system has become unstable due to over relaxed over sight of financial institution" - George Magnus - Senior Economic Advisor, UBS Investment Bank, London. The US economy is at critical juncture. It is suffering from weekend consumer spending as fallout of financial and credit market crises. The US share of world wide gross product - US GDP - as a percentage of World Gross Product declined just from 32% to 27%. - The Analyst, August 2008 (Report on 'Global Economic Crisis'). During the same period, the BRIC nations (Brazil, Russia, India & China) combined share of world wide gross product increased from 8.33% to 11.6%. In terms of growth in real GDP from 2001 to 2006, the US economy's 16% growth was well below than the leading performers. China at over 60%, India at 45%, Russia 37% and Ireland 28% (United Statistics Division, August 2008). In real GDP growth per capita from 2001 to 2006, China grew over 50%, Russia by over 40%, India by over 33%, while US grew up less than 10%. From 2001 to 2006, exports from China grew over 250%, from India 230%, from UK 170%, from Brazil 160%, while it grew less than 30% in the US. US FDI investment overseas percentage of GDP is also well below the worldwide average i.e., 1.6% compared.

Inflation, food shortage, LPG & Diesel crisis, record trade & fiscal deficits, huge subsidy bills, crumbling stock markets etc. are the real challenges the economy face with. Combining together with a host of other problems such as global warming & population explosion, global food crisis is plunging humanity into the gravest of crisis in the 21st century raising food prices & spreading hunger and poverty from rural areas into cities. More than 73 million people in 78 countries that depend on food handouts from the United Nations World Food Programme (WFP) are facing reduced rations this year – CSR June 2008 (Report on Global Food Crisis). Higher food cost means higher inflation, which will reduce consumption, savings & investment.

More about Indian Economy (CSR June 2008 – Special Report)

According to the latest data related by the Ministry of Commerce on May 2008, the cumulative of Indian exports registered a growth of 23.02 percent in dollar terms at $155.51 billion (i.e., 9.93 percent in rupee terms at 6,25,471.22 Crores) in 2007-2008 as against $126.41 billion (Rs.5,71,779 crores) in 2006-2007.

On the other hand, imports for the said period were valued at $235.91 billion (Rs.9,49,133.82 Crores) as against $185.74 billion (Rs.8,40,506 Crores) registering a growth of 27.01 percent in dollar terms and 12.92 percent in rupee terms.

For March 2008, exports were valued at $16.28 billion (i.e., Rs.65,710.71 Crore), registering an impression growth of 26.59 percent compared to $12.86 billion in March. Imports were valued at $23.17 billion, an increase at 35.24 percent over the level of imports in March 2007. The trade deficit sourced to an estimated

$80.39 billion in 2007-2008 against $59.32 billion in 2006-2007, mainly due to oil imports that went up by 38.25 percent.

According to the Bank for International Settlements, average daily turnover in global foreign exchange markets is estimated at $3.98 trillion. Trading in the world's main financial markets accounted for $3.21 trillion of this. This approximately $3.21 trillion in main foreign exchange market turnover was broken down as follows:

- $1.005 trillion in spot transactions
- $362 billion in outright forwards
- $1.714 trillion in foreign exchange swaps
- $129 billion estimated gaps in reporting

India's Export - Import Position by October 2008 (As per Report in Business Line- October 2008)

Although India's export juggernaut slowed down distinctly in October 2008 by 12 percent in dollar terms amid the slowdown of the global economy, overall export growth during the first seven months of the current fiscal - April to October - continues to cruise on a high growth of 23.7 percent in dollar terms and 32 percent in rupee terms.

Provisional foreign trade figures, compiled by the Directorate of Commercial Intelligence & Statistics (DGCI&S) and released by the department of Commerce, show that exports during October 2008 at $12.82 billion were 12.1 per cent lower than the level of $14.58 billion in October 2007. However the cumulative value of exports during the first seven months of the current fiscal continues to show salubrious trends with exports amounting to $107.79 billion, against $87.14 billion in April - October 2007.

The slowdown is a sequel to the world economic slowdown and labour - intensive export industries such as textiles, gem and jewelry and leather had all taken the hit in growth.

A particularly noteworthy feature on the export front is the persistent depreciation of the Indian rupee vis-à-vis the US dollar, in which a dominant share of Indian export receipts are dominated has also helped in a higher export growth of 8.2 per cent in rupee terms at Rs.62,387 crores in October 2008, against Rs.57,641 crores in October 2007. India's exports fetched Rs.4,67,505 crores during the period under review, against Rs.3,54,064 crores in the corresponding period of 2007, reflecting the beneficial fallout of the depreciating currency on export earnings.

Imports during October 2007 at $23.36 billion were 10.6 per cent higher over the level of imports valued at $21.12 billion in October, while cumulatively imports during April-October 2008 at $180.78 billion were 36.2 percent higher than $132.78 billion in the corresponding period of 2007.

In rupee terms, India's imports at Rs.1,13,659 crores during April 2008 were 36.2 percent higher than similar imports valued at Rs.83,472 crores in October 2007, while cumulatively imports during the first seven months of the current fiscal at Rs.7,86,059 crores were 45.6 per cent higher than the value of such imports at Rs.5,39,879 crores in April-October 2007.

The high growth in import both in the latest month and also cumulatively is the result of a depreciating currency which is computed to have depreciated by 20 per cent since the beginning of this year, making imports expensive.

Forex Reserves declined by $663 million (RBI Report May 2008)

According to the RBI's weekly statistical supplement released on May 2, 2008, India's forex reserves declined by $663 million to $312.871 billion during the week ended April 25, 2008 from a record $313.534 billion a week earlier.

RBI announces Annual Monetary Policy Statement for 2008-2009 (on April 29, 2008) which laid down emphasis on giving high priority to price stability and maintaining an orderly condition in financial markets while sustaining the growth momentum.

The RBI stated that two most important aspects to be kept in mind while pursuing financial inclusion were credit quality and credit delivery. The CRR was hiked to 8.25% with effect from May 24, 2008 while other key rates Bank rate (at present 6.0%) Reverse Repo Rate (at present 6.0%) and Repo Rate (at present 7.75%) left unchanged. Whereas present SLR is 25% and prime lending rate is 12.25 to 12.5% and Savings Bank rate is 3.5%.

Petroleum Ministry reports released on April 16, 2008 revealed that India's Crude oil import bill has jumped over 38% to $61.16 billion in the first 11 months of 2007-2008 fiscal in the wake of surge in global oil prices. India imported 111.089 million tones of crude oil in April - February 2007-2008 for Rs. 2,43,205.5 crores ($61.165 billion) as against 101.213 million tones crude oil imported a year ago for Rs.200,321 crore (i.e., $44.124 Billion). Besides crude oil India also imported 20.19 million tones of products, mainly Naphtha, LPG, Kerosene and diesel for Rs.54,180 crore (i.e., $13.4 billion).

The country's fuel consumption grew 64% to 116.711 million tones in April. February 2007-2008 due to double digit growth in diesel demand at 43.27 million tones.

The financial systems have gone much faster than the real output since 2000. When geographical integration of financial markets was the outstanding feature during eighties, Functional Unification across the various types of financial institutions within individual market became the feature during nineties Deregulation became the hallmark feature during 2000 permitting foreign financial institutions to enter into national markets and compete on equal footing with domestic institution. Securitisation and Disintermediation helped the borrowers to approach investors directly by issuing their own primary securities thus depriving the bank of their role and profits as intermediaries.

The explosive pace of deregulation & innovation the financial engineering has given rise to serious concerns about the viability & stability of the system.

Emerging Challenges

The responsibilities of today's financial managers can understood by examining the principal challenges they are required to cope with. The following key categories of emerging challenges can be identified with: To keep up to date with significant environmental changes and analyse their implications for the firm.

The variable to be monitored includes:

* Exchange rates
* Interest rates
* Credit condition at home and abroad
* Changes in international policies & trend
* Change in tax
* Foreign trade policies
* Stock market trends

* Fiscal & monetary developments
* Emergence of new financial products etc.

To understand and analyse the complex interrelationship between relevant environmental variable & corporate responses - own and competitive.

Especially,

* What would be the impact of stock market crash on credit conditions in the International Financial Market?
* What opportunities will emerge if infrastructure sectors are opened up to private investment?
* What are the potential threats from liberalisation of foreign investment?
* How will a takeover of major competitor by an outsider affect competition within the industry?
* How will a default by a major debt country affect competition within the industry?

To Adapt finance function to significant changes in the firm's own strategic posture. i.e.,

* Major changes in the product mix
* Opening a new sector/industry
* Significant changes through a take over
* Significant changes in operating result
* Major financial restructuring
* Changes in dividend policies
* Asset sales to overcome temporary cash shortage etc.

To take in stride past failures and mistakes to minimize their adverse impact

Eg:-

* A wrong take over decision
* A floating rate financing obtained when interest rate is low and since have been rapidly raising
* A fix price supply contract when there comes a substitute at lower price
* A wrong dividend declaration
* A large foreign loan in a currency that has since started appreciating made faster than expected.

To design and implement effective solution to take advantage of the opportunities offered by the markets and advances in financial theory

Eg:-

* Entering into exotic derivative transactions
* Swaps and futures for effective risk management
* Innovative funding technique

"The finance manager of the new century cannot afford to remain ignored about international financial markets & instruments and their relevance for the treasury function, wealth management and risk management. The financial markets around the world are fast integrating & evolving a whole new range of financial products and markets. As national economies are becoming closely knit through cross border trade and investment, the global financial system must innovative to carter to the ever changing needs to the real economy. The job of the finance manager set to become increasingly more challenging, demanding & exciting" - Prakash G Apte, IIM Bangalore (A report on International Financial Management in a Global Context)

FUNDAMENTALS OF FOREIGN EXCHANGE

Forex Market/Foreign Exchange Market

Forex Market is a market in which currencies are bought and sold against each other or it is the market for converting the currency of one country into that of another country. It is the largest market in the world. Bank for International Settlement (BIS) survey specifies that over USD $1500 billion were traded world wide every day, on an average basis. Bulk of the transactions are in currencies - US Dollar, Euro, Yen, Pound Sterling, Swiss franc, Canadian dollar & Australian dollar. Forex market is an OTC market. This means there is no single physical/electronic market place/an organised exchange (like stock exchange) with a cultural trade clearing mechanism where traders meet and exchange currencies.

The market itself is a world wide network of inter-bank traders, consisting primarily of banks, connected by telephone lines and computers. While a large part of inter bank trading takes place with electronic trading systems such as Reuters Dealing 2000 and Electronic Booking System, Banks and large commercial (i.e., corporate consumers) still use the telephone to negotiate prices and consummate the deal.

After the transaction, the resulting market bid/ask price is then fed into the computer terminates provided by official market reporting service companies. (i.e., network such as Reuters®, Bridge Information Systems® and Telerate). The prices displayed on official Quote Screens reflect one of, may be, dozens of simultaneous deals that took place at any given movement. New technologies such as Interpreter 6000 Voice Recognition System (VRS) allow forex traders to enter orders using spoken commands, along with online trading systems.

The financial market functions virtually 24 hours enabling a trader to offset a position created in one market using another market. The five major centers of interbank currency trading, while handle more than two thirds of all forex transactions are London, New York, Zurich, Tokyo Frankfurt. Trading in currencies takes place during 24 hours a day except weekends. For example, if trading in currencies starts at 9.a.m in Tokyo, it begins an hour later in Hong Kong and Singapore. When the Asian trading centers closes, transactions begin in European trading centre's; and as the European trading centre's win up their operations, the trading centre's in the U.S. begins operating. As Los Angles ends its day at 5 p.m., Tokyo center open. Thus there is at least one center open for business somewhere in the world at any time of the day or night. As the Forex market is a global market operating 24 hous of the day, it is the largest market in terms of volume of transactions. The large volume of transactions, continuous trading and global dispersal ensures a high level of liquidity in the market.

STRUCTURE OF FOREX MARKET

Retail Market

It is a market in which travelers & tourists exchange one currency for another in the form of currency notes/travelers cheques.

Wholesale Market/Interbank Market

These are markets where commercial banks, investment institutions, non-financial corporations and central banks deal in foreign currency.

PARTICIPANTS

Primary Price Makers

Primary price makers/professional dealers make a two way market to each other and to their clients. i.e., on request, they will quote a two way price–a price to buy currency X against Y and a price to sell X against Y–and be prepared to take either the buy/ the sell side. This role will be done by large commercial banks/ large investment dealers/large corporations who have the right to do it.

Thus a primary dealer will sell US dollar against rupees to one corporate customer, carry the position for a while and offset it by buying US dollars against rupees from another customer/ professional dealer. In the mean while, if the price has moved against the dollar, he bears the loss.

Secondary Price Makers

In the retail market, there are entities who quote foreign exchange rate, for example, restaurant, hotels and shops catering to tourists who buy foreign currency in payment of bills. Some entities specialize in retail business for travelers and buy & sell foreign currencies & travelers' cheques with a wider bid-ask spreads. They are secondary price makers.

Foreign Currency Brokers

Foreign currency brokers acts as a middleman between two markets by providing information to the market both banks and firms.

Price Takers

Price takers are those, who take the prices Quoted by primary price makers and buy or sell currencies for their own purposes.

For example, corporations use the foreign exchange market for variety of purposes:-

(a) payment for imports

(b) Payment of interest on foreign currency loan.

(c) Placement of surplus funds and so on..

Many do not take active position in the market to profit from exchange rate fluctuations.

Central Bank

Central bank intervenes in the market from time to time to attempt to move exchange rates in a particular directions or moderate excessive fluctuations in the exclusive rate.

Of total volume of transactions, about two-thirds is accounted for by inter-bank transactions and the rest by transactions between bank and their non-bank customers. Foreign exchange flows crisis out of cross borders exchange of goods and services account for very small proportion of the turnover in forex market.

Need/Uses of FEM

International businesses have four main uses of FEM:

* First, the payments a company receives for its exports, the income it receives from foreign investments, or the income it receives from licensing agreements with foreign firms, in foreign currencies must be converted.
* Second, when they must pay a foreign company for its products or services in its country's currency.
* Third, when they have spare cash that they wish to invest for short terms in money market.
* Finally, for *currency speculation* which involves short term movement of funds from one currency to another in the hopes of profiting from shifts in exchange rate.

FUNCTIONS OF FEM

Main Functions

1. Currency Conversion
2. Insurance against Foreign Exchange risk

Other Functions

1. Provision of credit
2. Provision of Hedging
3. Transfer of purchasing power

Currency conversion

Each country has its own currency in which prices of goods and services are quoted so that within the borders of a particular country one must use the national currency. For example, an US tourist who walks into a store of Edinburgh, Scotland cannot use

US dollar to buy a bottle of Scotch whisky as dollars are not recognised as legal tender in Scotland. So the tourist must use British pounds for which he/she must go to a bank and exchange the dollar for pounds to buy whisky. Thus he has to participate in the FEM. The exchange rate is the rate at which the market converts one currency into another, which allows comparing the relative price of goods and service in different countries.

Provision of Credit

FEM also deals with credits & credit obligation in an international deal and hence it requires not only line of credit/ loan like any business transaction which are ultimately piped through FEM

Provision of Hedging

A foreign Exchange Market also deals with mechanisms to guard the importers & exporters against losses arising out of fluctuations in exchange rates

Transfer of Purchasing Power

When agreed sum of domestic currency is exchanged for equivalent sum of foreign currency, based on exchange rate, it ultimately affects the transfer of purchasing power of one currency to other (as all the countries have paper currency system, which is based on the statutory promise of respective government endowed in such currency paper).

TO PROVIDE INSURANCE AGAINST FOREIGN EXCHANGE RISK

Foreign Exchange Rate

An exchange rate is simply the rate at which one currency is converted into another

Types of Exchange Rates

Separate rates may be applicable in the Spot market and the Forward market known as Spot exchange rate and Forward exchange rate.

Spot Exchange rates

When two parties agree to exchange currency & execute the deal immediately the transaction is referred to as spot exchange. Exchange rates governing such 'on the spot' trades are referred to as spot exchange rates. In other words, spot exchange rate is the rate at which a foreign exchange dealer converts one currency into another currency on a particular day. When US tourist in Edinburgh goes to a bank in Scotland to convert his dollars into pounds, the exchange rate is the spot rate for that day. These rates are reported daily in financial pages of newspapers. An exchange rate can be quoted in two ways: as a price of the foreign currency in terms of dollars/as the price of dollars in terms of foreign currency. Dollar per foreign currency will be in direct terms and foreign currency per dollar is in indirect terms and spot rate changes continuously, often, on a day to day basis. The value of currency is determined by the interaction between the demand & supply of that currency related to the demand & supply of other currencies.

If lots of people want US dollar & dollars are in short supply, and a few people want British pounds & pounds are in plentiful supply, the spot exchange rate for converting dollars into pounds will change. The dollars is likely to appreciate against the pound/ conversely, the pound will depreciate against the dollar. Imagine the spot exchange rate is £1 = $1.50, when the market opens. As the day progresses, dealers demand more dollars and fewer pounds and by the end of the day the spot exchange rate might be £1 = $1.48. Thus the dollar appreciated and the pound has depreciated

Forward Exchange Rate

The fact that spot exchange rates continuously change as determined by the related demand & supply for different currencies can be problematic for international business. Suppose a US company that import laptop computers from Japan knows that in 30 days it must pay Yen to Japanese supplier when a shipment arrives.

The company will pay Japanese supplier ¥2,00,000 for each laptop computer and the current dollar/Yen spot exchange rate is $1 = ¥120. At this rate, each computer costs the US importer $1667 (i.e., 2,00,000/120). The importer knows she can sell the computer at the day they arrive for $2000 each which yields a gross profit of $333 on each computer. However, the US importer doesn't have funds to pay the Japanese exporter as the computers have not sold. If over the next 30 days the dollar unexpectedly depreciates against Yen, say $1 = ¥ 95, the importer will have to pay Japanese company $2105 per computer (i.e., 2,00,000/95) which is more than she can sell the laptop for.

Thus, a depreciation the value of dollar against Yen from $1 = ¥120, to $1 = ¥95 would transform a profitable deal into unprofitable for the US importer.

To avoid this risk the US importer might engage in a Forward Exchange contract. A Forward Exchange contract occurs when two parties agree to exchange currency and execute the deal at some specific date in future. Exchange rates governing such Future contracts are quoted for 30, 90 and 180 days into the future. Returning to our computer importer example, let us assume that a 30 days Forward Exchange rate for converting dollars into yen is $1 = ¥110. So, the US importer enters into a 30day forward exchange transaction with a foreign exchange dealer at this rate and thereby guarantee is that she will have to pay not more than $1818 (i.e., 2,00,000/110) for each laptop computer (guaranteeing him a profit of $182 per computer.

Forward exchange rates are offered in three ways:

* At par:- If forward rate and spot rate are same.
* At premium:- a currency is set to be at premium with respect to Spot, if it is able to buy more units of domestic currency at a later date.

For example; spot rate is U.S.$ 1= Rs.43.51 and 3 months forward is U.S. $ 1= Rs.43.96; the U.S. $ is at a *forward premium* (by Re. 0.45/45 paise).

* At discount:- it is set to be at discount, if it is able to buy less units of domestic currency at a later date.

For example; spot rate is £1 = Rs.69.45 and 3 months forward is £1 = Rs.68.75; the sterling is at a forward discount of Re.0.70 or by 70 paise.

The spot and the forward foreign exchange market is an OTC (Over-the-Counter) market, i.e., trading does not take place in a central market place where the buyers and sellers congregate. Rather, the Forex market is a worldwide linkage of the bank currency traders, non-bank dealers and FX brokers who assist in trades connected to one another via a network of telephones, telex machines, computer terminals and automated dealing systems of Reuters or Telerate or Bloomberg.

EXCHANGE RATE QUOTATIONS (BASE CURRENCY AND COUNTER CURRENCY)

The currencies of the world are usually represented by a three letter code which is internationally accepted by the ISO. E.g.: USD for US Dollar, INR for Indian Rupee etc. In the three letter ISO code, the first two letters refer to the country and the third letter to the currency. Currencies are traded against one another. For e.g., US Dollar may be exchanged for Euro, which is denoted by EUR/USD, where the price of Euro is expressed in US Dollars as 1EUR = 1.350 USD. The first currency in the pair is the base currency and the second currency is the counter currency. Usually the stronger currency in the pair is used as the base currency and the weaker currency as the counter currency. E.g., EUR/USD.

There are two methods for quoting the exchange rate between two currencies, the *Direct method and the Indirect method.*

Direct Quote

The direct method expresses the number of units of the home currency required to buy one unit of a foreign currency.

Example: 1 U.S. $ = Rs.43.5125

This means that Rs.43.5125 is needed to buy one U.S. Dollar. Thus it is the home currency price of a foreign currency. Exchange rate is expressed up to four decimal places; where the last decimal place is known as Point/Pip where the first three digits will be known as the Big Figure. If the dollar-rupee exchange rate moves from Rs.43.5125 to Rs.43.5128, the rate is said to have moved up by three points or pips.

Indirect Quote

The indirect method of quoting expresses the number of units of a foreign currency that can be bought with one unit home currency or with one hundred units of home currency. Example: Re.1 = U.S. $ 0.022982 or Rs.100 = U.S. $ 2.2982

This means that with rupees Rs.100 we can buy U.S. $ 2.2982. Thus indirect quote is the reciprocal of the direct quote or vice versa. In India all the banks are now required to quote foreign exchange rate in the direct method.

The rate quoted to the exporters will be the buying rate and the rate quoted by the dealer to the importers is the selling rate, for selling dollars to the importers who need them to make payments abroad for their import consignments.

In the spot market, dealers arrange the settlement for immediate delivery; usually settlement takes place on the second working date after the date of the transaction. In the forward market, the purchase or sale of a foreign currency is arranged today at an agreed exchange rate, but with delivery scheduled to take place at a later date in the future; usually from one, three, six or twelve months from the date of the transaction as explained in the laptop settlement case explained above.

When the home currency price of a foreign currency increases or moves up, there is appreciation in the value of foreign currency and the foreign currency is said to be appreciated against the home currency. For example, if the dollar-rupee exchange rate is 1 U.S. $= Rs. 42.35 and it moves up to Rs.43.75, it signifies appreciation in the value of the dollar. *This is known as foreign currency appreciation.* In such a case, when the dollar- rupee exchange rate is Rs.42.35/U.S.$, the value of the rupee in terms of U.S. Dollars would be U.S. $ 0.0236, being the reciprocal of Rs.42.35. When the exchange rate moves up to Rs. 43.75, the value of the rupee declines to U.S. $ 0.0229. *This is known as home currency depreciation.* Thus, when there is foreign currency appreciation there is a corresponding home currency depreciation and vice versa.

Bid and Offer Rates

Foreign exchange dealers usually quote two prices, one for buying and the other for selling the currency. The buying rate is termed as *Bid Rate,* while the selling rate is termed as the *Offer Rate* or *Ask Rate*. Usually the offer rate would be higher than the bid rate. The difference between the offer rate and the bid rate is termed as *bid-offer spread* and it is one of the sources of profit for the foreign exchange dealers.

In the direct method of quotation, the first rate quoted would be the buying rate or bid rate and the second rate quoted would be the selling rate or the offer rate. For e.g., if the dollar – rupee exchange rate is 1 U.S. $ = Rs.43.35 – 43.66 , it means that the dealer quoting the rate is prepared to buy one U.S. Dollar for Rs.43.35 ; but he is prepared to sell one U.S. Dollar for Rs.43.66. By buying US dollars at Rs.43.35 and selling them at Rs.43.66, the dealer makes a profit of Re.0.31 per dollar traded. The exchange rate of 1 US $ = Rs.43.505 is the middle quote which is halfway between the sell and buy price. The spread percentage is calculated using the following formula:

Ask - Bid X 100

Ask

i.e. 43.66 - 43.35 X 100 = 0.71%

43.66

CROSS RATES

The exchange rate between two currencies is based on the demand and supply of the respective currencies. Exchange rates are readily available for currencies which are frequently transacted. However, exchange rate may not be available for currencies which have only limited transactions. In such a situation, the home currency can be converted into common currency into a common currency and trade on the basis of three-way transaction. For e.g., the Indian Rupee-Canadian Dollar exchange rate is not available because of the limited transactions. In such a case, it can be worked out through a common currency US Dollar or the EURO. Let us take the base a US Dollar which the third currency. i.e., US $1 = Rs.40.00 - 40.30 and

US $1 = Can $ 0.76 - 0.78

Here in order to buy Canadian Dollars we have to buy US Dollars at Rs.40.30 (which is the offer rate of the dealer) and then sell these US Dollars at Canadian Dollar 0.76/US Dollar (which is the bid rate of the dealer) for buying the Canadian dollars. In effect, we can get Can $0.76 for Rs.40.30. Hence, Can. $1 = Rs.53.03 (i.e., Rs.40.30/Can. $0.76). This is the rate offered by the dealer for selling the Canadian dollars.

Thus, to obtain the offer rate of the desired currency from a dealer, we need to divide the offer rate of the common currency (expressed in the unit of the home currency) by the bid rate of the common currency (expressed in the units of the desired currency). (i.e., Rs.40.00/Can.$0.78, which is Rs.51.28)

Thus, the cross exchange rate between the Rupee and the Canadian Dollar is:

Can. $1 = Rs.51.28 - 53.03

Daily in the Wall Street Journal 45 cross exchange rates for all pair combinations of nine currencies calculated versus the US$ will be published.

TRIANGULAR ARBITRATION

Certain banks specialize in making a direct market between non-dollar currencies pricing at a narrower bid-ask spread than the cross rate spread which is known as Triangular Arbitration. It is the process of trading out of the US Dollars into a secondary currency , then trading it for a third currency , which is in turn traded for US Dollars. The purpose is to earn an arbitrage profit via trading from the second to the third currency when the direct exchange rate between the two is not in alignment with the cross exchange rate.

The interbank market is a network of correspondent banking relationship, with large commercial banks maintaining demand deposit accounts with one another, called as Correspondent Bank Accounts. The CBA networks allow for efficient functioning of the foreign exchange market. The Society for World Wide Interbank Financial Telecommunications (SWIFT) allows international commercial banks to communicate instructions to one another in the networking process through a message transfer system. SWIFT is a private non-profit organization with its head quarters in Brussels, with intercontinental switching centers in Netherlands and Virginia. Similarly CHIPS (the Clearing House Interbank Payment System) which is in cooperation with the US Federal Reserve Bank system provides a clearing house for the interbank settlement of US dollar payment between international banks. Another international organization which acts as clearing house for settling interbank Forex transaction is ECHO (Exchange Clearing House Ltd.); which is a multilateral netting system that on each settlement date, nets a client's payment and receipts in each currency, regardless of whether they are due to or from multiple counter parties.

The rates quoted by the banks to their non-bank customers will be called as *Merchant Rates*. Sometimes bank may quote a variety of exchange rates called as *TT Rates (Telegraphic Transfer Rates)* which are applicable for clean inward and outward remittances. For instance, suppose an individual purchases from Citi Bank in New York, a b $2000 drawn on Citi Bank, Mumbai.

The New York bank will credit the Mumbai bank's account with the amount immediately. When the individual sells the draft to the Citi Bank, Mumbai the bank will buy the dollars at TT Buying Rate. Similarly, TT Selling Rate is applicable when the bank sells a foreign currency draft.

FACTORS INFLUENCING EXCHANGE RATE (BASED ON EXCHANGE RATE THEORIES)

Since demand & supply conditions of goods, services, investment transactions etc., will differ, the supply & demand conditions of currencies will also differ from time to time. Thus, the exchange rate of two currencies is determined on the respective elasticities of demand & supply. If the supply is easily available (elastic), then the value of that currency will depreciate. On the other hand, if the supply of a currency is relatively less when compared to its demand, its value will appreciate. A country having unfavorable balance of trade will find its value of currency going down in international market. Thus, the demand for, and the supply of foreign exchange are derived from the underlying demand for domestic and foreign goods, services & investment opportunities. However, the rates of exchange do not fluctuate under the gold standard as it is fixed by references to the gold contents of the two currency units (mint par of exchange).

Unilateral transfers (compensations paid, donations etc.,), credit transactions & delayed payments will make it difficult to identify the total foreign exchange transactions with the BOP. Thus this imbalance will bring changes in the exchange rates. Further factors for the changes are :

* Disequilibrium in the Balance of Trade
* Changes in the Monetary policy - Inflationary policy through Deficit Financing/Contraction policy
* Capital movements for short periods and long periods.
* Speculative Activities.

EXCHANGE RATE DETERMINATION

Exchange rates are determined by the demand for and supply of one currency relative to the demand and supply of another which can be referred as demand and supply theory of exchange rate. This simple explanation doesn't specify what factors underlie for the demand and supply of the currency or under what conditions a currency is in demand/not in demand. Only if we understand how exchange rates are determined we may be able to forecast exchange rate movements.

The transaction in foreign exchange market, i.e., buying and selling foreign currency take at a rate, which is called 'Exchange Rate'. *Exchange Rate is the price paid in home currency for a unit of foreign currency.* The exchange rate can be quoted in two ways.

- One unit of foreign money to a number of units of domestic currency.

E.g., US $1 = Rs.50

- A certain number of units of foreign currency to one unit of domestic currency.

E.g., Re.1 = US $0.02

Exchange in a free market is determined by the demand for and supply of exchange of a particular country. The Equilibrium Rate is the rate at which the demand for foreign exchange and supply of foreign exchange are equal. i.e., it is the rate which over a certain period of time, keeps the balance of payment in equilibrium.

The demand for foreign exchange is determined by the countries'

- Import of goods and services.
- Investment in foreign countries. (i.e., outflow of capital to other countries.)
- Other payments involved in international transactions like payments by Indian government to various foreign governments for settlement.
- Other types of outflow of foreign capital like giving donations, contributions, etc.

Thus, the demand curve in an exchange determination graph represents the amount of foreign exchange demanded.

The supply of foreign exchange is determined by the countries'

- Export of goods and services to foreign countries.
- Investment from foreign countries. (i.e., inflow of foreign capital.)
- Other payments made by foreign governments to Indian government.

- Other types of inflow of foreign capital like remittances by the non resident Indians and foreigners by way of donations, contributions, etc.

The supply curve of foreign exchange is shown by 'SS'. The equilibrium exchange rate is determined at the point 'P', where the demand curve 'DD' intersects the supply curve, 'SS'. If the demand for foreign exchange is in excess of supply i.e., the demand is at the point of 'b' on the demand curve and the supply is at the point of 'a' on the supply curve, it indicates demand is greater than supply.

In contrast, if the demand is less than the supply, then the demand will be at point 'c' on demand curve at the supply will be at point 'd' on the supply curve. Thus, the excess demand over supply results in the exchange rate higher than the equilibrium exchange rate and vice versa, if the demand is less than the supply. Exchange rate policy can be Fixed Exchange Rate or Flexible Exchange Rate.

FIXED AND FLEXIBLE EXCHANGE RATE

Under Fixed Exchange Rate system, the government used to fix the exchange rate and the central bank to operate it by creating 'exchange stabilization fund.' The central bank of the country purchases the foreign currency when the rate falls and sells the foreign exchange when the exchange rate increases. Fixed exchange rate is also known as pegged exchange rate or par value.

Advantages of Fixed Exchange Rate System

(Why do countries go for Fixed Exchange Rate System?)

- Fixed exchange rate ensure certainty and confidence and thereby promote international business
- Fixed exchange rates promote long term investments by various investors across the globe.
- Most of the world currency areas like US dollar areas and sterling pound areas prefer fixed exchange rates.
- Fixed exchange rates result in economic stabilization.
- Fixed exchange rates stabilize international business and avoid foreign exchange risk to a greater extent. As such the small but international business oriented countries like the UK and Denmark prefer a fixed exchange rate system.

Despite these advantages, most countries of the world at present are not in favour of this system, though the IMF aimed of maintaining stable or pegged exchange rates.

Disadvantages of Fixed Exchange Rate System

- Fixed exchange rate system may result in a large scale destabilizing speculation in foreign exchange markets
- Long term foreign capital may not be attracted as the exchange rates are not pegged permanently.
- This system neither provides advantages of complete fixed rate system nor flexible exchange rate system.
- The economic policies and foreign exchange policies of the countries are rarely coordinated. In such cases, the pegged exchange rate system does not work.
- Deficit of balance of payments of the countries increases under a fixed exchange rate system as the elasticities in international markets are too low for exchange rate changes.
- Due to the problems with the fixed exchange rate system, IMF permits occasional changes in the system. This system is changed into 'managed flexibility system.' The managed flexibility system needs large foreign exchange reserves to buy or sell foreign exchange in order to manage the exchange rate. Maintenance of greater reserves aggravates the problem of international liquidity.

Flexible Exchange Rates are determined by market forces like demand for and supply of foreign exchange. Flexible exchange rates are also called floating or fluctuating exchange rate. Either the government or monetary authorities do not interfere or intervene in the process of exchange rate determination. Under this system, if the supply of foreign exchange is more than that of demand for the same, the exchange rate is determined at a low rate and *vice versa*.

Advantages of Flexible Exchange Rate System

- This system is simple to operate. This system does not result in deficit of surplus of foreign exchange. The exchange rate moves automatically and freely.
- The adjustment of exchange rate under this system is a continuous process.

- The system helps for the promotion of foreign trade.
- Stability in exchange rate in the long run is not possible even in a fixed exchange rate system. Hence, this system provides the same benefit like the fixed exchange rate system for long term investments.
- This system permits the existence of free trade and convertible currencies on a continuous basis.
- This system also confers more independence on the governments regarding their domestic policies.
- This system eliminates the expenditure of maintenance of official foreign exchange reserves and operation of the fixed exchange rate system.

Disadvantages of Flexible Exchange Rate System

- Market mechanism may fail to bring about an appropriate exchange rate. The equilibrium exchange rate may fail to give the necessary signals to correct the balance of payment position.
- It is rather difficult to define a flexible exchange rate.
- Under the flexible exchange rate system, the exchange rate changes quite frequently. These frequent changes result in exchange risks, breed uncertainty and impede international trade and capital movements.
- Under flexible rate system, speculation adversely influences fluctuations in supply and demand for foreign exchange.
- Under this system, a reduction in exchange rates leads to a vicious circle of inflation.

Despite the advantages of fixed exchange rate and the disadvantages of floating exchange rate system, it is viewed that the flexible exchange rate system is suitable for the globalization process. In addition, the convertibility also helps the floating rate system and the globalization of foreign exchange process.

Most economic theories of exchange rate movements seem to agree that three factors have an important impact on future exchange rate movements in a country's currency.

(i) The country's price inflation

(ii) Its interest rate

(iii) Market psychology and Bandwagon Effect.

THEORIES OF EXCHANGE RATE

Mint par of Exchange Theory

The rate of exchange does not fluctuate under the gold standard as it is fixed by references to the gold contents of the two currency units which is known as Mint par of exchange. Suppose India & US are on the gold standard, the rupee being equal to 0.001gram of gold and the dollar equal to 0.04gram of gold. The rate of exchange between two currencies will be,

$1=0.04/0.001 = 40/1 = Rs.40

Thus, the exchange rate is determined in a direct manner by comparison between the gold contents of two currencies. So that an Indian who wants to convert his rupee into dollar can get $1 for Rs.40. Suppose, the shipping & insurance charges for sending gold from India to America come to Re.1 per 0.04 gram of gold. The banks which deal in foreign exchange can then charge a commission of Re.1 per 0.04 gram for converting rupees into dollars. Thus the dollar will cost Rs.41 to an Indian. The market rate of exchange can deviate from the Mint par of exchange only by this difference. Therefore, the market rate in the FEM will be, $1=Rs.40 (specie point or gold point) to Rs.41

Free Paper currencies- PPP Theory

(GUSTAV CASSEL- Swedish Economist- "Abnormal Deviations in International Exchange"- Economic Journal - 1918)

If two countries are on free paper currencies, (nothing common between two currencies) the rate of exchange between the two currencies can be determined by reference to their purchasing power in their respective countries. Purchasing power of a unit of currency is measured in terms of tradable commodities; which is equivalent to the amount of goods and services that can be purchased with one unit of that currency.

Eg:- If a bale of cotton is sold for Rs. 4,000 in India and if the same bale is sold for $100 in the U.S.A, the rate of exchange (ignoring transport costs) will be ; $ 100 = Rs.4000 or $1= Rs. 40. If the price of the cotton moves up to Rs.4,400 in India on account of 10% inflation, the exchange rate will adjust to equate the purchasing power of the two currencies. Arbitrageurs will enter the market to make profit if the exchange rates are not adjusted accordingly, because they can buy the same commodity in the U.S.

for US $ 100 & sell it in India for Rs. 4,400. Hence, the dollar-rupee exchange rate will, therefore, move to a new equilibrium level to avoid such price disparity or arbitrage opportunity.

PPP theory also specifies that the purchasing power of a currency (value of the currency) will depend upon the price level in that country. The Absolute Version of PPP theory *states that the exchange rate between the currencies of two countries would be equal to the ratio of the price levels of the two countries measured by the respective consumer price indices. If the level of prices rises, the purchasing power of the currency would fall and its rate of exchange would also fall and if the price level in a country falls the purchasing power of the currency would rise and consequently its rate of exchange would also go up.* Thus we can determine the rate of exchange of one currency in terms of another, provided we know the purchasing power of two currencies in terms of common commodity traded in both the countries. This theory will hold good only if the same commodities are include in the same proportion in a basket of goods being used for the calculation of price indices in both the domestic and foreign countries.

Thus, Current Exchange Rate = Price level in the home country

Price level in the foreign country.

i.e., the consumer price index in India is 2856 and in USA, it is 136 the dollar-rupee exchange rate would be US $1 = Rs.21 (i.e., 2856/136)

Many Economists object to this method of comparison between the purchasing power of the two currencies through the medium of one commodity which is traded in both the countries.

They argue that if proper comparison of the purchasing power of two currencies has to be made, it is necessary to take the prices of all goods and services which money helps to purchase. In such case comparison will be made with the help of general price index numbers. This is the extended version of PPP theory.

By comparing the prices of identical products in different countries, it would be possible to determine the real or PPP exchange rate that would exist if markets were efficient.(An efficient market has no impediments to the free flow of goods and services)Thus if a basket of goods costs $200 in the US & Yen20,000 in Japan , PPP theory predicts that the Dollar/Yen rate should be $200/Y20,000;I.e., $1= Yen 100. The Relative Version of PPP Theory attempts to explain how exchange rate between two currencies fluctuates over the long run. According to this version one of the factors leading to change in exchange rate between currencies is *inflation* in the respective countries. *As long as the inflation rate in the two countries remains equal, the exchange rate between the currencies would not be affected. When a difference or deviation arises in the inflation levels of the two countries, the exchange rate would be adjusted to reflect the inflation rate differential between the countries.*

Thus PPP theory holds that any change in the equilibrium between the price levels of two countries due to different inflation rates between the countries tents produce an equal but opposite movement in the spot exchange rate between the currencies of the two countries over the long run. Accordingly, a country with higher exchange rate will experience depreciation in the value of its currency and vice versa. But if inflation in different countries is equal, Ceteris paribus, exchange rate do not change.(only if inflation of a country is higher than the other countries its currency tends to depreciate)

Many Economists object to this method of comparison between the purchasing power of the two currencies through the medium of one commodity which is traded in both the countries.....?

They argue that if proper comparison of the purchasing power of two currencies has to be made, it is necessary to take the prices of all goods and services which money helps to purchase. In such case comparison will be made with the help of general price index numbers. This is the extended version of PPP theory.

By comparing the prices of identical products in different countries, it would be possible to determine the real or PPP exchange rate that would exist if markets were efficient. (An efficient market has no impediments to the free flow of goods and services)Thus if a basket of goods costs $200 in the US & Yen20,000 in Japan , PPP theory predicts that the Dollar/Yen rate should be $200/Y20,000;I.e., $1= Yen 100.

Criticism of the PPP Theory

- No direct link between Purchasing Power and Rate of Exchange.
- Difficult in comparing price Indices I.e., problem as to which index number should be used. The wholesale price

index/agricultural price index or raw material price index/ cost of living index etc.,

- Index number problems because of :
  * different types of goods used in the calculation;
  * difference in goods used for domestic trade and International trade;
  * differences in prices in International markets due to differences in transportation costs;
- False assumption that changes in the exchange rate has no influence over the price level.
- This theory ignores Capital Flows between countries.
- This theory do not consider the extraneous factors such as interest rates, govt. interference, Business Cycle, political influence, BOP adjustments, decline in foreign exchange reserves etc., which may influence exchange rates.
- This theory applies only to product markets and not suitable for financial markets.

THE LAW OF ONE PRICE

The law of one price states that in competitive markets free of transportation costs and barriers to trade(such as tariffs), identical products sold in different countries must sell for the same price when their price is expressed in terms of the same currency. For e.g., if the exchange rate between the British pound and the U.S Dollar 1 pound = $1.50, a jacket that retails for $75 in New York should sell for £50 in London.

Consider what would happen if the jacket costs 40 pounds in London ($60 in the U.S.); at this price , it would pay a trader to buy jackets in London and sell the in New York(Arbitrage). The trade would initially make a profit of $15 on jacket by purchasing it for 40 pounds in London and selling it for $75 in New York. However, the increased demand for jackets in London would raise the price in London and the increased supply of the same would lower their prices there. This would continue until prices were equalized.

Thus, prices might equalize when the jacket costs 44 pounds ($66) in London & $66 in New York (assuming no change in the exchange rate of $1=£ 1.50)

The International Fisher's Effect

According to the Relative Version of PPP Theory one of the factors leading to change in exchange rate between currencies is inflation in the respective countries. As long as the inflation rate in the two countries remains equal, the exchange rate between the currencies would not be affected. When a difference or deviation arises in the inflation levels of the two countries, the exchange rate would be adjusted to reflect the inflation rate differential between the countries.

Irwin - Fisher's Effect states that Nominal interest rate comprises of Real interest rate plus expected rate of inflation. So the nominal interest rate will get adjusted when the inflation rate is expected to change. The nominal interest rate will be higher when higher inflation rate is expected and it will be lower when lower inflation rate is expected.

Mathematically, it is expressed as $r = a + i + ai$

i.e., Nominal rate of interest = Real rate of interest + expected rate of inflation + (Real rate of interest x expected rate of inflation)

Since interest rates reflect expectations about inflation, there is a link between interest rates and exchange rates. Fisher's Open Proposition or International Fisher's Effect or Fisher's Hypothesis articulates that the exchange rate between the two currencies would move in an equal but opposite direction to the difference in the interest rates between two countries.

A country with higher nominal interest rate would experience depreciation in the value of its currency. Investors would like to invest in assets denominated in the currencies which are expected to depreciate only when the interest rate on those assets is high enough to compensate the loss on account of depreciation in the currency value.

Conversely, investors would be willing to invest in assets denominated in the currencies which are expected to appreciate even at a lower nominal interest, provided the loss on account of such lower interest rate is likely to compensate by the appreciation in the value of the currency. Thus Fischer's effect articulates that the anticipated change in the exchange rate between two currencies would equal the inflation rate differential between the two countries, which in turn, would equal the nominal interest rate differential between these two countries.

EXCHANGE RATE REGIMES

An exchange rate is the value of one currency in terms of another. What is the mechanism for determining this value at a point in time? How are exchange rates changed? These are defined in an *exchange rate regime* which refers to the mechanism, procedures and institutional framework for determining exchange rates at a point in time and changes in them over time, including factors which induce the changes. In theory, a very large number of exchange rate regimes are there. At the two extremes is the Perfectly Rigid or Fixed Exchange Rates and the Perfectly Flexible or Floating Exchange Rates. Between them are Hybrids with varying degrees of limited flexibility. The regime that existed during four decades ago of 20th century is the Gold Standard. This was followed by a system in which a large group of countries had fixed but adjustable exchange rates with each other. This system lasted till 1973. After a brief attempt to revive it, much of the world moved to a sort of "non-system" where in each country chose an exchange rate regime from a wide menu depending on its own circumstances and policy preferences.

Some History on Exchange rate system.......

Bimetallism....(Before 1875)

Prior to 1870s, many countries had bimetallism which was having double standard in the free coinage period both maintained by gold and silver; which were used as international means of payment and the exchange rate among countries were determined either by their gold and silver contents. Countries that were on the bimetallic standards often experienced the well known phenomenon referred to as Gresham's Law which articulates that "bad money (abundant money) drives out good money (scarce money)". For example, when gold from newly discovered mines in California and Australia poured into the market in 1850's, the value of the gold became depressed, causing overvaluation of gold under French official ratio, which resulted to a gold Franc to silver Franc 15.5 times as heavy. As a result Franc effectively became a gold currency.

International Gold Standard 1875- 1914

(Oldest system which was in operation till the beginning of the First World War).

Though in Great Britain currency notes from the Bank of England were made fully redeemable for gold during 1821, the first full-fledged gold standard was adopted by France (as mentioned in the bimetallic period) in 1878. Later on United States adopted it in 1879 and Russia and Japan in 1897, Switzerland, and many Scandinavian countries by 1928.

An international Gold Standard is said to exist when;

- Gold alone is assured of unrestricted coinage
- There is a two way convertibility between gold and national currencies at a stable ratio
- And gold may be freely imported and exported.

In order to support unrestricted convertibility into gold, bank notes need to be backed by gold reserve of a minimum stated ratio. In addition, the domestic money stock should rise and fall as gold flows in and out of the country.

In a version called *Gold Specie Standard,* the actual currency in circulation consists of gold coins with a fixed gold content.

In a version called *Gold Bullion Standard,* the basis of money remains a fixed rate of gold but the currency in circulation consists of paper notes with the monetary authorities. i.e., the central bank of the country standing ready to convert on demand, unlimited amounts of paper currency into gold and vice versa, at a fixed conversion ratio. Thus a Pound Sterling note can be exchanged for say, X ounces of gold while a Dollar note can be converted into say, Y ounces of gold on demand.

Finally, under the version *Gold Exchange Standard,* the authorities stand ready to convert, at a fixed rate, the paper currency issued by them into paper currency of another country which is operating a gold specie or gold bullion standard. Thus if Rupees are freely convertible into Dollars and Dollars in turn into gold then Rupee can be said to be on gold exchange standard.

The exchange rate between any pair of currencies will be determined by their respective exchange rates against gold. This is called as Mint Parity Rate of Exchange.

Under the true gold standard, the monetary authorities must obey the following three rule of the game:

* They must fix once-for-all the rate of conversion of the paper money issued by them into gold.

* There must be free flows of gold between countries on gold standard
* The money supply in the country must be tied to the amount of gold the monetary authorities have in reserve. If this amount decreases, money supply must contract and *vice versa.*

The gold standard regime imposes very rigid discipline on the policy makers. Often, domestic policy goals such as reducing the rate of unemployment may have to be sacrifices in order to continue operating the standard and the political cost of doing so can be quite high. For this reason, the system was rarely allowed to work in its pristine version. During the Great Depression the gold standard was finally abandoned in form and substance.

Gold standard system had many short comings. First of all, the supply of newly minted gold is so restricted that the growth of world trade and investment can be seriously tampered for the lack of sufficient monetary reserves. The world economy can face deflationary pressures.. Second, whenever the government finds it politically necessary to pursue national objectives that are inconsistent with maintaining the gold standard, it had the freedom to abandon the gold standard.

Most of the countries gave priority to stabilization of domestic economies and systematically followed a policy of Sterilization of Gold by matching inflows and outflows of gold respectively with reductions and increases in domestic money and credit.

THE BRETTON WOODS SYSTEM

Bretton Woods is the name of the town in the state of New Hampshire, USA, where the delegations from over forty five countries met in 1944 to deliberate on proposals for a post-war international monetary system. The two main contending proposals were "the White plan" named after Harry Dexter White of the US Treasury and the "Keynes plan" whose architect was Lord Keynes of the UK. Following the Second World War, policy makers from victorious allied powers, principally the US and UK, took up the task of thoroughly revamping the world monetary system for the non-communist world. The outcome was the so called "Bretton Woods System" and the birth of new supra-national institutions, the International Monetary Fund (the IMF or simply the "Fund") and the World Bank.

Under this system US Dollar was the only currency that was fully convertible to gold; where other countries currencies were not directly convertible to gold. Countries held US dollars, as well as gold, for use as an international means of payment.

The system proposed an international clearing union that would create an international reserve asset called "bancor". Countries would accept payment in bancor to settle international transactions without limit. They would also be allowed to acquire bancor by using overdraft facilities with the clearing union.

In return for undertaking this obligation, the member countries were entitled to have access to credit facilities from the IMF to carry out their intervention in the currency markets.

The novel feature of regime which makes it an *adjustable peg* system rather than a fixed rate system like the gold standard was that the parity of a currency against the dollar could be changed in the face of a fundamental equilibrium. ***A fundamental equilibrium* is said to exist when at the given exchange rate, the country repeatedly faces balance of payment disequilibria, and has to constantly intervene and sell foreign exchange (persistent deficits) or buy foreign exchange (persistent surpluses) against its own currency. The situation of persistent deficits is much more difficult to deal with and calls for a devaluation of the home currency. Changes of upto 10% in either direction could be made without the consent of the Fund and obtaining their approval.

Under the Bretton Wood System, the US dollar in effect became international money. Other countries accumulated and held dollar balances with which they could settle their international payments; the US could in principal buy goods and services from other countries simply by paying with its own money.

This system could work as long as other countries had confidence in the stability of the US dollar and in the ability of the US treasury to convert dollars into gold on demand at the specified conversion rate.

Professor Robert Triffin warned that gold exchange system was programmed to collapse in the long run. To satisfy the growing needs of reserves, the US had to run BOP deficits continuously which would eventually impair the public confidence in the dollar, triggering a run on the dollar. If reserve currency country runs BOP deficits to supply reserves, they can lead to a crisis of confidence in the reserve currency itself causing the down fall of the system. This dilemma is known as Triffin Paradox.

The system came under pressure and ultimately broke down when this confidence was shaken due to various political and some economic factors starting in mid-1960s. On August 15, 1971, the US government abandoned its commitment to convert dollars into gold at the fixed price of $35 per ounce and the major currencies went on a float.

An attempt was made to resurrect the system by increasing the price of gold and widening the bands of permissible variation around the central parity. This was the so called *Smithsonian Agreement*. That too failed to hold the system together, and by early 1973, the world moved to a system of floating rates.

After a period of wild fluctuation in exchange rates - accentuated by real shock such as the oil price crises in 1973 - policy makers in various countries started experimenting with exchange rate regimes which were hybrids between fixed and floating rates. A group of countries in Europe entered into Bretton Woods like engagement of adjustable pegs within themselves. This was the European monetary system. Other countries tried various mixed versions.

FEATURES OF THE BRETTON WOODS INTERNATIONAL DOLLAR STANDARD

Four main features of the Bretton Woods system was as follows.

First, it was a *US dollar-based system*. Officially, the Bretton Woods system was a gold-based system which treated all countries symmetrically, and the IMF was charged with the responsibility to manage this system. In reality, however, it was a US-dominated system with the US dollar playing the role of the key currency (the dollar's dominance still continues today).

The relationship between the US and other countries was highly asymmetric. The US, as the center country, provided domestic price stability which other countries could "import," but did not itself engage in currency intervention (this is called *benign neglect*; i.e., the US did not care about exchange rates, which was desirable). By contrast, all other countries had the obligation to intervene in the currency market to fix their exchange rates against the US dollar.

Second, it was an *adjustable peg system*. This means that exchange rates were normally fixed but permitted to be adjusted infrequently under certain conditions. As a consequence, exchange rates were supposed to move in a stepwise fashion. This was an arrangement to combine exchange rate stability and flexibility, while avoiding mutually destructive devaluation. Member countries were allowed to adjust "parities" (exchange rates) when "fundamental disequilibrium" existed.

However, "fundamental disequilibrium" was not clearly defined anywhere. In reality, exchange rate adjustments were implemented far less often than the builders of the Bretton Woods system imagined. Germany revalued twice, the UK devalued once, and France devalued twice. Japan and Italy did not revise their parities.

Third, *capital control* was tight. This was a big difference from the Classical Gold Standard of 1879-1914, when there was free capital mobility. Although the US and Germany had relatively less capital-account regulations, other countries imposed severe exchange controls.

Fourth, *macroeconomic performance was good*. In particular, global price stability and high growth were simultaneously achieved under deepening trade liberalization. In particular, stability in tradable prices (wholesale prices or WPI) from the mid 1950s to the late 1960s was almost perfect and globally common. This macroeconomic achievement was historically unprecedented.

Bretton Woods: US Dollar at Center

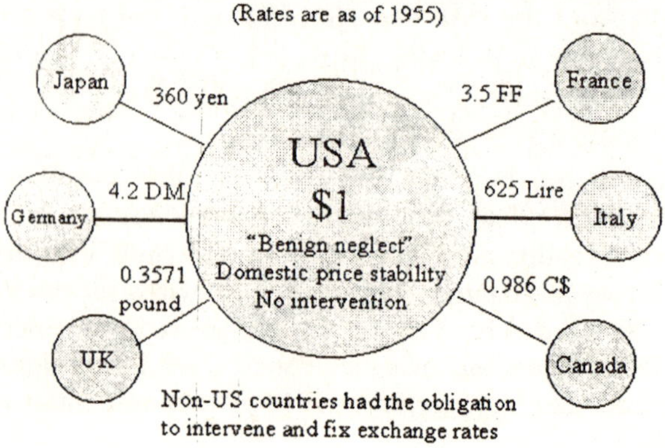

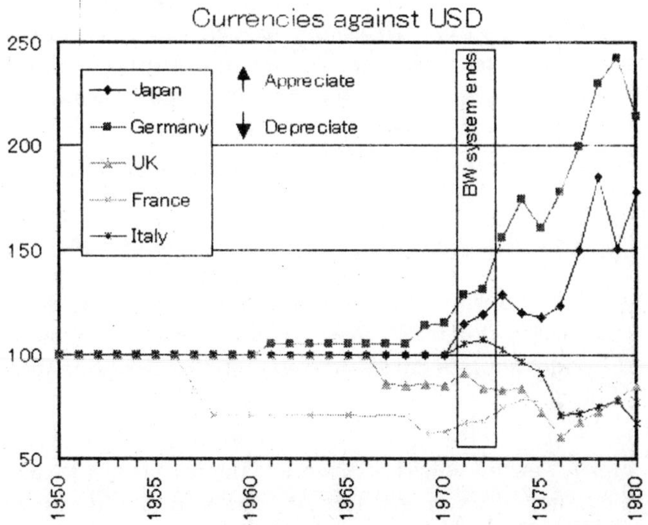

The exchange rate regime that was put in place can be characterized as the Dollar Based Gold Exchange Standard where:

The US government undertook to convert the US dollar freely into gold at a fixed parity of $35 per ounce. (In other words, each country established a par value in relation to the US dollar, which was pegged to gold at $35 per ounce.)

Other member countries of the IMF agreed to fix the parties of their currencies vis-à-vis the dollar with variation within 1% on either side of the central parity being permissible. However a member country with a ***fundamental disequilibrium* may be allowed to make a change in the par value of its currency.

If the exchange rate hit either of the limits, the monetary authorities of the country were obliged to "defend" it by standing ready to buy or sell dollars against their domestic currency to any extend required to keep the exchange rate within the limits.

How did the Bretton Woods system collapse?

With such an excellent macroeconomic record, why did the Bretton Woods system collapse eventually? Economists still debate on this question, but it is undeniable that there was a nominal anchor problem. The collapse of the Classical Gold Standard was externally forced (i.e., by the outbreak of WW1), but the collapse of the Bretton Woods system was due to internal inconsistency. The American monetary discipline served as the nominal anchor for the Bretton Woods system. But when the US started to inflate its economy, the international monetary system based on the US dollar began to disintegrate.

Let us follow the history of the Bretton Woods system, step by step.

The 1950s was a period of *dollar shortage*. Europe and Japan wanted to increase imports in the process of recovery from war damage. But the only internationally acceptable money at that time was the US dollar. So their capacity to import was severely limited by the availability of foreign reserves denominated in the US dollar.

However, by the late 1960s, there was a *dollar overhang* (oversupply) in the world economy. This turnaround was due to the US balance of payments deficit, which in turn was caused by expansionary fiscal policy. The spending of the US government increased for three reasons: (i) the war in Vietnam; (ii) welfare expenditure; and (iii) the space race with the USSR (send humans to the moon by the end of the 1960s).

In the late 1950s, the IMF felt the need to create a new international currency to supplement the dollar. But the international negotiation took a long time, and the artificial currency (called the Special Drawing Rights, or SDR) was created only in 1969. By that time, there was no longer a dollar shortage; in fact there was a dollar glut! (Today, SDR plays only a minor role, mainly as the IMF's accounting unit.)

In the mid 1960s, US domestic inflation (as measured in WPI) began to accelerate, which strained the Bretton Woods system. When the US was providing price stability, other countries were willing to give up monetary policy independence and peg their currencies to the dollar. Through this operation, their price levels were also stabilized. But when the US began to have inflation, other countries gradually refused to import it.

There was a downward pressure on the dollar. In 1968, the fixed linkage between dollar and gold was abandoned. The *two-tier pricing of gold* was introduced whereby the "official" gold-dollar parity was de-linked from the market price of gold. The market price of the dollar immediately depreciated. This was similar to the situation of multiple exchange rates: an overvalued official rate vs. a more depreciated market rate.

Finally, in 1971, the fixed linkage between dollar and other currencies was given up. On August 15, 1971, US President Richard Nixon appeared on TV and declared that the US would no longer sell gold to foreign central banks against the dollar. This completely terminated the working of the Bretton Woods system and major currencies began to float. At the same time, President Nixon also imposed temporary price controls and stiff import surcharges. These measures were all supposed to fight inflation and ameliorate the balance of payments crisis that the US was facing. This was called the "Nixon Shock." [If any country adopted such a policy package today, it would be severely criticized by the IMF, WTO and the international community. It would be told to tighten the budget and money first.]

For 11 trading days that followed, the Bank of Japan intervened heavily in the currency market to fight off massive speculative attacks, losing 4 billion dollars of foreign reserves. Then, it gave up and let the yen appreciate. European central banks gave up much sooner before losing a lot of foreign reserves.

Between 1971 and 1973, there was an international effort to re-establish the fixed exchange rate system at adjusted levels (with a more depreciated dollar). In December 1971, the monetary authorities of major countries gathered in Washington, DC to set their mutual exchange rates at new levels (the Smithsonian Agreement). But these rates could not be maintained very long. In early 1973, under another bout of heavy speculative attacks, the Smithsonian rates were abandoned and major currencies began to float.

Triffin's dilemma

Prof. Robert Triffin offered a famous explanation as to why the Bretton Woods system had to collapse inevitably. He noted that there was a fundamental liquidity dilemma when some country's national currency was used as an international money.

His argument went something like this. As the world economy grew, more international money (dollar) was demanded. To supply that, the US had to run a balance-of-payments deficit (how else can the rest of the world get more dollars?)

But if the US continued to run a BOP deficit, it would lose credibility as a sound currency country. The amount of gold that the US had would soon be much less than the amount of dollars held by other countries. This meant that the US could not guarantee conversion of international dollars into gold, if all foreign central banks tried to cash in.

To supply global liquidity, the US must run a deficit. But to maintain credibility, the US must not run a deficit. That was the fundamental dilemma. In the end, the US opted to run a BOP deficit, which led to the loss of credibility and the collapse of the Bretton Woods system.

According to Prof. Triffin, the US should not be blamed for the collapse of the Bretton Woods system, because there was no way to get out of this impossible situation. But is Prof. Triffin right?

The issue is controversial. My personal view is that Prof. Triffin was not necessarily right, that there was a logical way out of this "dilemma." First, de-link dollar from gold so the US government is relieved of the obligation to exchange gold for dollar. Second, supply just the right amount of dollar to the world to avoid global inflation or deflation (this requires adjustments in fiscal and monetary policies, just as the IMF would recommend). If these revisions were adopted, I think the Bretton Woods system could have continued much longer. Obviously, this would have required a lot of hard thinking, political maneuvering, and consensus building. Whether that was possible at that time was another matter.

Gold and money

At this point, we may stop and ask why gold is needed at all for the design of the international monetary system. Why can't a wise central bank (or a group of them) manage money supply without any reference to gold? In fact, this was exactly the question raised by Keynes.

Perhaps the most fundamental answer is: central bankers are (were) not so wise. If you tie the value of money to gold, it may fluctuate due to the shifting demand and supply conditions of gold. But that would be much better than hyperinflation or deep devaluation caused by a huge budget deficit or irresponsible monetary policy. Gold is needed to discipline the monetary and fiscal authorities. Even though macroeconomics has advanced, we cannot trust every central banker, even to this date.

But at the same time, there are problems associated with the rigid gold-money linkage.

First, short-term price fluctuation is unavoidable. In the 19th century, when a new gold mine was discovered in California or Alaska, the supply of gold increased greatly and the world had an inflation. But when there was no such big gold discovery, there was a deflation. No one could ensure that the speed of gold discovery matched the increase in global money demand.

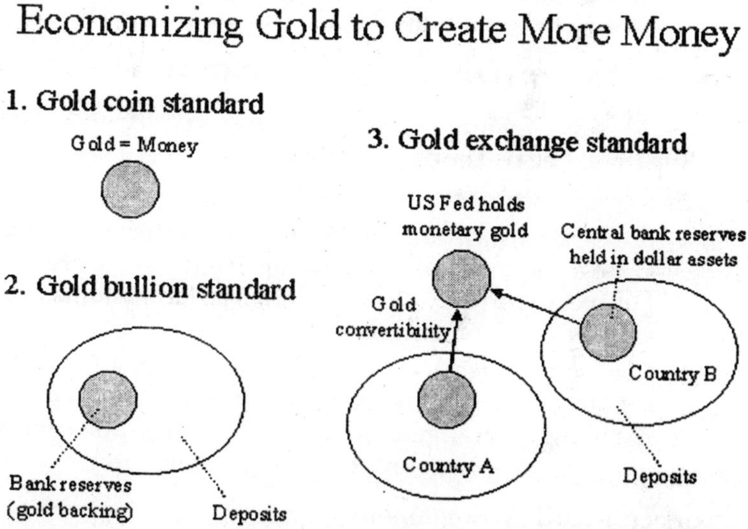

Second, the more serious problem is long-term shortage of monetary gold. Over the years, the growth of the rapidly industrializing world economy was faster than the pace of gold discovery. In order to supply the needed money, the gold standard was gradually transformed so that a small amount of gold could back a much greater amount of money. The gold standard evolved in the following steps.

(1) *Gold coin standard*: only gold coins circulate as money, and no paper money or bank deposits are used. The amount of monetary gold is equal to money supply. All money has intrinsic value.

(2) *Gold bullion standard*: as the banking system creates deposit money, people begin to carry paper notes for convenience. But paper money can be exchanged for gold at any time. Most monetary gold is accumulated at bank vaults in the form of gold bullions (gold bars). Through the money multiplier process, money supply is much greater than the amount of gold held by banks.

(3) *Gold exchange standard*: if gold shortage persists, further saving of gold becomes necessary. Gold can be held only by the center country (US Federal Reserves) while other central banks hold dollar reserves, not gold. Their dollar holdings are guaranteed to be converted to gold by the US.

SUBSEQUENT INTERNATIONAL MONETARY DEVELOPMENTS

No Separate Legal Tender Arrangement

This group includes

a) Countries which are members of a currency union and share a common currency like the twelve members of the European Currency Union (ECU), who have adopted Euro as their common currency or

b) Countries which have adopted the currency of another country as their currency. IMF's 1999 Annual Report on Exchange Arrangements and Exchange Restrictions indicates that 37 countries belong to this category.

Currency Board Arrangement

A regime under which there is a *legislative commitment* to exchange the domestic currency against a specific foreign currency at a fixed exchange rate coupled with restrictions on the monetary authority to ensure that this commitment will be honored. This implies constraints on the ability of the monetary authority to manipulate domestic money supply. In its classification referred to above, IMF has classified eight countries – Argentina, Bosnia, Brunei, Bulgaria, Djibouti, Estonia, Hong Kong, and Lithuania – as having a currency board system. However, Hanke (2002) argues that none of these countries can be said to conform to all the criteria of an orthodox currency board system. According to him, legislative commitment to convert home currency into a foreign currency at a fixed rate is just one of the six characteristics of an orthodox currency board arrangement.

Conventional Fixed Pegs Arrangement

This is identical to the Bretton Woods system where a country pegs its currency to another or to a basket of currencies with a band of variation not exceeding +1% around the central parity. The peg is adjustable at the discretion of the domestic authorities. 39 IMF members had adopted this regime as of 1999. Of these thirty had pegged their currencies to a single currency and the rest to a basket.

Pegged Exchange Rates within Horizontal Bands

Here there is a peg but variation is permitted within wider bands. It can be interpreted as a sort of compromise between a fixed peg in the floating exchange rate. 11 countries had adopted such wider band regimes in 1999

Crawling Peg

This is another variant of limited flexibility regime. The currency is pegged to another currency or a basket, but the peg is periodically adjusted to a well specified criterion or is discretionary in response to changes in inflation rate differentials. 6 countries come under crawling peg regime in 1999.

Crawling Bands

The currency here is maintained within certain margins around a central parity which 'crawls' in a pre-announced fashion or in response to certain indicators.9 countries are having such regimes under an agreement in 1999.

Managed Floating with no Pre-announced Path for the Exchange Rate

Here, the central bank influences the exchange rate by means of active intervention in the foreign exchange market through buying and selling foreign currency against home currency without any commitment to maintain the rate at any particular level. 27 countries joined to this group in 1999.

Independently Floating

Here, the exchange rate is market determined, where the central bank intervening is only to moderate the speed of change and to prevent excessive fluctuations but not attempting to maintain the rate at any particular level. 48 countries including India joined as independent floaters in 1999.

Is there an Optimal Exchange Rate Regime?

Starting from the gold standard regime of fixed rates, passing through the adjustable peg system after the Second World War, it has finally ended up with a system of managed floats after 1973. Since 1985, the pendulum has started swinging, though very slowly and erratically, in the direction of introducing some amount of fixity and rule based management of exchange rates.

Despite these empirical facts, there is a school of thought within the professional which argues that in the years to come there will be only two types of exchange rate regimes: truly fixed rate arrangements like currency unions or currency boards, or truly market determined, independently floating exchange rates. The "middle ground" - regimes such as adjustable pegs, crawling pegs, crawling bands and managed floating - will pass into history. Some analysts even predict that three currency blocks - the US dollar block, the Euro block and the Yen block - will emerge with currency union within each and free floating between them. The argument for the impossibility of the middle ground refers to the "impossibility trinity" i.e., it asserts that a country can achieve any two of the following three policy goals but not all three:

1. A stable exchange rate
2. A financial system integrated with the global financial system i.e., an open capital account; and
3. Freedom to conduct an independent monetary policy

Of these, (1) and (2) can be achieved with a currency union board, (2) and (3) with an independently floating exchange rate and (1) and (3) with capital control.

As of now, there is no consensus either among academic economists or among policy makers or among businessmen and bankers as to the ideal exchange rate regime. The debate is extremely complicated and made more so by the fact that it is very difficult if not impossible to sort out the effects of exchange rate fluctuations on the world economy from those of other shocks, real and monetary (oil price gyrations, Mid East wars, political developments in East Europe, disagreements over trade liberalisation, developing country debt crisis etc.).

INTERNATIONAL TRADE FINANCE

Financing international trade is a complex process, involving many variables, ranging from corporate policy and marketing strategy to exchange risk and general borrowing conditions. The reason behind this complexity is that trade involves two countries with different currencies and jurisdictions. In addition, payments must be made at a distance and across time, so the exporter, the importer, or both need credit during part or all of the period form the initial manufacture of goods by the exporting firm to the time of the final sale and collection by the importer. The main objective of a good corporate export financing policy should be financing the greatest possible amount of sales with the greatest possible management simplicity and with minimal risk.

Following are among the important considerations in the choice of a strategy for trade financing:

The nature of good in question. Capital goods usually require medium to long-term financing while consumer goods, perishable products, etc. require short term finance.

A buyers' market favours the importer and the exporter may have to offer longer credit terms, bear the currency risk and possibly some credit risk. A sellers' market on the other hand, favours the exporter.

The nature of the relationship between the exporter and the importer. For example, if both are members of the same corporate family (affiliated to the same MNC) or have had a long standing relation with each other, the exporter may agree to sell on open account credit while absence of confidence may require a letter of credit.

The availability of various forms of financing, government regulations pertaining to the sale transaction, etc.

The crucial question is who will bear the credit risk? When an exporter sells on open account or consignment basis, the exporter bears the entire credit risk. On the other hand, in cases when the importer makes advance payment at the time of placing the order, he bears the credit risk. Most often, given the complexities in cross-border transactions and the absence of detailed knowledge regarding the financial status of the two parties, credit risk will be shifted to an intermediary who specialises in evaluating and undertaking such risks. This may be a government institution such as an EXIM bank or commercial banks, factors or others.

The nature of the relationship between the exporter and is critical for understanding the methods of import-export financing utilised. There will be usually three categories of relationships in an international trade:

1) Unaffiliated unknown: - where a foreign importer with which the term has not previously conducted any business.
2) Unaffiliated known: - where a foreign importer with which the firm has previously conducted business successfully.
3) Affiliated: - where a foreign importer is a subsidiary business unit of the firm (intra firm trade)

There are three basic elements for an import export transaction:

1) Contracts: - where all contracts shall include the definition and specification for the quality, grade, quantity with reference to published prices/catalogs and associated descriptions/blueprints/diagrams and other technical detail aspects or characteristics.
2) Prices: - prices should clearly indicate with reference to quantity, discounts, advance payment, extra charges in case of deferred payment, transportation charges, insurance fee, surcharge of any other fee levied by the relative country.
3) Documentation: - Documentation involves a variety of issues of particular importance from a financial management perspective; including shipping deadline, payment instructions (where various methods of payment are there), packing and marketing, warranties, guarantees and inspections. The methods of payment includes Open Account Credit, Consignment, Forfaiting, Factoring, Guaranteeing, Lines of Credit, Letter of Credit, Documentary Draft, Cross Border Leasing, Cash Down (CBD, COD), Buyers' Credit, Suppliers' Credit etc.

METHODS OF PAYMENT

In any international trade transaction, credit is provided either by the supplier (exporter), or the buyer (importer), or one or more financial institutions, or any combination of these. The important methods of payment in international trade transaction are:

Letter of Credit

A letter of credit (L/C) is a written guarantee given by the importer's bank to honour an exporter's draft or any other claims for payment provided by the exporter has fulfilled all the conditions specified in the L/C. The L/C is opened by the importer's bank at the request of the latter. It is the issuing or opening bank. The issuing bank forwards the L/C to a correspondent bank (its own branch) in the exporter's country (the advising bank) who in turn forwards it to the exporter who is the beneficiary under the L/ C. since the documentation is quite elaborate and the written clause require careful interpretation, the International Chambers of Commerce have evolved a standard code called Uniform Customs and Practices for Documentary Credits to deal with documentary disputes in international trade. The L/C by itself is not a financing instrument; it is only a bank's commitment to pay. Financing depends upon how the related draft is disposed off. Payment under a L/C is either against a Sight or Demand Draft or a Usance Draft.

To cater to the wide variety of transactions and customers, different types of letters of credit have evolved.

A Revocable L/C is issued by the issuing bank and contains a provision that the bank may amend or cancel the credit without the approval of the beneficiary. It provides least protection to the exporter

An Irrevocable L/C cannot be so amended or cancelled without the exporter's prior approval.

A Confirmed, Irrevocable L/C contains an extra protection; in addition to the issuing bank's commitment, a confirming bank adds its own undertaking to pay provided all conditions are met. The confirming bank (which may be but need not be the same as the advising bank) will pay even if the issuing bank cannot or will not honour the exporter's draft.

A Revolving L/C is used when the exporter is going to make shipments on a continuing basis and a single L/C will cover several shipments. A Transferable L/C permits the beneficiary to transfer a part or whole of the credit in favour of one or more secondary beneficiaries. This type of L/C is used by trader exporters who act as middlemen between the importer and the manufacturers of the goods. The trader intends to profit from the difference between the original amount of credit and the amount transferred to the secondary beneficiaries.

In a Back-to-Back L/C, the beneficiary of the original L/C requests a bank (usually the advising bank to the original L/C) to open an irrevocable L/C in favour of another party who may be the ultimate manufacturer or supplier of the goods. The original L/C is a guarantee against the second L/C.

In a Red Clause L/C, a clause is printed in red ink, on a normal L/C authorizing the advising bank to make clean advances to the exporter which is offset against the export proceeds when the documents are finally presented. In effect the importer makes unsecured loans to the exporter in the latter's currency. This type of L/C is used when there exists a close relationship between the importer and the exporter.

A Standby L/C, actually a term covering a wide variety of arrangements, provides a fallback guarantee to the supplier in case the primary obligor fails to pay.

Draft

A draft or a bill of exchange is an order written by an exporter that requires an importer to pay a specified amount of money at a specified time. Through the use of drafts, the exporter may use its bank as the collection agent on accounts that the exporter finances. The bank forwards the exporter's drafts to the importer directly or indirectly (through a branch or a correspondent bank) and then remits the proceeds of the collection back to the exporter.

A draft involves three parties:

1. The drawer or maker: - The drawer is the person or business who issues the draft. This person is usually the exporter who sells and ships the merchandise.
2. The drawee: - The drawee is the person or business against whom the draft is drawn. This person is usually the importer who must pay the draft at maturity.
3. The payee: - The payee is the person or business to whom the drawee will eventually pay the funds.

If the draft is not a negotiable instrument, it designates a bank or a person to whom payment is to be made. Such a person, known as the payee, may be the drawer himself or a third party such as the drawer's bank.

However, this is generally not the case because most drafts are a bearer instrument. Drafts are negotiable if they meet a number of conditions:

(1) They must be in writing and signed by the drawer-exporter.
(2) They must contain an unconditional promise or order to pay an exact amount of money.
(3) They must be payable on sight or at a specified time.
(4) They must be payable on sight or at a specified time.
(5) They must be made out to order or to the bearer.

Bill of Lading

The third key document for financing international trade is the Bill of Lading or B/L. The bill of lading is issued to the exporter by a common carrier transporting the merchandise. It serves three purposes: a receipt, a contract, and a document of title.

As a receipt, the bill of lading indicates that the carrier has received the merchandise described on the face of the document. The carrier is not responsible for ascertaining that the containers hold what is alleged to be their contents, so descriptions of merchandise on bills of lading are usually short and simple. If shipping charges paid in advance, the bill of lading will usually be stamped "freight paid" or freight prepaid". If merchandise is shipped collect – a less common procedure internationally than domestically – the carrier maintains a lien on the goods until the freight is paid.

As a contract, the bill of lading indicates the obligation of the carrier to provide certain transportation in return for certain charges common carriers cannot disclaim responsibility for their negligence through inserting special clauses in a bill of lading. The bill of lading may specify alternative ports in the event that delivery cannot be made to the designated port, or it may specify that the goods will be returned to the exporter at the exporter's expense.

As a document of title, the bill of lading is used to obtain payment or a written promise of payment before the merchandise is released to the importer. The bill of lading can also function as collateral against which funds may be advanced to the exporter by its local bank prior to or during shipment and before final payment by the importer.

CHARACTERISTICS OF BILL OF LADING

Bills of lading are either *straight* or *to order.*

A Straight Bill of Lading provides that the carrier deliver the merchandise to the designated consignee only. A straight bill of lading is not title to the goods and is not required for the consignee to obtain possession. Therefore, a straight bill of lading is used when the merchandise has been paid for in advance, when the transaction is being financed by the exporter, or when the shipment is to a subsidiary.

An Order Bill of Lading directs the carrier to deliver the goods to the order of a designated party, usually the shipper. An additional inscription may request the carrier to notify someone else of the arrival. The order bill of lading grants title to the merchandise only to the person to whom the document is addressed, and surrender of the order bill of lading is required to obtain the shipment.

International trade and Foreign Exchange

International trade is exchange of capital, goods, and services across international borders or territories. In most countries, it represents a significant share of gross domestic product (GDP). While international trade has been present throughout much of history, its economic, social, and political importance has been on the rise in recent centuries. Industrialization, advanced transportation, globalization, multinational corporations, and outsourcing are all having a major impact on the international trade system. Increasing international trade is crucial to the continuance of globalization. International trade is a major source of economic revenue for any nation that is considered a world power. Without international trade, nations would be limited to the goods and services produced within their own borders.

International trade is in principle not different from domestic trade as the motivation and the behavior of parties involved in a trade does not change fundamentally depending on whether trade is across a border or not. The main difference is that international trade is typically more costly than domestic trade.

The reason is that a border typically imposes additional costs such as tariffs, time costs due to border delays and costs associated with country differences such as language, the legal system or a different culture.

International trade uses a variety of currencies, the most important of which are held as foreign reserves by governments and central banks.

Another difference between domestic and international trade is that factors of production such as capital and labor are typically more mobile within a country than across countries. Thus international trade is mostly restricted to trade in goods and services, and only to a lesser extent to trade in capital, labor or other factors of production. Then trade in good and services can serve as a substitute for trade in factors of production. Instead of importing the factor of production a country can import goods that make intensive use of the factor of production and are thus embodying the respective factor. An example is the import of labor-intensive goods by the United States from China. Instead of importing Chinese labor the United States is importing goods from China that were produced with Chinese labor. International trade is also a branch of economics, which, together with international finance, forms the larger branch of international economics.

As specified early, according to the Bank for International Settlements, average daily turnover in global foreign exchange markets is estimated at $3.98 trillion. Trading in the world's main financial markets accounted for $3.21 trillion of this. This approximately $3.21 trillion in main foreign exchange market turnover was broken down as follows:

- $1.005 trillion in spot transactions
- $362 billion in outright forwards
- $1.714 trillion in foreign exchange swaps
- $129 billion estimated gaps in reporting

RISKS IN INTERNATIONAL TRADE

The risks that exist in international trade can be divided into two major groups

Economic risks

- Risk of insolvency of the buyer,

- Risk of protracted default - the failure of the buyer to pay the amount due within six months after the due date
- Risk of non-acceptance
- Surrendering economic sovereignty
- Risk of exchange rate
- Susceptibility to changing standards & regulations within other countries

Political risks

- Risk of cancellation or non-renewal of export or import licenses
- War risks
- Risk of expropriation or confiscation of the importer's company
- Risk of the imposition of an import ban after the shipment of the goods
- Transfer risk - imposition of exchange controls by the importer's country or foreign currency shortages
- Risk of different tax rates
- Surrendering political sovereignty
- Influence of political parties in importer's company
- Relations with other countries

Gains from International Trade

There are various gains which international trade brings to participating countries. However the three most commonly expressed gains are:

It allows countries to import goods which they may be unable to produce themselves, in exchange for those that they can produce. For example Bangladesh may produce excess amounts of rice, which they can exchange for more luxurious goods such as chocolate.

Secondly, it allows a country to specialise in the production of goods in which it has some form of advantage - possibly from the natural resources available. It is also important to highlight that the specialisation of production will implicate lowered costs as that particular country is able to invest the necessary funds for production.

Furthermore, international trade often results in the total world production level increasing - which is beneficial for the world economy as currency values are stimulated.

INTERNATIONAL TRADE THEORIES

Global trade in a liberalized environment is a trade in investments and technology apart from simple trade in goods and services. The main questions on which international trade theory focus are:

i. Why do countries export and import the sort of products they do and at what relative prices/terms of trade?

ii. How are these trade flows related to the characteristics of a country and how do they affect domestic factor prices?

iii. What are the gains from trade and how are they divided among trading countries?

THE BASIS FOR INTERNATIONAL TRADE & INTERNATIONAL TRADE THEORIES

Differences in prices/costs are the basic cause for trade. But why should costs differ from country to country. Lower costs for products because of lower wages only seem to be plausible enough reason. Yet a country with lower wages imports labor intensive products from the other country having high wages. So differences in wages cannot explain trade pattern. An enduring two way flow of goods must be traced to systematic international differences in the structure of costs and prices. Some products may be cheaper to produce abroad and will be imported from other countries. This generalization is the basic to the theory of foreign trade and is known as 'The principle of Comparative advantage'. It asserts that a country will export products which it can produce at lower costs.

A nation's comparative advantage and trade pattern are highly affected by its resource endowment both natural and manmade because some countries may be rich in copper, some may be in petroleum, some may have huge water resources or fertile plains etc., A nation rich in people but poor in skills may be suited to certain tasks, but not in all. A nation that has very few persons per square mile but has lavished its energies on technical training is likely to enjoy a comparative advantage in the production of certain precision goods.One part of nation's capital stock is embodied in its labor force for agricultural activities and scientific skills and another part is embodied in capital intensive equipments. The given below trade theories explain why it is beneficial for a country to engage in international trade and the pattern of international trade in the world economy.

INTERNATIONAL TRADE THEORIES

Mercantilism Theory (English Mercantilist: *THOMAS MUN-1630)*

The first theory of international trade emerged in England in the mid 16th century. Its principle assertion was that gold and silver were the mainstays of national wealth and essential to vigorous commerce. At that time, gold and silver were the currency of trade between countries; a country could earn gold and silver by exporting goods. Similarly importing goods from other countries would result in an outflow of gold and silver to those countries. The main tenet of mercantilism was that it was in a country's best interests to maintain a trade surplus, to export more than it imported. By doing so a country could accumulate gold and silver and consequently increase its national wealth and prestige. According to David Hume, the classical economist, in the long run no country would sustain a surplus on the *Balance of Trade* and so accumulate gold and silver as the mercantilism had envisaged. The flaw of mercantilism is that it was viewed as a *Zero Sum game* ie, a game in which a gain in one country results in loss by another. For example, if England has a Balance of Trade surplus with France, the resulting inflow of gold and silver would swell the domestic money supply and generate Inflation in England and the latter would have an opposite effect. i.e., as a result of outflow of too much gold and silver money supply would contract and its prices would fall. This change in relative prices between two countries would encourage the French to buy fewer goods from English (because goods will become more and more expensive day by day) and the English would start buying goods from France. The result would be deterioration in Balance of trade of English and improvement in France's trade balance unless the English's surplus is totally eliminated.

Theory of Absolute Advantage(ADAM SMITH –*'The wealth of Nations'*-1776)

Adam Smith argued that countries differ in their ability to

produce goods efficiently and they should specialize in the production of goods for which they have an absolute advantage and then trade for these goods produced by other countries. In other words a country should never produce goods at home that you can buy at a lower cost from other countries. A tailor doesn't make his own shoes, he exchange a suit for shoes. Thereby both the tailor and the shoe maker will gain. In the same manner Smith argued that a whole country can gain by trading with other countries. A country has an absolute advantage in the production of a product when it is more efficient in producing it than any other country. According to Smith countries should specialize in the production of goods for which they have an absolute advantage and then trade them for goods produced by other countries. Here we can see a positive sum game i.e., it produces net gains for all involved. For example, English should specialize in the production of textiles while France would specialize in wine so that England could get quality wine by selling its textiles to France and buying wine in exchange.

Consider the effects of trade between two counties England and France given below:

- If it takes 10 labour units to produce one unit of good- A- in Country - I -England; &
- If it takes 20 labour units to produce one unit of same good– A- in country –II France &
- If it takes 20 labour units to produce one unit of good-B- in country – I - England &
- If it takes 10 labour units to produce one unit of same good- B- in country- II -France;

It would be better that if two countries exchange both the goods at the ratio of 1:1 , both of them would have more of both the goods within a given effort by trading with each other which is a *Positive Sum game* as it produces net gains for all invoved.

Theory of Comparative Advantage (DAVID RICARDO- 'Principles of Political Economy'-1817)

David Ricardo took Adam Smith's theory one step further by exploring what might happen when one country has an absolute advantage in the production of all goods. Smith's theory suggests that such a country might derive no benefits from international trade. But Ricardo in his book 'Principles of political economy' specifies that this was not the case. According to Ricardo's theory of comparative advantage it makes sense for a country to specialize in the production of those goods that it produces most efficiently and to buy the goods that it produces less efficiently from other countries, even if this means buying goods from other countries that it could produce more efficiently by itself. Ricardo points out that even if one country is more productive than another country in all lines of production still it benefits the country to trade. Because so long as the country is not equally less productive in all lines of production it still pays both the countries to trade. The basic message of this theory is that potential world production is greater with unrestricted free trade than it is with restricted trade. Ricardo's theory suggests that consumers in all nations can consume more if there are no restrictions on trade.

This occurs even in countries that lack an absolute advantage in the production of any good. In other words to an even greater degree than the theory of absolute advantage, the theory of comparative advantage suggests that international trade is a positive sum game in which all countries that participate realize economic gains. Thus it encourages a strong rationale for free trade.

Consider the effects of trade between two counties Ghana and South Korea given below:

- If it takes 10 unit resources to produce one ton of good- Cocoa - and 13.5 unit resources to produce one ton of another good- BT Rice in country –I-Ghana &
- If it takes 40 unit resources to produce one ton of good- Cocoa - 20 unit resources to produce one ton of good- BT Rice in country –II-South Korea ;

Here Ghana have *Absolute advantage* in the production of both the goods Cocao and BT Rice but the former have *Comparative advantage* only in the production of Cocoa.

What is this Comparative advantage?

The production of any good requires resources or inputs such as land, labour and capital. Consider the effects of trading between Ghana and South Korea. Assume that 200 units of resources are available in each country. With this given limited resources Ghana could then produce 20 tons of cocoa (200/10) and no BT Rice or

15 tons of BT Rice (200/13.5) and no Cocoa or in any combination on its PPF i.e., Production Possibility Frontier. And with the given same limited resources South Korea could produce 5 tons of Cocoa(200/40) and no BT Rice or 10 tons of BT Rice (200/20) and no Cocoa or in any combination on its PPF. Here Ghana can produce 4 times as much as Cocoa as South Korea, but only 1.5 times as much BT Rice. Thus Ghana is comparatively more efficient at producing cocoa than it is producing BT Rice. By engaging in trade, the two countries can increase their combined production of Cocoa and BT Rice and consumers in both nations can consume more of both the goods. The basic message of the Theory of Comparative Advantage is that *"Potential world production is greater with unrestricted free trade than it is with restricted trade". "It is a Positive – Sum games in which all countries that participates realizes economic gains", which provides a strong rationale for encouraging free trade.*

Factor Endowment Approach/Heckscher Ohlin Theory

(ELI HECKSHER-1919) and BERTIL OHLIN (1933)

When Ricardo's theory stress that comparative advantage arises from differences in productivity,(as he stressed labour productivity and argued that differences in labour productivity between nations underlie the notion of comparative advantage.) Swedish economist Eli Heckscher and Bertil Ohlin argues that the pattern of international trade is determined by differences in factor endowments ie, the extent to which a country is endowed with such resources as land, labour and capital. Nations have varying factor endowments and different factor endowments explain differences in factor costs. The more abundant a factor the lower will be its cost. Thus this theory proceeds from three assumptions.

(a) Products differ in factor requirements. Cars require more time per worker than cotton, furniture etc.

(b) Countries differ in factor endowments. Some have large amount of capital per worker(Capital abundant countries) and some have very little capital but more labour.(Labour abundant countries)

(c) Technologies are same across the countries.

One could make cars by several methods either use small machine shop/an automated plant etc. The choice of technique will depend upon the factors of production, Wages to labour, rental to machines etc. The factor endowment theory assumes that the product which is capital involve at one set of factor prices is also most capital intensive at way other set. The theory argues that capital abundant countries will tend to specialize in capital intensive goods like cars aircrafts and will export some of their specialties in order to import labour intensive goods. Similarly labour intensive goods and will export their own specialties in order to import capital intensive goods. To put the proposition in general terms. Trade will be based on differences in factor endowments and will serve to relieve each country's factor shortages.

Leontief Paradox (WASSILY LEONTIEF-1953)

Wassily Leontief raised questions about the validity of Heckscher Ohlin theory. Leontief postulated that even though the U.S was relatively abundant in capital-intensive goods (being relatively abundant in Capital compared to other nations); (he found that) U.S exports were less Capital intensive than U.S imports. One possible explanation is that the U.S has a special advantage in producing new products/goods with innovative technologies and hence such products may be less Capital intensive than products whose technology had time to mature and become suitable for mass production. Thus U.S may be exporting goods that heavily use skilled labour and innovative entrepreneurship, while importing heavy manufactures that use large amount of capital. This leaves economists with a difficult dilemma. The key assumption in Heckscher-ohlin theory is that technologies are same across the country. Leontief Paradox points out that, 'this may not be the case 'and *difference in technology may lead to differences in productivity, which in turn, drives international trade patterns.* Japans success in exporting automobiles was not just on the relative abundance as capital, but also on its development of innovative manufacturing technology that enabled it to achieve higher productivity levels in automobile production than other countries that also had abundant capital. However many economists specifies that Richardo's theory of comparative advantage, actually predicts trade patterns with greater accuracy.

Product Life Cycle Theory/Vernon's Theory (RAYMOND VERNON-1960)

Raymond Vernon's theory was based on the observation that for most of the 20th century a very large proportion of the world new products had been developed by U.S firms & sold first in the U.S market (e.g. mass produced automobiles, television, instant cameras, photocopiers, personal computers, semiconductor chips etc) To explain this Vernon argued that the wealth and size of U.S market gave us firms a strong incentives to develop new consumer products & the high cost of U.S labor gave U.S firms an incentive to develop new consumer products with cost- saving process innovations(as labor cost is very high). The new product as first sold in the U.S it could be produced abroad at some low -cost location, then exported back into the U.S. However, Vernon argued that most new products were initially produced in America. Apparently, the pioneering firms believed that it was better to keep production facilities close to the market, and to the firm's center of decision making, given the uncertainties & risk inherent in introducing new products. Consequently firms can relatively charge higher prices for new products, which obviate the need to look for low cost production sites in other countries

LIFE CYCLE CONCEPT

Vernon went on arguing that early in the life cycle of a typical new product, while demand is starting to grow rapidly in U.S, demand in other advanced countries is limited to high -income groups. This limited initial demand in other advanced countries doesn't make it worthwhile for firms in those countries to start producing the new product which necessitate some exports from the U.S to those countries.

Overtime demand for the new products start to grow in the other advanced countries like U.K, France, Germany and Japan. As it does, it become worthwhile for foreign producers to begin producing for the home markets.In addition U.S firms may set up production facilities in those advanced countries begins to limited the potential for exports from the U.S.

As the market in the U.S and other advanced nations matures, the product becomes more standardized, and price becomes the main competitive weapon. As this occurs, cost consideration starts to play a greater role in the competitive process. Producers based in advanced countries where labors cost are lower than in the U.S might now be able to export to the U.S.

If cost pressures become intense the process might not stop there. The cycle by which the U.S lost its advantage to other advanced countries might be repeated once more, as developing countries like Thailand begin to acquire a production advantage over the other advanced countries. Thus the locus of global production initially switches from the U.S to other advanced countries and then from those nations to developing countries.

The consequence of these trends for the pattern of world trade is that overtime the U.S switches from being an exporter of the product to an importer of the product as production becomes concentrated in lower - cost foreign locations. The figure in the next page shows the growth of production & consumption over time in the U.S, other advanced countries and developing countries.

The Flaws

Vernon's arguments that most new products are developed & introduced in the U.S seem ethnocentric. Although it may be true that during U.S. global dominance (1945 to 1975) most new products were introduced in the United States, there have always been important exceptions.

With the increased globalization and integration of the world economy, a growing number of new products are now simultaneously introduced in the U.S, Japan & other advanced European nations. This may be accompanied by globally disbursed production, with particular components of a new product being produced in those locations around the globe where the mix of factor costs and skills is most favorable.

Consider the case of Laptop computers which where simultaneously introduced in a number of major international markets by Toshiba. Although various components for Toshiba Laptops were manufactured in Japan (e.g., display screens, memory chips) , other components were manufactured in Singapore and Taiwan and still others (hard drives and microprocessors) were manufactured in the U.S..All the components were later on shipped to Singapore for final assembly and the completed products were shipped to the major markets around the world.This pattern of trade for a new product is both different from and more complex than the pattern predicted by Vernon.

Although Vernon's theory may be more useful in explaining the pattern of international trade during the brief period of American global dominance, its relevance in the modern world is limited.

The New Trade Theory-(1970)

This theory began to emerge when number of economists were questioning the assumption of "diminishing returns to specialization" used in international trade theory. They argued that "increasing returns to specialization" might exist in some industry. Economics of scale represent one particularly important source of increasing return. "Economics of scale" are the unit cost reduction associated with a large scale of output. If international trade results in a country specializing in the production of certain good & if the economics of scale in producing that good and then as output of that good expands, unit costs will fall. In such a case these will be increasing returns to specialization & not diminishing returns. Put differently, as a country produces more of the good, due to realization of economics of scale productivity will increases and costs will fall.

New trade theory argues that if the output required realizing significant scale economics represents a substantial proportion of total world demand for the product, the world market may be able to support only a limited no. of firms based in a limited no. of countries producing that product. Thus those firms that enter the world markets first gain an advantage that may be difficult for the other firms to match with. In the other words, a country may dominance in the export of a particular product where scale economics are important & where the volume of output required gaining scale economics represent significance proportion of world output.

This argument is the notion of *first -mover advantages,* which are the economics & strategic advantages that occur to early entrants into an industry. Because they are able to *gain econonics of scale;* the early entrants into an industry may get a lock on the world market that discourages subsequently entry by other firms. The ability of first movers to reap economics of scale creates a barrier to entry. For e.g. in the commercial Aircraft Industry, the fact Boeing & Airbus are already in the Industry discourages new entry.

This theory thus suggests that a country may dominate in the exports of a good simply because it was lucky enough to have one/more firms among the first to produce that goods. Thus the new trade theorists argue that the U.S leads in exports of commercials Jet aircrafts not because it is better endowed with factors of production required to manufacture aircraft, but because of the first movers in the industry. Boeing & MC Donald Douglas were US firms. As economies of scale result in an increase in the efficiency of .resources utilization and home in productivity, the new trade theory identifies important sources of comparative advantages. Thus this theory stresses the role of Luck, Entrepreneurship and Innovation in giving a firm first mover advantages.

Michael Porters' (National Competitive Advantage) Theory - Harvard Business School.

Michael porter in his book "*The competitive Advantage of nations*" attempts to determine why some nations succeed and others fail in international competition", based on the study conducted in 100 industries in 10 nations. He theorizes that four broad attributes of a nation shape the environment in which local firms compete, and these attributes promote/impede the creation of competitive advantage.

These attributes are:

1) Factor Endowments: A nation's position in factors of production such as skilled labor/the infrastructure necessary to compete in a given industry.
2) *Demand conditions* – the nature of home demand for the industry's product and services.
3) *Relating & supporting industries*: the presence/absence of supplier industries and related industries those are internationally competitive.
4) *Firm strategy, structure and rivalry:* the conditions governing how companies are created, organized and managed and the nature of domestic/rivalry.

He argues that firms are most likely to succeed in industries/ industry segments where the diamond is most favorable, as it is a mutually reinforcing system. The affect of one attribute is contingent on the state of others. For e.g. favorable demand conditions will not result in competitive advantage unless the state of rivalry is sufficient to cause firms to respond to them. According to him additional two variables that can influence the national demand are: *chance and government*. Chance events such as major innovations can reshape industry structure and provide the opportunity for one nation's firms to supplement another. Government by its choice of polices can detract from/improve national advantage. E.g.: Govt. investments in education can change factor endowments.

Porter contents that the degree to which a nation is likely to achieve international success in a certain industry is a function of the combined impact of factor endowments, domestic demand conditions, related and supporting industries and domestic rivalry. He also conducts that the govt. influences each of the four components of diamond either positively/negatively. Factor endowments can be affected by subsidies polices towards capital markets, policies towards education and so on. Govt. can shape domestic demand through local standards/with regulations that mandate/influence buyer needs. Govt. policy can influence support and related industries through regulation and influence firm rivalry through such devices as capital market regulation, tax policy and antitrust laws.

If Porters' theory is correct, countries should be exporting products to those industries where all four components of the demand are favorable, while importing; in those areas the components are not favorable.

Why does all this matter for an international business? There are atleast three main implications for international business:

i. Location implication
ii. First- mover implication &
iii. Policy implication

GLOBALIZATION

Globalization (or globalization) describes an ongoing process by which regional economies, societies and cultures have become integrated through globe-spanning networks of exchange. The term is sometimes used to refer specifically to economic globalization: the integration of national economies into the international economy through trade, foreign direct investment, capital flows, migration, and the spread of technology.. However, globalization is usually recognized as being driven by a combination of economic, technological, socio-cultural, political and biological factors. The term can also refer to the transnational dissemination of ideas, languages, or popular culture. Looking specifically at economic globalization, it can be measured in different ways which centers around the four main economic flows that characterize globalization:

- Goods and services, e.g. exports plus imports as a proportion of national income or per capita of population
- Labor/people, e.g. net migration rates; inward or outward migration flows, weighted by population
- Capital, e.g. inward or outward direct investment as a proportion of national income or per head of population
- Technology, e.g. international research & development flows; proportion of populations (and rates of change thereof) using particular inventions (especially 'factor-neutral' technological advances such as the mobile or telephone, automobiles, broadband etc.,)

INTERNATIONAL CAPITAL FLOWS

International capital flows are the financial side of International trade. When someone imports goods or services, the buyer (the importer) gives the seller (the exporter) a monetary payment, just as in domestic transactions. If total exports were equal to total imports, these monetary transactions would balance at net zero: people in the country would receive as much in financial flows as they paid out in financial flows. But generally the trade balance is not zero. The most general description of a country's balance of trade, covering its trade in goods and services, income receipts, and transfers, is called its current account balance.

If the country has a surplus or deficit on its current account, there is an offsetting net financial flow consisting of currency, securities, or other real property ownership claims. This net financial flow is called its capital account balance.

When a country's imports exceed its exports, it has a current account deficit. Its foreign trading partners who hold net monetary claims can continue to hold their claims as monetary deposits or currency, or they can use the money to buy other financial assets, real property, or equities (stocks) in the trade-deficit country. Net capital flows comprise the sum of these monetary, financial, real property, and equity claims. Capital flows move in the *opposite* direction to the goods and services trade claims that give rise to them. Thus, a country with a current account deficit necessarily has a capital account surplus. In balance-of-payments accounting terms, the current-account balance, which is the total balance of internationally traded goods and services, is just offset by the capital-account balance, which is the total balance of claims that domestic investors and foreign investors have acquired in newly invested financial, real property, and equity assets in each others' countries.

While all the above statements are true by definition of the accounting terms, the data on international trade and financial flows are generally riddled with errors, generally because of undercounting. Therefore, the international capital and trade data contain a balancing error term called "net errors and omissions."

Because the capital account is the mirror image of the current account, one might expect total recorded world trade—exports plus imports summed over all countries—to equal financial flows—payments plus receipts.

But in practical, suppose for example in a particular year assume that the capital account balance was $17.3 trillion, more than three times the latter, at $5.0 trillion.What it indicates?. There are three explanations for this. First, many financial transactions between international financial institutions are cleared by netting daily offsetting transactions.

For example, if on a particular day, U.S. banks have claims on French banks for $10 million and French banks have claims on U.S. banks for $12 million, the transactions will be cleared through their central banks with a recorded net flow of only $2 million from the United States to France even though $22 million of exports was financed.

Second, since the 1970s, there have been sustained and unexplained balance-of-payments discrepancies in both trade and financial flows; part of these balance-of-payments anomalies is almost certainly due to unrecorded capital flows. Third, a huge share of export and import trade is intrafirm transactions; that is, flows of goods, material, or semi finished parts (especially automobiles and other non- electronic machinery) between parent companies and their subsidiaries.

Compensation for such trade is accomplished with accounting debits and credits within the firms' books and does not require actual financial flows.

COMPOSITION OF CAPITAL AND FINANCIAL FLOWS

Trade imbalances are financed by offsetting capital and financial flows, which generate changes in net foreign assets. These payments can be any combination of the following:

Capital investments

Portfolio investments in either debt or equity securities

Direct investment in domestic firms (FDI) including start-ups

Changes in International Reserves

Balance of Payments

Countries trade with one another their exports paying for imports. Balance of payment refers to the value of imports and exports on commodities i.e., visible items only. Movement of goods between the countries is known as visible trade because the movement is open and can be verified b officials. If exports and imports are exactly equal for a given period of time, is said to be balanced. If the value of exports exceeds imports, the country has favorable balance of trade. If the excess of imports over exports is there, it is adverse balance of trade.

Balance of payment is more comprehensive. In India, it is classified into two:

1. Balance of Payment on current account
   a. Visible trade relating to imports & exports
   b. Invisible items, for example, receipts and payments for such services as shipping, banking travel etc.
   c. Unilateral transfers such as donations
2. Balance of Payment on capital account

Current account shows whether India has a favorable balance or deficit balance in any given year. The balance of payment on capital account shows the implications of current transactions for the country's international finance positions. For example, surplus and deficit of current account are reflected in capital account through changes in foreign exchange reserves of a country, which are in index of current strength or weakness of country's international payment positions.

RBI defines BOP of a country as a systematic record of all economic transactions between the residence of a country and the rest of the world. It presents a classified record of all receipts on account of goods exports, service rendered and capital received by residence and payments made by them on account of goods exported and services received from the capital transactions to non residence or 'foreigners'.

BOP - Double Entry Concept

BOP is a standard double entry accounting record. As in all matters it is related with rules of double entry book keeping. i.e., for every transaction, there must be one credit and one debit leaving errors and omissions adjustment where the totals of credit must exactly match with the total of debit.

Rules (Accounting Principles in BOP)

1. A transaction which results in increase in demand of foreign exchange is to be recorded as debit entry, while a transaction which results in increase in supply of foreign exchange must be recorded as credit entry. Thus, increase in foreign assets or reduction in foreign liability is a debit aspect while increase in foreign liability or reduction in foreign assets is a credit aspect. In a nutshell, capital outflow is a debit and capital inflow is a credit.
2. All transactions which relate to immediate or prospective transactions from the rest of the world (ROW) to the country should be recorded as credit entries. The payment themselves should be recorded as offsetting debit entries. Conversely all transactions which results in actual or prospective payment from the country to the ROW should be treated as debits and the corresponding payments as credits.

DEFICIT & SURPLUS

Equilibrium and Disequilibrium in BOP

In economic sense, BOP equilibrium occurs when a surplus or deficit is eliminated, from the BOP. Concept of BOP is based on the concept of accounting equilibrium; i.e., current account + capital account = 0.

But normally such equilibrium is not found. Rather, normally such equilibrium is not found. Rather, it is disequilibrium in the balance of payment which is a normal phenomenon. The deficit/

surplus in BOP in economic terminology is disequilibrium in BOP. Though several external variables influence the BOP and give rise to disequilibrium, domestic economic variables like national output and national spending, money supply, exchange rate and interest rate are more significant causative factors. It could be explained as follows:

- If national income exceeds national spending, the excess amount will be invested abroad resulting in capital account deficit and conversely excess of national spending over national income causes borrowings from abroad which would push the capital account into surplus. Thus, disparity in national income and national spending influences the capital account via current account. If national output exceeds national spending, the difference manifests itself in exports causing current account surplus. This surplus is invested abroad which again means capital account deficit. Likewise, the excess of national spending over national output leads to import. The country borrows to meet the current account deficit and the borrowing results in capital account surplus.
- Increase in money supply rises the price level, where exports turn uncompetitive and fall in exports leads to deficit in current account.
- Higher prices of domestic goods make the price of imported commodities competitive, as a result of which imports rise and deficit again rises in current account.
- If currency of a country depreciates exports become competitive and import becomes costlier, as a result of which imports will be restricted. If imports are not restrained deficit will again appear in the trade account.
- An increase in domestic interest causes capital inflow in search of high returns and capital account turns surplus and the reverse in case of interest rate falls.

INDIA'S BALANCE OF PAYMENT POSITION

First Five Year Plan (1951-52 - 1955-56)

India had adverse BOP which extends to Rs.42 crores.

Reason: affected by Korean War and American recession of 1953

Second Five Year Plan (1956 - 1961)

Severe deficit extends to Rs.2339 crores.

Reasons:

a) Heavy import of capital goods to develop heavy & basic industries.

b) The failure of agriculture production

c) Inability of the economy to increase exports

Third Five Year Plan (1951 - 1966)

Invariable balance (extends to Rs.1951 crores) because of:

a) Imports were expanding faster to overcome domestic shortages especially food grains.

b) Exports were extremely sluggish.

Forth Five Year Plan (1967 - 1974)

Trade deficit which extended to Rs.1564 crores and surplus was there in net invisible which extended to Rs.1664 crores. For the first time surplus was there, though it was nominal to the extent of Rs.100 crores.

Fifth Five Year Plan (1975 - 1979)

India was able to have huge surplus BOP, which extended to Rs.3082 crores by showing a comfortable position to external account.

Reasons:

a) Stringent to measure taken against smuggling and illegal payment transaction.

b) Increase in earnings from foreign tourists.

c) Increase in number of Indians going abroad for employment and larger remittances send by them in India.

d) Relative stability in the external value of rupee.

Sixth & Seventh Plan (1956 - 1961)

6th Plan - adverse BOP extended to Rs.11,385 crores and 7th plan is like to Rs.41,047 crores.

Reasons:

Tremendous growth of imports and comparatively much lower rate growth of exports and excessive withdrawals from IMF through extended credit facility arrangements using SDR.

Eighth Five Year Plan (1992 - 1997)

During 8th plan trade deficit reach their record level of Rs.52,561 crores.

Ninth Five Year Plan (1997 - 2002)

The trade deficit was whipped out to the extent of 78% by invisible account surplus by invisible account surplus. Dr. C Rangarajan (former Governor of RBI), who headed the high level committee on BOP came with the report on June 4, 1993 for correcting the adverse BOP system with the following findings and recommendations:

1) Government should exercise caution against extending concessions of facilities to foreign investors.
2) Efforts should be made to replace dead flows with equity flows
3) Stable exchange rate should be kept through restrictions on trade and invisibles and close control over capital transactions.
4) Strong recommendations were made for disinvestment
5) Debt should be linked to equity and should be limited in the ratio of 1:2

CAUSES OF ADVERSE BALANCE OF PAYMENT IN INDIA

The main reason for adverse BOP was evaluated which were as follows:

a) Import Liberalisation

   Import liberalisation for automatic and electronic industry created a damper on indigenous production
b) Adverse effect on the gross of capital goods in India.
c) Import policy mainly hit small scale industries and majority SSIs were in the shut down stage.
d) Dumping:- Technological dumping in the name of technological upgrading
e) Raising level of import of capital intensive goods, raw materials and space parts.
f) High import of defense equipments & infrastructure supportive equipments and machineries
g) High import of consumer goods and packed food items

h) Seasonal short term disequilibrium caused by
i) Increase in the price of petroleum, oil and lubricants.
j) Rapid population growth
k) High external debt principal and internet
l) Inflationary pressure in the economy
m) Bad quality of exports
n) Neo-protectionism :- Even though quantitative restrictions are being completely eliminated under WTO, developing countries are restricting exports from India by adopting a variety of non-tariff barriers like VER (Voluntary Export Restraints) and technical regulations
o) Business cycle

MEASURES TO CORRECT ADVERSE BOP

a) Monetary Policy: - Measures adopted by Central Bank/ Monetary authority to increase/decrease the money supply and availability of credit. Monetary policy aimed at increase the monetary supply and availability of credit to the public is called 'expansionary monetary policy' or 'easy money policy' and policy aimed at decreasing money supply & availability of credit to the public is called 'contraction monetary policy' or 'dear money policy'.
b) Fiscal Policy: - it refers to the deliberate changes the government makes in its expenditure and taxation policies or both.

METHODS OF CORRECTING ADVERSE BOP

Deflation & Adverse Balance

Deflation means fall in prices rise in the value of money. This attempt is to restrict demand for foreign goods by restricting consumption. The fundamental cause of adverse BOP is excessive demand for foreign goods. To correct this, it is essential to curtail demand for foreign goods by restricting consumption. RBI may adapt policy of deflation, which will result in fall in prices and income. Reduction of money income will be followed by reduction in demand and imports. Similarly exports may be stimulated. Indians will attempt to buy goods within India rather than from abroad as internal prices are lower than prices elsewhere.

Exchange Depreciation & Adverse Balance

Exchange depreciation means decline in the rate of one currency in terms of another. In such a case, price of dollar will appreciate in value while appreciation in Dollar will reduce India's demand for American goods.

Thus, imports will decline. As Indian currency is cheap, Americans will buy more from Indian market.

Devaluation & Adverse Balance

Devaluation is the reduction in the value of currency by government, where depreciation stands for automatic reduction in the value of currency market forces.

Exchange Control & Adverse Balance

It may be adopted to overvalue or undervalue its exchange rate or to avoid fluctuation in exchange rate. It may also be adopted to freeze the assets of foreign nationals so that they might not be able to use them.

THREE METHODS OF EXCHANGE CONTROL

Pegging Operations

Pegging up or pegging sown the currency of a country to a chosen rate of exchanges. Pegging operation takes place through buying and selling of home currency either by the government or Central bank of the country in exchange for the foreign currency in foreign exchange market. If pegging operations are carried out to maintain the exchange rate at higher level, they are known as 'Pegging up' and if they are done to keep the exchange rate at a lower level, they are termed as 'Pegging down'

Restrictions

Restrictions means the policy by which government restricts the supply of its currency coming into the exchange market by

* Centralizing all trading in foreign exchange with central bank of the country
* Prevention of exchange of national currency against foreign currencies without the permission of central government.
* Make all foreign exchange transactions through the agency of the government.

Exchange Clearing Agreements (ECA)

Under this, two countries engaged in trade, pay their respective central banks the amount payable to their respective foreign creditors. The central banks then use the money in offsetting the corresponding claims. Suppose India have ECA with US, the RBI will open an account with itself in the name of Federal Reserve Bank of America, which in turn, will open an account in the name of RBI. All Indians who had imported goods from America will pay in Rupees to the credit of FRBA in the RBI and all Indian exporters of goods to US will receive payment from RBI out of the account in the name of FRB. This system is essentially one of all setting each others payments and the basic assumption is that the countries entering into such an agreement will see that imports and exports are more or less equal and that there is no necessity for either taking payments to or reviewing payments from the other country.

Import Duties and Quotas & Adverse Balance

Import quotas cut down the demand for imports and there by eliminate adverse BOP, where the central government may fix maximum quantity of commodity to be imported during a given period.

All these five methods are available to government for correcting the adverse BOP with the least amount of delay for curtailing imports and stimulating exports.

BALANCE OF PAYMENT: CLASSICAL VS. ELASTICITY APPROACH

Classical View

Classical economists view that disequilibrium in the BOP is self adjusting through 'price-specie-flow mechanism'.

Price-specie-flow mechanism specifies that an increase in money supply raises domestic prices, exports become uncompetitive, exports drop, foreign goods become cheaper and imports rise. As a result, current account balance goes deficit. Precious metals flow out of the country to finance imports, there by the quantity of monetary drops that lowers the price level. Lower prices in the economy lead to increased exports resulting in the trade balance regaining equilibrium. It also points out that a country could achieve lasting balance of trade surplus through trade protection and export promotion.

Elasticity Approach

This is based on partial equilibrium analysis; where everything is held constant except the effects of exchange rate changes on export/import. It explains that depreciation in the currency leads to greater export and diminished import.

It is assumed that the elasticity of supply of output is infinite, so that neither the price of export in home currency rise as demand increases nor the prices of import fall with a squeeze in demand for imports.

There will be 'pass through effect' which refers to contraction in imports due to rising cost on account of devaluation of currency.

There will be 'J-curve effect' which refers that devaluation of the currency first rises trade deficit then lowers it.

Where 'Ex' is the price elasticity for demand for export, and 'Em' is the price elasticity of demand for import devaluation helps improving current account balance only if Em + Ex >1.

If elasticity of demand is greater than unity, devaluation will lead to contraction of import in the wake of escalated cost of import (which is known as 'pass through effect') and increase in import as a result of lower prices of export in the international market.

Elasticity approach does not consider supply and cost changes as a result of devaluation or income and expenditure effect of exchange rate changes.

SWIFT (Society for World wide Inter-bank Financial Telecommunications)

Communications pertaining to international financial transactions are handled mainly by a large network called 'SWIFT, which is a non-profit Belgium Cooperative Society (1973) with main and regional centers around the world connected by data transmission lines, which links banks and brokers in every financial centers. It is the largest of the world's financial telecommunication networks.

Depending on the location a bank can access, a regional processor or main centre which transmits the information to appropriate location. This computer based communication links banks and brokers in every financial center.

INTERNATIONAL MONETARY FUND (IMF)

Origin

The IMF also called the Fund is an International monetary institution/supranational financial institution established by 45 nations under the Bretton Woods Agreement of 1944. Such an institution was necessary to avoid repetition of the disastrous economic policies that had contributed to Great depression of 1930's. The principal aim was to avoid the economic mistakes of the 1920s and 1930s.

It started functioning from March 1, 1947. In June, 1996, the Fund had 181 members. The IMF was established to promote economic and financial co-operation among its members in order to facilitate the expansion and balanced growth of world trade. It performs the activities like monitoring national, global and regional economic developments and advising member countries on their economic policies (surveillance); lending member hard currencies to support policy programmes designed to correct BOP problems; offering technical assistance in its areas of expertise as well as training for government and central bank officials.

Objectives

The fundamental purposes & objectives of the Fund had been laid down in Article 1 of the original Articles of Agreement and they have been upheld in the two amendments that were made in 1969 & 1978 to its basic charter. They are as under:

1. To promote international monetary co-operation through a permanent institution which provides the machinery for consumption & collaboration in international monetary problems.
2. To facilitate the expansion and balanced growth of international trade.
3. To promote exchange stability, to maintain orderly exchange arrangements among members, and to provide competitive exchange depreciation.
4. To assist in the establishment of a multilateral system of payments in respect of current transactions between

member and in the elimination of foreign exchange restrictions which hamper the growth in the world trade.

5. To lend confidence to members by making the Fund's resource available to them under adequate safeguards.
6. In accordance with the above, to shorten the duration and lessen the degree of disequilibrium in the international balance of payments of members.

Functions

To fulfill the above objectives, The IMF performs the following functions:

1. The IMF operates in such a way as to fulfill its objectives as laid down in the Bretton Woods Articles of Agreements. It's the Fund's duty to see that these provisions are observed by member countries.
2. The Fund gives short term loans to its members so that they may correct their temporary balance of payments disequilibrium.
3. The Fund is regarded "as the guardian of good conduct" in the sphere of balance of payments. It aims at reducing tariffs and other trade restrictions by the member countries.
4. The Fund also renders technical advice to its members on monetary and fiscal policies.
5. It conducts research studies and publishes them in IMF staff papers, Finance and Development, etc.
6. It provides technical experts to member countries having BOP difficulties and other problems.

Organisation and Structure

The Second Amendment of the Articles of Agreement made important changes in the organization and structure of the Fund. As such, the structure of the fund consists of a Board of governors, an Executive Board, a Managing Director, a council and a staff with its headquarters in Washington, U.S.A. There are ad hoc and standing committees appointed by the Board of Governors and the Executive Board. There is also an Interim Committee appointed by the Board of Governors. The Board of Governors and the Executive Board are decision making organs of the Fund. The Board of Governors is at the top in the structure of the Fund. It is composed of one Governor and one alternate Governor appointed by each member. The alternate Governor can participate in the meeting of the Board but has the power to vote only in the absence of the Governor.

The Board *of Governor* which has now 24 members meets annually in which details of the Fund activities for the previous year are presented. The annual meeting also takes few decisions with regards to the policies of Fund.

The Executive Board has 21 members at present. Five Executive Directors are appointed by the five members (USA, UK, W. Germany, France and Japan) having the largest quotas)

There is a *Managing Director* of the Fund who is elected by the Executive Directors.

The Executive Board is the most powerful organ of the Fund and exercise vast powers conferred on it by the Articles of Agreement and delegated to by the Board of Governors. So its power relates to all Fund activities, including its regulatory, supervisory and financial activities.

The Interim Committee (now IMFC) was established in October 1974 to advice the Board of Governors on supervising the management and adaptation of the international monetary in order to avoid disturbances that might threaten it. It currently has 22 members.

The Development Committee was also established in October 1974 and consists of 22 members. It advices and reports to the Board of Governors on all aspects of the transfer of real resources to developing countries and makes suggestions for their implementation.

FINANCIAL RESOURCES

IMF's resources mainly come from two sources Quotas and Loans. The capital of the Fund includes quotas of member countries, amount received from the sale of gold, General Arrangements to Borrow (GAB), New Arrangements to Borrow (NAB) and loans from members nations.

Quotas and Loans and their Fixation: The Fund has General Account based on quotas allocated to its members. When a country joins the Fund, it is assigned a Quota that governs the size of its subscription, its voting power, and its drawing rights. The country will be assigned with an initial quota in the same range as the quotas of existing members that are broadly comparable in the economic size and characteristics. At the time of the formation of the IMF, each member is required to pay its subscription in full or on joining the Fund – of which 25 percent of its quota in gold/SDR/widely accepted currencies such as USD/Euro/Yen/UK Pound and the rest in their own currencies. In order to meet the financial requirements of the Fund, the quotas are reviewed every five years and are raised from time to time. Loans from members and non-members constitute another major source of funds for the IMF. Since 1980 IMF has been authorized to borrow from commercial capital markets too. Quotas are denominated in Special Drawings Right , which is the IMF'S Unit of account. IMF has a weighted voting system. the larger a country's Quota in the IMF (determined broadly by its economic size) the more the vote the country has, in addition to its basic votes of which each member has an equal number.

FUND BORROWINGS

Besides performing regulatory and consultative functions, the Fund is an important financial institution. The bulk of its financial resources come from quota subscriptions of member countries. Besides, it increases its funds by selling gold to members. While Quota subscriptions of member countries are its major source of financing, the IMF can activate supplementary borrowing arrangements if it believes that resources might fall short of the members' needs. Through the General Arrangements to Borrow (GAB) and the New Arrangements to Borrow (NAB), a number of member countries and institutions express their readiness to lend additional funds to the IMF. GAB and NAB are credit arrangements between IMF and group of members and institutions to provide supplementary resources of up to US$54 billion to cope with the impairment of the international monetary system or deal with an exceptional situation that poses threat to the stability of the system. The GAB enables the IMF to borrow specified amount of currencies from 11 developed countries or their Central Banks under certain circumstances at market related interest rates. Whereas the NAB is a set of credit arrangement between the IMF and 26 Members and Institutions. The NAB is the first and principal resource in the event of a need to provide supplementary resources to the IMF.

Commitments from individual participants are based predominantly on relative economic strength as measured by the IMF Quotas. Like other financial institutions IMF also earns income from the interest charges and fees levied on its loans.

FUND LENDING

The Fund has a variety of facilities for lending its resources to its member countries. Lending by the Fund is linked to temporary assistance to members in financing disequilibrium in their balance of payments on current account. Reserve tranche and Credit tranche facilities are two basic facilities available for meeting BOP deficits.

Reserve tranche: Every member country is entitled to borrow without any conditions a part of its Quota (i.e., the subscription paid by the member country to the IMF). If a member has less currency with the Fund than its quotas, the difference is called Reserve tranche. It can draw up to 25 percent on its reserve tranche automatically upon representation of the Fund for its balance needs. It is not charged on any interest on such drawings, but is required to repay within a period of three to five years.

Credit Tranche: A member can draw further annually from balance quota in 4 installment up to 100% of its quota from credit tranche. Drawings from credit tranches are conditional because the members have to satisfy the Fund adopting a viable programme to ensure financial stability.

OTHER CREDIT FACILITIES

Buffer Stock Financing Facility (BSFF)

It was created in 1969 for financing commodity buffer stock by member countries. The facility is equivalent to 30 percent of the borrowings member's quota.

Extended Fund Facility (EFF)

It is another specialized facility which was created in 1974. Under EFF, the Fund provides credit to member countries to meet their balance of payments deficits for longer periods, and in amounts larger than their quotas under normal credit facilities.

Supplementary Financing/Reserve Facility (SFF/SRF)

It was established in 1977 to provide supplementary financing under extended or stand-by arrangements to member countries to meet serious balance of payments deficits that are large in relation to their economies and their quotas.

Structural Adjustment Facility (SAF)

The Fund setup SAF in March 1986 to provide concessional adjustment to the poorer developing countries.

Enhanced Structural Adjustment Facility (ESAF)

The EASF was created in December 1987 with SDR 6 billion of resources for the medium term financing needs for low income countries. The objectives, eligibility and basic programme features of this facility are similar to those of the SAF.

Compensatory & Contingency Financing Facility (CCFF)

The CCFF is created in August 1988 to provide timely compensation for temporary shortfalls or excesses in cereal import costs due to factors beyond the control of the member and contingency financing to help a member to maintain the momentum of Fund-supported adjustment programmes in the face of external shocks on account of factors beyond its control.

Systematic Transformation Facility (STF)

In April 1993, the IMF established STF with $6billion to help Russia and other Central Asian Republics to face balance of payments crisis.

Emergency Structural Adjustment LOAN (ESAL)

The Fund established ESAL facility in early 1999 to help the Asian and Latin American countries inflicted with the financial crisis.

Contingency Credit Line (CCL)

The CCL was created in 1999 to protect fundamentally sound countries from the contagion of financial crisis occurring in other countries, rather than from domestic policy weaknesses.

Poverty Reduction and Growth Facility (PRGF) and Exogenous Shock Facility (ESF)

These are concessional lending arrangements to low income countries and are unpinned by comprehensive country -owned strategies, delineated in their Poverty Reduction Strategy Papers (PRSP). In recent years PRGF has accounted for the largest number of IMF loans. The interest levied on these loans is 0.5% only and the repayment period is over 5-10 years.

Stand- By Agreements (SBA)

SBA is designed to help countries having deficit BOP with an extended repayment period of 2 to 4 years. Under Stand-By and Extended Arrangements a member can borrow up to 100% of its quota annually and 300% cumulatively.

EXCHANGE RATE

The original Fund Agreement provided that the par value of each member country was to be expressed in terms of gold of certain weight and fineness or US dollars. The underlining idea was to create a system of stable exchange rates with ordinary cross rates. But the Fund was obliged to agree to changes in exchange rates which did not exceed +/- 1 percent of the initial par value. A further change of +/- 1 percent required the permission of the Fund.

OTHER FACILITIES

The IMF advices its member countries on various problems concerning their BOP and exchange rate problems and on monetary and fiscal issues. It sends specialists & experts to help solve BOP and exchange rate problems of member countries.

The Fund has setup three departments to solve banking and fiscal problem of member countries:

a) There is the Central Banking Service Department which helps member countries with the services of its experts to run and manage their central banks and to formulate banking legislation.

b) The Fiscal Affairs Department renders advice to member countries concerning their fiscal matters.

c) The IMF institutes conducts short-term training courses for the officers of member countries relating to monetary, fiscal, banking and BOP policies.

Criticisms

Fund conditionality: The Fund has developed conditionality over the last five decades or so which a country has to fulfill for generation a loan from the Fund.

The Fund has laid down the following conditionalities:

a) To liberalise trade by removing exchange & import controls.

b) To eliminate all subsidies so that the exporters are not in a advantageous position in relation to the other trading countries.

c) To treat foreign lenders on an equal footing with domestic lenders. Besides, the Fund insists on good governance.

High interest rates: Besides, these hard conditionalities, the Fund charges high interest rates on loans of different types. They are a great burden on the borrowing countries.

Secondary role. The Fund has been playing only a secondary role rather than the central role in international monetary relations.

It does not provide facilities for short term credit arrangements. This hard resulted in "swap" developed countries.

Lack of resources: The IMF has not enough resources for immediate future. But these are not sufficient to meet the future needs of its members.

Failure to maintain exchange rate stability. The Fund has failed in its objective of promoting exchange stability and to maintain orderly exchange arrangements among members.

Failure to eliminate foreign exchange restrictions. One of the objectives of the Fund has been to eliminate foreign exchange restrictions which hamper the growth in world trade.

Discriminatory policies. The Fund has been criticized for its discriminatory policies against the developing countries and in favour of the developed countries. It is, therefore, characterized as "Rich Countries Club"

Despite these criticisms, the IMF has shown sufficient flexibility to mould itself in keeping with the changing international economic conditions.

The original Articles of Agreement were amended in 1978 to legalise flexible exchange rates, raise quotas to increase the Fund's resources and to dethrone the gold in Fund transactions. The Fund has been helping the developing countries in their balance of payments and other problems through such facilities as CFF, BSFF, EFF, SFF, SAF, ESAF, CCFF, etc.

SPECIAL DRAWING RIGHTS (SRDS)

Meaning

Special Drawing Rights (SDRs), also known as the *paper gold,* are a form of international reserves created by the IMF in 1969 to solve the problem of international liquidity. They are not paper notes or currency. They are international units of account in which the official account of the IMF are kept.

Origin

SDRs were created through the First Amendment of the Fund Articles of Agreement in 1969 following persistent US deficits in balance of payments to solve the problem of liquidity. Until December 1971, an SDR was linked to 0.88867 gram of gold and was equivalent to US $1. With the break down of fixed parity system after 1973 when the US dollar and other major currencies were allowed to float, it was decided to stabilize the exchange value of the SDR. Accordingly, the value of SDR was calculated each day on the basis of a basket of 16 most widely used currencies of the member countries of the Fund. Each country was given a weight in the basket in accordance with its importance in international trade and financial markets.

After the Second Amendment of the Fund Articles of Agreement in 1978, the SDR became an international unit of account. To facilitate its valuation, the numbers of currencies in the "basket" were reduced to five in January 1981. They include the US dollars, the German Deutsche Mark, the British Pound, the French Franc and the Japanese Yen. The present currency composition and weighting pattern of the SDR is revised every five years beginning January 1, 1986. The revision of weights is based on both the values of the exports of goods and services and the balances of their currencies held by other members. In 1977, they were US dollar (39%), German DM (21%), UK Pound and French Franc (11% each) and Japanese Yen (18%). The value of one SDR was equal to US $1.35610 on October 1, 1997.

Uses

SDR is an international unit of account which is held in the Fund's Special Drawing Account. The quotas of all currencies in the Fund General Account are also valued in terms of the SDR. SDRs are used as a means of payment by Fund members to meet balance of payments deficits and their total reserve position with the Fund. They cannot be used for any other purpose. Thus SDRs act both as an international unit of account and a means of payment.

There are three principal uses of SDRs:

Transactions with Designation

Under it, Fund designates a participant in the SDR scheme who has a strong balance of balance of payments and reserve position to provide currency in exchange for SDRs to another participant needing its currency.

Transactions with General Account

SDRs are used in all transactions with the General Account of the Fund. Participants pay charges in SDRs to the General Account for the use of the Fund resources and also to repurchase their own currency from it.

Transactions by Agreement

The Fund allows sales of SDRs for currency by agreement with another participant. In order to further widen the uses of SDRs, the Second Amendment empowered the Fund to lay down uses of SDRs not otherwise specified. Accordingly, the following additional uses of SDRs are:

i) in swap arrangements,
ii) in forward operations,
iii) in loams,
iv) in the settlement of financial objections
v) as security for the performance of financial obligations
vi) in dominations or grants.

The Fund pays interest on all holdings of SDRs kept in the Special Drawing Account and charges internet at the same rate on allocations to participants.

Merits

Despite these weaknesses, the SDRs scheme possesses the following merits:

a) SDRs are a new form of international monetary reserves which have been created to free the international monetary system from its exclusive dependence on the US dollar.

b) They have rid the world of its dependence on the supply of gold and fluctuations in gold prices.

c) They cannot be demonetised like gold or become scare when the demand for dollar increases in the world.

d) Unlike gold, SDRs are costless to produce because production of gold requires resources to mine, refine, transport and guard it.

e) SDRs have been created to improve international liquidity so as to correct fundamental disequilibria in balance of payments of Fund members. Under this scheme, the participants receive SDRs under *transactions with designation and transaction by agreement* unconditionally.

f) Fund members are not required to change their domestic economic policies as they are expected under the Fund aid programmes.

g) The payment and repayment of SDRs out of the Special Drawing Account is easier and more flexible than under the Fund schemes.

h) Last but not the least, SDRs act both as a unit of account and a means of payment of international monetary system.

CRITICISMS

Despite these merits, the SDR scheme has been criticized in the following grounds:

Not Linked with Development Finance

SDR scheme does not link the creation of international reserves in the form of SDRs with the need for development finance on the part of developing countries.

Failure to Distribute Social Saving.

Williamson and others have criticized the SDR scheme for its failure to distribute social saving of SDRs to the developing countries. The present rules for allocation distribute the social saving to a participant country in proportion to his contribution or its demand for SRDs.

Failure to Meet International Liquidity Requirement

The Fund has failed in its objective of increasing international liquidity through SDRs.

THE WORLD BANK (IBRD)

The International Bank for Reconstruction and Development (IBRD) or the World Bank was established on December 27, 1945 following international ratification of the Bretton Woods Agreement of 1944 , which emerged from the United Nations Monetary and Financial Conference (July 1-22,1944).to assist in bringing about a smooth transition from a war time to peace time economy. It is the sister institution of IMF. Since its inception in 1944, the World Bank has expanded from a single institution to an associated group of coordinated development institutions. The Bank's mission evolved from a facilitator of post-war reconstruction and development to its present day mandate of worldwide poverty alleviation, social sector funding and comprehensive development framework. The term 'World Bank' now refers to World Bank Group which includes

- International Bank for Reconstruction and Development (IBRD) established in 1945 for providing debt financing on the basis of sovereign guarantees.
- International Financial Corporation (IFC) established in 1956 for providing various forms of financing without sovereign guarantees primarily to the private sector.
- International Development Association (IDA) established in 1960 for providing concessional financing (interest free loans, grants etc.) usually with sovereign guarantees.
- International Centre for Settlement of Investment Disputes (ICSID) established in 1966 which works with various governments of various countries to reduce investment risks.
- Multilateral Investment Guarantee Agency (MIGA) established in 1988 for providing insurance against certain types of risks including political risks primarily to the private sector.

Functions

The IBRD also called the World Bank performs the following functions:

1. To assist in reconstruction and development of territories of its members by facilitating the investment of capital for productive purpose and to encourage the development of

productive facilities and resources in less development countries.

2. To promote private foreign investment by means of guarantees on participation in loans and other investment made by private investors.
3. To promote the long range balanced growth of international trade and the maintenance of equilibrium in the balance of payments of member countries by encouraging international investments for the development of their productive resources.
4. To arrange the loans made or guaranteed by it in relation to international loans through other channels so that more useful and urgent small and large projects are dealt with first.

Membership

World Bank is like a cooperative where its 185 member countries are its shareholders. The shareholders are represented by a Board of Governors, which is the ultimate policy making body of the World Bank. Generally governors are member countries ministers of finance or ministers of development who will meet once in a year at the Annual Meeting of the Board of Governors of the World Bank Group and IMF

The members of International Monetary Fund are the members of the IBRD. If a country resigns its memberships, it is required to pay back all loans with interest on due dates. If the Bank incurs a financial loss in the years in which a member resigns, it is required to pay its share of the loss on demand.

Organisation

Like the IMF, the IBRD has a three-tier structure with a President, Executive Directors and Board of Governors. The President of the World Bank Group (IBRD, IDA and IFC) is elected by the Bank's Executive Directors whose number is 21. Of these, 5 are appointed by the five largest shareholders of the World Bank. They are the US, UK, Germany, France and Japan. The remaining 16 are elected by the Board of Governors. There are also Alternate Directors. The first five belong to the same permanent member countries to which the Executive Directors belong. But the remaining Alternate Directors are elected from among the group of countries who cast their votes to choose the 16 Executive Directors belonging to their regions.

The President of the World Bank presides over the meetings of the Board of Executive Directors regularly once a mouth. The Executive Directors decide about policy within the framework of the Articles of Agreement. They consider and decide on the loan and credit proposal made by the President. They also present to the Broad of Governors at its annual meetings audited accounts, an administrative budget, and Annual Report on the operations and policies of the Bank. The President has a staff of more than 6000 persons who carry on the working of the World Bank. He is assisted by a number of Senior Vice-Presidents and Directors of the various departments and regions. The Board of Governors is the supreme body. Every member country appoints one Governor and an Alternate Governor for a period of five years. The voting power of each Governor is related to the financial contribution of its government.

Workings

The World Bank operates under the leadership and direction of the President, Vice Presidents and other senior management staffs who will look after the functions like Fund generation, Loans, Grants and other analytical and advisory services.

- Fund Generation: IBRD lending to developing countries is primarily financed by selling AAA rated bonds in the world financial markets. It earns a small margin on this lending where major proportion of its income comes from lending of its own capital which consists of, reserves built over the years and money paid to the Bank from its 185 member countries. International Development Association (IDA) provides interest free loans and grant assistance to poorest countries which is replenished every three years by 40 donor countries. Additional funds are generated through repayments of loan principle on 35 to 40 years interest free loans which are then available for relending. IDA accounts for nearly 40% of total lending of the World Bank.
- Loans: Through IBRD and IDA, the bank offers two basic types of loans and credits- Investment Loans and Development Policy Loans. Investment Loans are made to

countries for goods, works and services in support of economic and social development projects in a broad range of economic and social sectors.

- Development Policy Loans on the other hand provide quick disbursing financing to support countries policy and institutional reforms. IDA provides long term interest free credits at a small service charge of o.5 %to 0.75%
- Grants: Grants are designed to facilitate development projects by encouraging innovation and co- operation between organizations and local stakeholders participation in projects.; which are either funded directly or managed through partnerships used mainly to relieve debt burden of heavily indebted poor countries, improve sanitation and water supplies, support vaccination and immunization programs to reduce the occurrence of communicable diseases ,combat HIV/AIDS pandemic, support civil society organizations and create initiatives to cut the emission of green house gases.
- Analytical and Advisory Services: Through economic research on board issues such as the environment, poverty ,infrastructure, trade, social safety, and globalization the Bank evaluates a country's economic prospects and assists in the following activities:

THE ASIAN DEVELOPMENT BANK (ADB)

During the 1950s, it was strongly felt that there should be a bank for Asia like the World Bank to meet the development needs of this region. This view was suggested for the first time at the ministerial Conference on Asian Cooperation held at Manila in December 1963. The Conference constituted a working group of experts which submitted its report to the UN Economic commission for Asia and Far East (ECAFE) at its session held at Wellington in March 1965. It was on the basis of this report that an Agreement Establishing the Asian Development Bank was drafted and adopted at the Second Ministerial Conference on Asian Economic Cooperation at Manila in November-December 1965. By January 1966, 33 countries had signed its Charter and the Asian Development Bank was set up on December 19, 1966 with its headquarters at Manila in the Philippines.

Objectives

The main aim for the establishment of ADB was to supplement the work of the World Bank in Asia.

Its objectives are:

1. To promote public and private investment for economic development in the ECAFE region and Developing Member Countries(DMCs)
2. To utilize the available resources for financing of economic development.
3. To help the regional members in the coordination of their plans and policies for economic development to enable them to achieve a better utilization of their resources
4. To provide technical assistance for the preparation, financing and implementation of projects and programme for economic development, including the formulation of specific projects.
5. To co-operate with the United Nations and its organs and subsidiaries, including, in particular, the ECAFE and other international institutions and organizations and national entities in the investment of development funds in the region.
6. To undertake all such activities and provide such services which may fulfill the above objectives.

Membership

The membership of ADB is open to the following:

1. Members of the ECAFE.
2. Associated members of ECAFE.
3. Other countries of the ECAFE region which are the members of the United Nations or any of its specialized agencies. It has a membership of 56 countries at present. Any country can become its member when two-third members of the Board of Governors cast their vote in its favour.

Management

The ADB is managed by a President, Vice-President, and a Board of Governors along with an administrative staff. The President is the administrative head of the Bank. The Vice-President performs the duties of the President in his absence. Each member country nominates a Governor and an Alternate Governor to the Board of Governors. At least one meeting of the Board of Governors is held every year. The Board of Governors has delegated its executive power to the Board of Directors. The Board of Directors consists of ten members of whom seven belong to regional countries and three to non regional countries.

The Board of Directors takes all decisions relating to the Bank, passes its annual budget and presents the accounts of the Bank to the Board of Governors for approval.

There are certain functions which only the Board of Governors has to perform. They are:

a) Entry of new member.

b) Change in the authorized capital of the Bank.

c) Election of the President and administrators

d) Amendment in the Charter of the Bank.

FINANCIAL RESOURCES

The Bank started its operations with an authorized capital of $ 2.9 billion which was raised to $25 billion in 1992. Output of this, 50% had been contributed by Japan and the remaining by member countries. To increase its resources, the Bank issues debentures and accepts deposits from the special funds. To augment its resources further, the Bank borrows from the capital markets of the world.

Functions

The ADB performs the following functions:

Financial Assistance

The Bank provides financial assistance in the form of grants & loans. It gives three types of loans: project loans, sector loans and programme loans. Project loans are tied to specific projects. Sectors loans are given to a number of related projects in a given sector. Programme loans cover more than one sector and relate to the implementation of a policy or programme for bringing about certain changes.

The Bank advances loans out of its Ordinary Funds Reserves/ Ordinary Capital Reserves and Special Fund Reserve. The Ordinary

Funds Reserve refers to the Bank's ordinary capital resources OCR's out of which direct loans are given for development projects or specific projects. For sector lending, the Bank has established a Special Funds such as the Asian Development Funds, Multipurpose Special Funds and Agriculture Special Funds.

Technical Assistance

The ADB also provides technical assistance to member countries out of the Technical Assistance Special Fund. The technical assistance is provided to the member in ECAFE region through their governments, agencies, regional institutions and private firms. It may be in the form of grants and loans or both.

The Bank's technical assistance has two main objectives:

a) To prepare and finance and implement specific national and/or regional development plans and projects.
b) To help in the working of existing institutions and/or the creation of new institutions on a national or regional basis in such areas as agriculture, industry, public administration, etc.

Surveys and Research:

One of the ADB is to conduct surveys and research in order to formulate policies for the future and to promote regional economic integration.

Poverty Reduction:

Since the 1990s, Bank's greater emphasis has been to promote employment and reduce poverty through improved efficiency, sustainable pro-poor economic growth and better development opportunities for the poor. In promoting economic growth, the Bank stresses the importance of increasing productivity also.

The ADB now pays more attention to human resources development, poverty reduction, social infrastructure development, urban environmental improvement and development, comprehensive economic and structural reforms, etc.

Bibliography

Bardsley, N., Cubitt: *Assessing Experimental Economics*, Princeton, Princeton University Press, 2009.

Basu, Kaushik. *Analytical Development Economics, The Less Developed Economy Revisited*, Cambridge, Mass.: MIT Press, 1997.

Burke, Frank M., *Valuation and Valuation Planning for Closely Held Businesses*, Englewood Cliffs, NJ, Prentice Hall, 1981.

Clive W. J.: *Empirical Modeling in Economics, Specification and Evaluation*, London, Cambridge University Press, 1999.

Commons, J. R., *Institutional Economics-Its Place in Political Economy*, The University of Wisconsin Press, Madison, Wisconsin, 1934.

Cootner, Paul : *The Random Character of Stock Market Prices*, MIT Press, 1964.

Dimson, Elroy: *Stock Market Anomalies*, Cambridge University Press, 1988.

Harrigan, K. R.: *Strategies for Declining Businesses*. Lexington, MA: Heath, 1980

Hunt, E. K. *History of Economic Thought, A Critical Perspective*, New York, HarperCollins, 1992.

Jack Murrin, *Valuation: Measuring and Managing the Value of Companies*, New York, Wiley, 1994.

John A, Marcell, *Handbook of Small Business Valuation Formulas and Rules of Thumb*, Valuation Press, 1993.

Judy A.: *Feminism, Objectivity and Economics*, London and New York, Routledge, 1996.

Link, Albert N.: *Evaluating Economic Damages, A Handbook for Attorneys*, Westport, CT, Quorum Books, 1992.

Loomes, G.: *Current Issues in Microeconomics*, New York: St. Martin's Press, 1989.

Magnussen, L., *Evolutionary and Neo-Schumpeterian Approaches to Economics*, Kluwer, Boston, 1994.

March, J. G.: *A Behavioural Theory of the Firm*, Englewood-Cliffs, Prentice Hall, 1963.

Martin, Gerald D.: *Determining Economic Damages*, Santa Ana, CA: James Publishing, 1995.

Pesendorfer, W.: *The Foundations of Positive and Normative Economics*, New York, Oxford University Press 2008.

Plous, S.: *The Psychology of Judgement and Decision Making*, New York, McGraw-Hill, 1993

Santos, A.C.: *The Social Epistemology of Experimental Economics*, London, Routledge 2009.

Schotter, A.: *The Foundations of Positive and Normative Economics*, New York, Oxford University Press, 2008.

Scott, W. R.: *Organizations: Rational, Natural, and Open Systems*, Englewood Cliffs, 1981.

Smith, V. L.: *Papers in Experimental Economics*, Cambridge, Cambridge University Press, 1991.

Towse, Ruth ed.: *A Handbook of Cultural Economics*, Edward Elgar, 2003.

Warwick, D. P.: *A Theory of Public Bureaucracy*, Cambridge, MA: Harvard University Press, 1975.

Weibull, J. W.: *Advances in Understanding Strategic Behaviour*, New York, Palgrave, 2004.

Wood, A.: *The Corporate Economy*, London: Macmillan, 1971.

Index

□□□